MAYA VEERAM
or
The Forces of Illusion

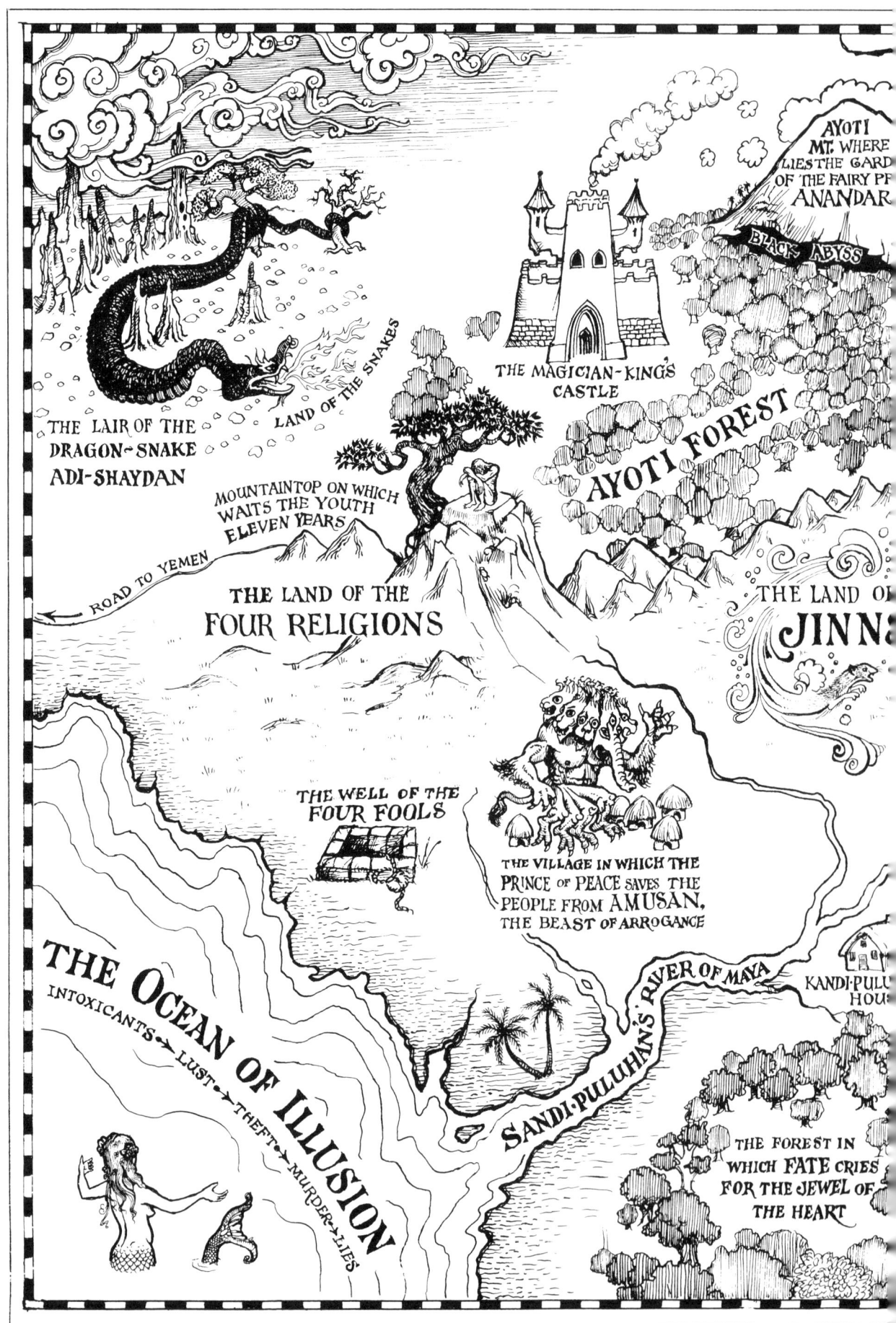

MAYA VEERAM
or
The Forces of Illusion

by

*His Holiness
M. R. Bawa Muhaiyaddeen*

SAMUEL WEISER, INC.
York Beach, Maine

Acknowledgements

Maya Veeram: The Forces of Illusion was originally spoken in Tamil by His Holiness M. R. Bawa Muhaiyaddeen and recorded by scribes in Jaffna, Sri Lanka in 1942. It was later published in Tamil in 1957. Then in 1980 it was translated into English by Dr. K. Ganesan, Mrs. R. Ganesan, and Mrs. Crisi Beutler, and edited by Ms. Sharon Marcus.

NOTE TO THE READER:

The following traditional supplications written in Arabic calligraphy will be found periodically throughout the text.

ﷻ following Allah stands for *Jalla Jalālah*—Exalted is His Glory!

ﷺ following Prophet Muhammad or Rasūlullāh stands for *Sallallāhu 'alaihi wa sallam*—Blessings and peace be upon him!

؏ following the name of a prophet or angel stands for *'alaihis-salām*—Peace be upon him!

Copyright © 1982 by The Bawa Muhaiyaddeen Fellowship

First published in 1982 by

Samuel Weiser, Inc.
P. O. Box 612
York Beach, Maine 03902

ISBN 0-87728-550-0

Library of Congress Catalogue Card Number: 82-61774

All rights reserved. No part of this publication may be reproduced, stored in a retrieval system, or transmitted in any form, or by any means, electronic, mechanical, photocopying, recording, or otherwise without prior permission of the copyright owner. Brief excerpts can be quoted for review purposes.

Printed in the United States by Maple-Vail, Binghamton, N.Y.

His Holiness M. R. Bawa Muhaiyaddeen

Contents

1. SANDAKUMARAN, THE PRINCE OF PEACE *1*

2. SANDAKUMARAN MEETS THE PULUHANS *15*

3. SANDAKUMARAN'S MISSION *33*

4. SANDAKUMARAN MEETS THE ANGEL OF DEATH *49*

5. SANDAKUMARAN LEARNS THE STORY OF THE DOG *67*

6. VANDI PULUHAN'S STORY *95*

7. THE FOUR FOOLS *117*

8. VANDI PULUHAN AND KANDI PULUHAN GO IN SEARCH OF THE CONQUEROR OF ALL THE CONQUERORS *133*

9. THE CITY OF SOKKU *157*

10. KUNAMAYJAYAN *171*

11. KAMAMOHASUNTARI *191*

12. SANDAKUMARAN MARRIES MUTAVALLI *205*

Preface to the English Edition

$\mathcal{M}$ay God help us.

This book was written for all the people in the world whose personal sorrow and suffering made them lose their faith in God, and for all the people who have been wondering whether a God would permit the terrifying murders, the treachery and evil they see in the world today. They have run away from faith in God, from faith in the religions, and from faith in worship and prayer. This book was written for them.

My brothers and sisters, we must have absolute faith that God exists always, forever. Seasons may change, time may change, the hours and minutes may change, desire, creation, and forms may change, but the truth never changes. Lies and falsehood are easily seen on the surface, but truth has to be seen within, truth has to be understood from within. We must open our hearts and try to see the truth as the truth within ourselves.

It was for this reason that we assembled *Maya Veeram*. What happened in the past has come and gone now, but by reading this book we can make some sense out of what happens today, and we can understand what will happen in the future. Religions, races, and the strife among them, the wars and the battles that have been fought because of them, all this can be understood if we look beneath the surface of the book. This story describes the present and the future, the destruction which is supposed to take place, and the peace which will follow.

Three types of people who have set out to conquer the world are distinguishable. One group categorically denies there is a God. Others say there is no God because of the poverty and the suffering they have endured. And there are others who still have some belief buried in their hearts, but they deny Him outwardly for worldly advantage or because of their doubts. Together, they have determined to rule the world with their lies, their treachery, their atomic bombs and weaponry. They attempt to influence the thinking of the world through the press and the media, trying to transform the good intentions of people, converting cities into forests and forests into cities, changing men into animals, and making animals their food or prey, making virtuous women prostitutes and prostitutes virtuous women, making decent people thieves and thieves decent people, good people bad and bad people good, making kings beggars and beggars kings, rich people poor and poor people rich, changing good to bad and bad to good. In this way they transform the world, turning everything upside down. Their leaders take over different countries, establish dictatorships, and enslave the body, mind, and soul of all the people. They ration food and clothing, and make the people labor by day and by night. Those who try to escape are food for their guns and their cannon.

In addition to this misery is the suffering caused by religious, racial, and caste or class discrimination. Everything that used to be valued—virtue, justice, honesty—is vanishing. A woman with ten children gives up her husband and children for a new, young husband. A man with ten children abandons his wife and children for a new, young wife. A mother consorts with her son, the son with his mother, a brother consorts with his sister and the sister with her brother, a father consorts with his daughter and the daughter with the father.

Maya Veeram describes many such irregularities which will occur in the future. On the surface it might seem to be a storybook, but if we examine it wisely, we will uncover all its inner secrets. The present, the future, and the possibility of imminent destruction, all these are examined. If we can understand this, strengthen our faith and have absolute certitude that God does exist, we can try to escape from the devastation which those who have no faith in God are heaping upon us. Every human being must strengthen his faith to understand that final destruction, to know how injustice will ultimately destroy injustice, and how truth and justice will save those with faith in God. As each person reads this book, he must comprehend its inner meaning. Even though it may appear to be just a story, it is filled with truth and meaning.

For anyone with the wisdom to read this book correctly, *Maya Veeram* will resemble a prophecy; it will account for the plight of the world today, it will indicate what will happen tomorrow, and if you want to know what will happen next year, it can tell you that too. Those who can read it this way, those who consider it deeply and penetrate the surface, plunging into the many different inner meanings will discover how to escape from the destruction that threatens us.

May we reflect on this. May we read this book and learn how to escape from the disaster threatening this world. God alone can protect us all.

M. R. Bawa Muhaiyaddeen

BISMILLĀHIR-RAHMĀNIR-RAHĪM

Author's Song

May the grace of Allah's divine Messenger,
And that prophet's divine grandson,
Filled with luminous wisdom, help everyone
Trusting this false world
Grow with melting love.

May the lamp of their hearts
Burn with bright purity.
May clarity grow in their hearts.
In this world of forms,
May they understand good and evil clearly.

Day by day in this false world,
May they realize that money and wealth are external things,
And that wife, children, house, and property
Will not join them in the hereafter.

May those with compassion
Know and see themselves truly,
With clear inner hearts
On judgment day.

May God's grace be given
To all who have been born with me,
To all who are my own life.
May they be protected.

May all these children
Receive Your grace, O Allah.
With Your love
Please dispel all the unbearable,
Ever increasing sorrows
Inherent in the actions and words
Of Your slaves, O God.

Yā Muhaiyaddeen, may Allah be pleased with him,
Yā Rasūl, O Messenger, blessings and peace be upon him,
Yā Rabbal-'alamīn, O Ruler of the universes.

Invocation to God

So that beautiful girls with melodious songs and captivating eyes,
So that these treasures of the god of love
Do not cause storms in my heart,
I seek refuge at Your feet,
In full surrender, with all my love.
O God from whom all sound emanates,
O God who is praised in songs,

O God who is praised in scriptures,
You are the One whose eyes are everywhere,
You are the One who rides the green peacock.
Live and vibrate in my heart,
So that this story may be sung by You
In sweet, flowing songs.

The Word of Grace and Beauty

There is a song with a hidden meaning,
A song which contains its own vibration,
A song of wisdom which comes
From the heart of that grace and love
Of *Allāhu ta'ālā,* God who is all mighty, the precious treasure.
Is it easy for me, with a black body,
Is it easy for me, wandering from land to land,
Is it easy for me, the blind one who does not know
The difference between right and wrong
To sing the song of One whose path is grace in this world,
Of One who is grace and beauty in the heart?

They say that great sages with *gnānam* or divine knowledge
Are submerged in the deep ocean, the blissful radiance
Of the highest awakened wisdom,
And that God who gently dwells
In clear, wise men
Reveals exalted words of grace through them,
Words which are that very mysterious, true religion.
I am so discarded,
Can that be why I sing about God?

Some people find fault, using words sharper
Than the point of a needle.
Please listen now to words
Of one whose head has felt the dust
Beneath the flower-like feet of wise men who have that light,
Who trust in the loving and incomparable
Great Prophet Muhammad, blessings and peace be upon him.

Those good people who write down
The words of my tongue
Which knows nothing,
Which does not even know good Tamil,
Write blissfully, knowing the inner meaning
Of these words.
Even if there are millions of faults in this world,
Please be patient,
Take what is good,
Have inner patience,
And correct the faults within yourself.

1

Sandakumaran, the Prince of Peace

Sandakumaran, the Prince of Peace, explains the ways of the ABCD world, the world of deception, arrogance, desire and pride.

Once upon a time in the suburban kingdom of a good country they call Destiny, there were four people named Owl, Monkey, Great One, and Ruler. Owl was the king, Monkey was his wife, Great One the king's honorable minister, and Ruler was the benefactor to everyone who came near him. For those with clear hearts, for those whose subtle wisdom had emerged, Ruler represented divine wisdom itself. He was a mystery to those who were themselves mysterious, and a *faqīr* from a long line of *faqīrs*. These four governed that land and apparently they all lived happily enough. However, King Owl did become quite blind at cockcrow every day, and not only *that*, at daybreak he could no longer see even a glimmer of light.

JUDGMENT: What does *that* mean?

SANDAKUMARAN: *That,* cousin? *That* doesn't know where its government, its wife or children are, nor does it have any idea where it is itself.

JUDGMENT: How can such an Owl run the government, cousin?

SANDAKUMARAN: That's why his government includes a store, a street bazaar, a washerman, a barber, and so on. Everything in this government is found in the ABCD.

JUDGMENT: What's this, my friend? You were talking about this and that earlier, and now you're talking about something else. What does it all mean?

SANDAKUMARAN: Look, is that what's worrying you? Let me tell you a story. Listen very carefully, and then you'll know what it means, cousin. This is a story which happens in the present.

JUDGMENT: Heavens cousin, first you were telling me a story about some king, and now you say it's a present-day story, a modern story.

SANDAKUMARAN: Cousin, you don't seem to understand the meaning of a modern story: today a king will become a beggar, and a beggar will become a king. That's how it is!

JUDGMENT: How's that?

SANDAKUMARAN: The world today will praise and exalt evildoers while degrading and humiliating good people. The tricks and devices of hypocrites rule the world. At any rate, no matter what I say or explain, my intellect is only equal to a buffalo's. But those who know, will know; those who don't know, won't.

JUDGMENT: Really? Oh well, tell me the story.

SANDAKUMARAN: Because they understand present-day trends, millionaires, rich men, and others put on the right costume and act in this passing drama with great skill. The drama, cousin, is essential for making a living, but something else is necessary to make the body flourish.

JUDGMENT: What's that, cousin?

SANDAKUMARAN: The ABCD mantra. That you must learn first and foremost! That alone will sustain the body.

JUDGMENT: And if you learn it, what's it good for?

SANDAKUMARAN: Don't you see? Laws, titles, honors, plans, influence, and power—all these are in that mantra.

JUDGMENT: Tell me cousin, is there any way for people like me who haven't learned the ABCD mantra to earn a living?

SANDAKUMARAN: Any way? No way!

JUDGMENT: Why cousin, what makes you say this? If that's true, shouldn't we just drown ourselves in the ocean, or take our lives by jumping in the nearest lake or pond? What do you say?

SANDAKUMARAN: Well, when you put it that way it makes me sad too, but I've learned so much in this ABCD world. Look, I'll tell you those stories later; right now I have an idea how you can earn your living in the world today. If you listen to this advice and follow it, you'll do well in the world. There is no better way.

JUDGMENT: What is it, cousin? You must tell me.

SANDAKUMARAN: Business. Business is proclaiming its own victory in this world of illusion. So listen carefully and concentrate deeply while I explain.

JUDGMENT: But cousin, how can I start a business when I don't even have a cent?

SANDAKUMARAN: That doesn't matter. I'll give you something to do business with right now.

JUDGMENT: What is that something cousin, how can I possibly do business with it, what is it, what is it?

SANDAKUMARAN: It's something very important, cousin. If you have it you can do anything. Now, your name is Judgment, isn't it? Well, its name is fate. If fate and Judgment get together they can carry on a modern business very successfully, and be respectable too. No one in this ABCD world can overcome the combination of Judgment and the thing called fate. Here's what's necessary: a mirror, a comb, a dish, soap, cream, vaseline, bracelets, decorated belts, and about half a yard of material to be half-clothed. These are the novelties that attract today's world, so it's best to do business with them. Now let me tell you about some other things: palmyra toddy, coconut toddy, arrack, whiskey, brandy, beer, marijuana, opium, and similar poisonous intoxicants; meat, fish, eggs, and other harmful, inedible foods, they must all be put together for business. In this ABCD world if business is conducted properly even people who have been starving for eight days will approach you with a desire to buy things. They will even offer their wives' jewelry and their household goods for them. If you do this business correctly millionaires and rich men will be reduced to blocks of wood, you will sit on them, and race, caste, religion, law, influence, plans, and titles will all be straw under your feet. This business cousin, this cure for the disease of poverty, if you do it properly, then you'll have something profitable.

JUDGMENT: Right, cousin, right. What you say sounds really splendid, and if I continue all this on a regular basis, it will bring great, great happiness.

SANDAKUMARAN: Not just that. Listen carefully and I'll tell you about the one thing in the ABCD world I desired. The need dawned in my heart to contract a marriage in this world of spurious energy, and I searched and wandered and looked all over the ABCD to find a good-natured girl with good qualities who would please my heart. But I didn't find such a girl in this drama, this world of today. I wandered far and wide, I was tired, exhausted, and dizzy, I saw darkness before my eyes, my body seized up, I lost my sight, and came to a halt. At that very moment up came a girl whose name was ABCD, cousin. The speed she came with tossed me up to six-and-three-quarters plus one-half plus one-quarter.

JUDGMENT: What's this, cousin? Your story is just like the man who wandered around the street bazaar asking for, "Ginger, ginger!" to show off his new gold teeth. Then someone slapped him, out fell the false teeth, and he had to wander about mumbling, "Om, mum."

SANDAKUMARAN: Now cousin, I've caught hold of you just like the rattlesnake caught the shrew. The snake couldn't swallow it and didn't dare let it go. I told you a story, but you've made a ginger-eating monkey out of me. Never mind, cousin, you have become the shrew, but it's not really like that. Listen carefully, I'll tell you that story of the modern world.

JUDGMENT: All right then, continue the story you started to tell. Yes, yes, cousin, about the six-and-three-quarters plus one-half plus one-quarter— did it take you far away, did you thrash about and roll around because of it, did it make you crazy, did it frighten you, did you run away? Oh well, we're even. What you said and what I say amounts to the same thing. Now tell your story.

SANDAKUMARAN: You asked if I rolled around or got caught or went crazy, didn't you? It was nothing like that. Listen, I'll tell you. The ABCD lady came running at me with four wheels and noises like *kada, muda, lada, puda, tada-tada, kudu-kudu*. She knocked me down and dragged me a long way.

JUDGMENT: For heaven's sake cousin, what kind of talk is this? Your words are like those of a man with a precious human body but no brains in his head. But let that be and explain the story you set out to tell me.

SANDAKUMARAN: It is what it is. It's seven-and-a-half.

JUDGMENT: Seven-and-a-half is only a number. What can it do?

SANDAKUMARAN: O ho! You seem ignorant of its strength. Listen, it can toss, it can catch, it can turn, roll and even torture good people, and it can do more. The full nature of this number will be revealed in the story I'm going to tell you now. Listen cousin.

Saneeswaran and Shiva

At one time long ago Saneeswaran, that is Satan, prayed endlessly to Shiva, and finally Shiva appeared saying, "My faithful devotee, what would you like?"

Saneeswaran said, "Grant me the right to be inside and outside all beings. Let me ruin those who love you by luring them over to my side."

To that Shiva replied, "I will give you what you ask, but on one condition, you cannot go near true devotees, chaste women, or mighty *gnānis*. If you do approach them you will be disgraced."

Saneeswaran immediately stared at Shiva and said, "O great Shiva, do not go. I want you as the first victim of your gift," and he came up close to him. Shiva became frightened, ran away, and jumped into a pond taking the form of a fish. Hoping to catch the frightened deity and torture him, Saneeswaran assumed the form of a crane and stood waiting. After some time Shiva rose to the surface as a fish, a *keliru* fish with a ridge of spines. When he saw that fish the crane seized it at once and swallowed it, but the fish caught in his throat causing him great suffering.

Shiva revealed himself and said, "You wretched crane possessed by Satan, why did you try to swallow that fish?" Saneeswaran was ashamed of himself and returned to his own form. From that day he has ruled in the seven-and-a-half way.

SANDAKUMARAN: Do you know the meaning of that?

JUDGMENT: I don't. Explain it to me.

SANDAKUMARAN: This is the seven-and-a-half year period of the planet Saturn's influence—that is Satan—which recurs three times in a man's life. It is also marriage, cousin. When marriage begins, Satan begins. Don't think, cousin, don't think for one moment that you alone will be spared the torments of that strong and powerful creature.

JUDGMENT: Ha! Now I begin to understand just how mighty he is. In fact, when I think about this my stomach churns and I can't even face the thought of food. So we must be careful. Right, tell me the rest of the story about the girl.

SANDAKUMARAN: There was a tent on four wheels, and something which looked like a girl got out and came towards me. When I saw her I stood up. She looked at me and said, "Bloody, bloody!" I immediately gave her a punch and a kick in the ribs. She fell down, got up, stood there and shouted, "Hey, what's this, fool?" So then I had to answer him.

JUDGMENT: Wait a minute, this is really strange! First it was a 'she' and now it's a 'he'.

SANDAKUMARAN: That's true. When the figure was standing up it appeared to have a woman's face, and when it fell down it seemed to be a man.

JUDGMENT: Well this is amazing! There are many differences between men and women. Don't you know them?

SANDAKUMARAN: I know, I know, but when I pondered deeply, when I thought and considered deeply and looked again, there was no difference.

JUDGMENT: Indeed, then where did it go?

SANDAKUMARAN: That's the point, but it is where it was. In those days everyone knew this sort of thing, and it was easy to tell male from female.

These days I believe it lives in the ABCD world. Listen, I'll tell you something else, a story about Kandan, our family god.

Kandan and the Peacock

Kandan, who is sometimes called Murugan, was fighting a demon named Padmasuran. Just as the demon was about to be killed, it surrendered, worshiped Kandan, and changed into a peacock. Kandan made that peacock his chariot. They say that Kandan who fills the hearts of his devotees as he travels through the world has one problem. In the words of the proverb, 'No matter what advice you give him, Kandan's attention is always fixed between his thighs.' There are some people in the world today who dedicate their bodies, their possessions, and their souls to that place. They actually worship there. Even if you tell them this is folly millions and millions of times, they won't give up what they feel the urge to do.

But there is an inner meaning to Kandan's attention being focused there: Surar and Asurar are two sons of illusion, and Asurar is held captive between Kandan's thighs as a peacock. The divine king Kandan must always look down to that area where the peacock form and its demonic qualities might reveal themselves unexpectedly at any moment. When such a situation arises it is Kandan's duty to destroy the demon, and that's why he has to watch that place continually. We must understand this is his duty. Aside from all this, a demon born as a man always focuses on his base desires.

SANDAKUMARAN: Cousin, do you realize the mystery of male and female?

JUDGMENT: What's this cousin, everything that's come from you bears down into the seventh level of the earth. All right, if that's the way it is, how can we tell the difference between male and female?

SANDAKUMARAN: It must be seen by stroking and feeling—that's how the difference can be realized.

JUDGMENT: That's right, cousin, that's right; that's what people of the world say.

SANDAKUMARAN: Right, you believe what I say? Yes, yes, I'm telling you the truth. Listen to my story with great concentration. Earlier when she and I were talking, many forms appeared with indescribable noises, *kada, muda, tada, puda, kudu-kudu, vidu-vidu*. I was so afraid that my nerves trembled and my heart shook. I took to my heels, but they came at me from all four directions shouting, "Bloody. Hit him with stones! Hit him in the head!" Suddenly I took a rock, threw it at their heads, and felt a great sense of relief. I saw a stick, took it in both hands, and beat them to my heart's content.

But those who had received my favors caught me, tied me up and took the lady and me together in a ladapuda-mobile to Owl, the ABCD king. He said to the guards, "We'll see about him tomorrow. Throw him in a dark room for now." The guards immediately locked me in a dark room.

JUDGMENT: Now cousin, you said something like *kada muda*. What's that?

SANDAKUMARAN: That's what is called modern machinery. There are many classes and divisions of these machines, such as horseless carriage, car, van, bus, *pudu-pudu* cycle, *kuru-kuru* aeroplane, and the steam carriage. I'm told there are others like that. Listen, there really is more to my story.

Sandakumaran at the King's Court

As soon as dawn broke, the guards took the ABCD lady and myself to the king's presence. When he became aware of us, the king looked in my direction and said, "Right, bloody fool, come on!"

"O king, what are you talking about?" I asked.

"Shut up!" said the king and resumed the inquiry. Because the king couldn't see in the light, he touched me from head to foot and said, "You are a male, aren't you?" I laughed aloud. "Shut up! Shut up!" yelled the king.

When the guards caught me and started to tie me up again, I noticed someone there with human qualities. I looked at him and said, "Sir, they are saying something like 'Shut up! Shut up!' What's that?"

"That, my son, is the lusty demon, the ABCD language which has fascinated the modern world. It is the mantra which turns men into women and women into men. That is why the king touched you and asked if you are male or female. That, my child, is why it is such a suitable language for today's world. But never mind that for now. If you ask the king's pardon, he will change his mind and send you back to your own country."

When I heard that I said, "Pardon? Never! You want me to ask pardon from a king who is blind to the truth?" Then I sang this song.

SONG FOR THE POOR PEOPLE

Before 1940 civilization flourished,
Then military might came into the world,
Reason and wisdom vanished.
The modesty of women
And the good qualities of children vanished.
There was endless misery and destruction.

When women and children suffer,
Must they, too, beg for pardon?
Those who see this happening in the world will laugh,
Great wise beings in days gone by have said.
Punishment is the work of God,
The saints of the Himalayas have said.

He is the divine Being
Who does not ever close His eyes for even a moment.
He is the conquering grace without daybreak or dusk,
He is the conquering action, the good action,
He is all treasures.

Stay in this heart my son,
Stay in this incomparable patience,
In the One with the terrifying gaze
Of the deadly Bengal tiger.

When I finished my song, that good man looked at me and said, "In that case you can never escape. But if I teach you a trick, will you do it?"

"What is that trick, Sir? Please tell me right away."

"Well, if you rant and rave like a lunatic you can escape from this ABCD place, and I will say something appropriate to make sure that you are set free."

"Ah, do those who trust in God as their only help need to act like lunatics in this ABCD world? That would never happen where I come from," I said angrily, and then sang another song.

SANDAKUMARAN'S SONG

If you have God's qualities
And the grace of an enlightened Sheikh
Your heart will be exalted.

The world is worthless.
Your only wealth, your only grace
In this world and the next
Is perfect peace of mind.
What else could you need?

If you have God's qualities
And the grace of an enlightened Sheikh
Your heart will be exalted.

Precious Treasure, may my heart know you.
Loving His devotees is the height of joy.
A true man has no pride.
A true man who knows His bliss is God.

If you have God's qualities
And the grace of an enlightened Sheikh
Your heart will be exalted.

A true man contemplates God
In thought and dream,
Unaffected by worldly sorrow.
A true man reflects on the word of God,
And knows the truth
In his heart.

If you have God's qualities
And the grace of an enlightened Sheikh
Your heart will be exalted.

What is the cause of suffering?
Your mind engulfs you and gathers in sorrow.
You fail to understand this wisely
O man, and conclude
These must be the trials of God.
The sorrow and torment, the demons that attack
And bring turbulence to your life
Will be destroyed
When wisdom cuts the schemes of your mind.
What suffering can there be then?
Analyze this and examine yourself,

*Then you will know the state
Of being one with God.
What other bliss can there be
But this?*

"Then how will you escape?" he asked as soon as I finished singing.

"Everything happens as God wills," I said.

"In that case, shall I do something on my own?"

"That's up to you," I replied, and at this point the good man went away.

The following morning the inquiry was resumed in the king's court. "What is your name?" asked the king.

"My name is Sandakumaran," I replied, as the defendant.

"Do you admit your guilt?" continued the king.

At that moment the good man, who was actually Murugan, stood up and addressed the king, "My lord, this is the court of the king's justice where you have investigated many odd and peculiar cases and given judgment, but in this situation you must consider the circumstances fully before pronouncing your verdict.

Let me tell you a little about Sandakumaran who stands accused. Please listen to this attentively. Even though there are many, many wise men in the world, those who lack wisdom also live here. Even though some have studied countless books in the pursuit of wisdom, all those without the wisdom to apply what they have learned live here in this world too. But Sandakumaran is a gem in a garbage heap, a red lotus that blooms in the mud. Although he is poor he has integrity, good character, great wisdom, and has given devoted service to his native land where he is looked upon as a precious son. Any punishment you ordered would be mere dust to a person of such flawless character, so completely free of any wrongdoing. A prison cell would be a palace to while away his days. He is a blessed man who has offered his life for his country many times, and I saw myself that he was unaware of the treacherous things which happened on that day. Therefore, I ask on behalf of the people that this man be set free."

SANDAKUMARAN: The king set me free because of the words of that good man.

JUDGMENT: Whew cousin! What happened after that? Were you the only accused, or was the ABCD lady also accused?

SANDAKUMARAN: Just me, cousin, just me.

JUDGMENT: In that case, was there no punishment for her?

SANDAKUMARAN: Punishment? It doesn't exist in the ABCD world.

JUDGMENT: Why not?

SANDAKUMARAN: Everything is contained in the ABCD. So what punishment can there be?

JUDGMENT: *Aday,* cousin, I don't understand anything you say.

SANDAKUMARAN: You don't understand? Listen, I'll explain. There isn't even an atom of virtue, justice, reason, or duty in the ABCD world, no good conduct, no worship, not even an atom of respect for parents. The exalted behavior of men and women has flown away.

JUDGMENT: When did this start?

SANDAKUMARAN: When Kalian was born.

JUDGMENT: And how long has it been since he was born?

SANDAKUMARAN: All the characteristics of this Kali yuga have been accumulating and growing in strength since Kalian was born forty-seven-and-a-half million years ago. And now one thousand years have passed since a special intensifying of these evil qualities began, and another thousand are nearly done.

JUDGMENT: Ah cousin, when will the other thousand be finished?

SANDAKUMARAN: Ah, that's how it is. It's in a hurry.

JUDGMENT: What do you mean?

SANDAKUMARAN: It is very old and therefore it's tottering. Its teeth have fallen out, its mouth has fallen in, and because of that, months, weeks, days, man, goat, cow, woman, race, religion, fanaticism, wise counsel, good language, good speech, good Tamil are all trembling, *kuda-tada, lotta-lotta, koda-koda,* and tottering along on its last legs. It cries, "Heaven, O God, O light of gracious bliss, You created me. This present-day, crazy ABCD madness together with damaged brains tried to dig a hole and put all of us, including You, into it. O my Creator," it says with tears flowing endlessly like an ocean, "O my God, is this my final destiny or is there a little more time? I do not know." Weeping, filled with sorrow, Time sings this song.

TIME'S SONG

There are tens of millions in the world who do not know the Sheikh,
There are many beings whose good qualities are not clear,
None of them know grace.
They will cry and pray, but their minds
And hearts will be without love.

Many will cry, "O King!"
Some will act with the qualities of the deadly Bengal tiger.
Many will think, "I have crossed the line."
They will walk on everything and trample the heads of others.
Cursing the mother and father who cradled and protected them
They pay allegiance to their wives,
Anointing them with milk, curds, and ghee,
Creating yet another injury for their parents.
With sticks in their hands,
They walk on their parents' heads.

Thus Time sang, then raising both hands he said, "O God, You are the One who created us. O Father, You must come and protect us this day." He stood looking at the sky.

JUDGMENT: What was the fate of Time after that?

SANDAKUMARAN: His fate? Only God can save him now.

JUDGMENT: And if He doesn't?

SANDAKUMARAN: We are lost.

JUDGMENT: Cousin! Aren't you married?

SANDAKUMARAN? Cousin, that's exactly the story I'm telling you. Listen carefully.

Do Not Believe Fate is Our Master

O mind, do not believe fate is our master.
If the remembrance of God returns,
You will be so close to Him.

Do not believe wealth and world and status are permanent,
Do not believe life is permanent.

O mind, do not believe fate is our master.
If the remembrance of God returns,
You will be so close to Him.

Do not believe the body is immortal,
Do not believe your life is all that matters.
Be unattached to the body,
Be unattached to women.

O mind, do not believe fate is our master.
If the remembrance of God returns,
You will be so close to Him.

Do not believe your home and your family are permanent,
Do not believe your farms,
Livestock, and wives are permanent.

O mind, do not believe fate is our master.
If the remembrance of God returns,
You will be so close to Him.

Do not believe
Your parents, your loving children,
Or your landowner status
Are permanent.
Do not believe what is seen without wisdom.

O mind, do not believe fate is our master.
If the remembrance of God returns,
You will be so close to Him.

2

Sandakumaran Meets the Puluhans

The Prince of Peace meets Vandi Puluhan who is one with no faith in God, Kandi Puluhan whose work it is to disguise all the lies and deceit of the world with sweet words, and Sandi Puluhan who sucks away all the good things inside people and fills them up with evil. This family of evil realizes that a true man cannot be affected by their evil qualities.

The man who had saved me from jail took me home. Then someone else came along and spoke very pleasantly to me. Expecting him to be a good person I went over, spoke to him, and asked his name. When he said it was Vandi Puluhan, which means great big liar, I started to laugh.

VANDI PULUHAN: Why are you laughing?

SANDAKUMARAN: I'm laughing at your name.

VANDI PULUHAN: Little brother, you have never seen anyone like me in the twice seven or fourteen worlds, but those who love me, prosper. Those who don't love me have to live without rice to eat, without clothes to wear, without a place to stay, wandering and roaming from street to street. You don't seem to know this, but there is really and truly no place in this world for those who aren't my friends. Now, you look at *me* with amazement, but if you were to see my friend, your surprise would be unimaginable. He is ten times more skillful than I am. Even if you wanted to stay here he wouldn't let you. In any case, if you just looked at him you would be so frightened you couldn't stay in this land. Do you know his name?

SANDAKUMARAN: I don't, tell me what it is.

VANDI PULUHAN: His name is Kandi Puluhan which means boastful liar, my name is Vandi Puluhan, and his son's name is Sandi Puluhan, the strutting liar.

SANDAKUMARAN: My dear fellow, are there only three of you or are there others?

VANDI PULUHAN: There are many like me. I'll tell you about that later. Now I'll just tell you one of the many small stories which illustrate my talent. Listen attentively because there's no one in this world of illusion who is more ingenious than I am. Back in the days when I lived with name and fame, Kandi Puluhan sought me out when he heard of me and the glory I had won in this land. At that time I used to ride around the world on a chameleon in half a second. Holding onto the bridle I traveled at the speed of one-and-three-quarter demons per minute, striking the sixty-four elephants in their frenzy of must, biting the ninety-six lions, tearing up the four thousand, four hundred and forty-eight soldiers, and destroying the four wild monkeys. Once while crawling into the two hundred and forty-eight bones, the bridle of my chameleon broke.

SANDAKUMARAN: It broke? What happened then?

VANDI PULUHAN: I jumped immediately into the eight compass points and the sixteen intermediate points tying them all up. I crushed and crunched them shouting, "I'm going to end the world!" jumping head over heels, staring, rolling my eyes. Then my steed, orbiting the twice seven or fourteen worlds, caught a rat, bit a cat, tortured some ants, chewed on some beetles, swallowed snakes, inhaled chickens through his nose, drank the waters of the seven oceans, leaped on any animal in his path, caught, bit, chewed, swallowed, digested it, and belched with a crunching, rustling, chewing sound. He leaped among the spheres of the wind, the spheres of the clouds and the rains, the spheres of the moon and the sun asking, "Are there any enemies of my master here?" He leaped rolling his eyes, tossing his head and twisting his neck.
"Hey! Where are you going?" I called out. "Don't go. Stop!"
"In half a second I'll destroy all your enemies in this world," he shouted back crawling into the mouth of a frog. He plucked out the frog's intestines and then crept out through the top of its head. He destroyed and scattered idols and climbed into a cactus. Then I took the skin of a good man, cleverly made it into a bridle, put it on my chameleon, mounted it, and came home. Next I started preparing food for this creature. Sir, no one could gather enough food for him. Have you ever seen or even heard of a mount like that?

SANDAKUMARAN: Ah! I haven't seen or heard of one anywhere, any time. Only now, from you, do I hear talk of a chameleon mount. Well sir, what kind of food do you give this incredibly talented beast?

VANDI PULUHAN: Don't even ask about his food! Others may go on searching and searching until this world is destroyed, but I'm the only one who can find enough for it, and even I have a lot of trouble satisfying the beast. Only that God with no eyes understands my problems.

SANDAKUMARAN: Sir, what does he eat then?

VANDI PULUHAN: Listen, I'll tell you. He crawls into the body of a man, ascends to his head, creeps into the countless pores on the scalp, squeezes and bites him without squeezing him, then sucks and drinks his blood. Sometimes I catch a louse named Singa Bahu, split a hair into seven parts and use one section for a bridle, then I mount the louse and orbit the world. I creep into a jungle of beans, catch a poet who lives in a bean seed, and bring him back as food for my chameleon-vehicle. It was while I was feeding my mount this way I met Kandi Puluhan one day.

SANDAKUMARAN: Hold on my friend, let's examine your first story. Now I notice you spoke of the louse named Singa Bahu. What is the meaning of that? You said it crawled into the body, squeezed without squeezing, and drank. That is . . . . . ?

VANDI PULUHAN: O ho! Don't you understand that? Listen, I'll tell you. In our ABCD world we crawl into people like you. Through the five great sins we devastate their hearts, fragment their ability to judge and make their destiny play games with them. We break up marriages, destroy families, ruin their good qualities, destroy their *dharma,* obliterate their sense of duty, and ruin their *gnānam*. We torture their dignity, wipe out their modesty, bury their realizations, and root out their intellect. Know that of the five great sins, falsehood is the louse named Singa Bahu.

Listen Sandakumaran, I'll explain a few other things. That falsehood named Singa Bahu takes possession of everyone in our kingdom. When I say one hair is split seven ways, those are the seven hells. There are four of us who climb on that louse and make the true people of today's world wither away. We destroy them. There is so much more we do besides, Sandakumaran, do you understand? Anyhow, you could be that jungle poet of liberation I mentioned. Our job is to suck you dry.

SANDAKUMARAN: I understand, my friend, I understand. Your words are clever, but I doubt if there has ever been anyone like you before.

VANDI PULUHAN: Why do you say that?

SANDAKUMARAN: Because if people had ever boasted like you before, they would have died of it, and if you had known that you wouldn't have gone on boasting that way, but you keep boasting fearlessly, so they couldn't have died, and therefore there couldn't have been anyone like you before. You *are* a clever boaster!

VANDI PULUHAN: *Appa,* you're calling me clever boaster, clever Puluhan, but my name is Vandi Puluhan.

SANDAKUMARAN: O ho! Is that so? Then tell me the rest of the story.

Vandi Puluhan Meets Kandi Puluhan

Let me tell you. Now, as I was walking along afterwards I saw Kandi Puluhan. He had pulled up eighteen palm trees by the roots and twisted them together as a staff in his hand. He came towards me carrying seven mountains on his head, and just to see who he was, I crawled up into his rear-end, into his stomach, and up into his nose where I peeped out at him. Because it seemed to him that an ant had crawled into his nose he blocked off one nostril and sneezed so hard I was hurled seventy cubits down into the earth. While Kandi Puluhan was looking down at me and thinking, "What's this, can a little bug be so skillful?" I jumped into his mouth, bored through his skull, and moved into his brain. Kandi Puluhan reflected with confusion to himself, "Hmm! Who in this world is cleverer than I? I can't do anything, my head is heavy, my brains are scrambled." Then he asked, "Who are you?"

I said, "I'm Vandi Puluhan. Who are you?"

"My name is Kandi Puluhan. Hey, are you greater than I am?"

"Hey, when you know the state I live in, you'll know."

"Hey, lunatic! Don't you know me? I pulled up the eighteen *purānas* by the root, and twisted them together for a staff. I'm the clever one who swallowed the eight heavens while carrying the seven hells on my head. You paltry little ant, do you presume to speak to me as though you were my equal?"

So I said, "You! You may very well swallow the eight heavens, the seven hells, and the eighteen *purānas,* but I can swallow your head! Listen, I'll tell you how clever *I* am. I have the ability to be both inside and outside all the worlds at the same time, I ride on illusion at the speed of an ass, I beat up the sixty-four arts and sciences, pummel the arrogance of an elephant in must, bite the ninety-six powers, and rip open the four thousand, four hundred and forty-eight diseases. I annihilate the four monkeys of the mind, break open divine analytic wisdom, and shatter the inner meanings of the six corners. I eradicate the three hundred and thirty million heavenly beings and make the ABCD world quake. There are many more things I do. You're a little boy, have you really come to compete with me? Just wait and see what I'm going to do to you."

All this really scared Kandi Puluhan. His judgment was so hypnotized by my lying nonsense he decided it would be a good idea to go along with me somehow. So he said, "Hey, older brother, from now on let's the two of us be loving friends."

VANDI PULUHAN: I immediately agreed.

SANDAKUMARAN: You agreed too? What happened after that?

VANDI PULUHAN: Well I left his brain, came out through his eyes, and made friends with him. He invited me home for dinner.

SANDAKUMARAN: Then what happened?

When I went to Kandi Puluhan's house I noticed some very valuable things there, and immediately decided to steal them. Keeping him engaged in conversation, I stealthily took a box of jewels and tied it to my belly without his noticing it.

Kandi Puluhan said to his wife, "Cook a variety of good food for my elder brother Vandi Puluhan, and we'll rest a while in the garden before we come back to eat." Then he took me along to the part of the garden where the coconut palms grew and said, "Elder brother, stand under this tree a minute while I climb up and pick two juicy coconuts." But before he could even get up that one tree I climbed fifty others, drank all the coconut milk, ate all the coconuts, piled all the shells in one place, and came back to stand at the same tree trunk. He didn't know I had done any of this, so when he came back down with the two young coconuts and saw the piled up shells, he was a little embarrassed and stood there without saying anything for a while.

Then he said, "Elder brother, these coconut shells weren't here when I climbed this tree. Who picked them? Well," he continued, "It's all right, it doesn't matter, we'll let it go. Now drink this," and he cut the young coconuts and gave them to me. As I took them and raised my head to drink, Kandi Puluhan recovered the box I had tied around my belly. Then we both went back to his house. He told me to sit on the verandah while he went inside. In a flash I jumped to the roof, split it open, and hanging upside down, I watched Kandi Puluhan poke around in the kitchen hearth, put the box inside, cover it with ashes, and go back out. As quick as lightning I jumped down there without anyone seeing me, seized the box hidden in the fireplace, tied it around my waist again, and came back to the verandah.

Now his attention was caught by the expression on my face; he suspected me again and went to look for the box. When he discovered it wasn't there he came back. "Elder brother, come, let's eat," he called to me, and he told his wife to bring some water. When she brought it he offered it for my hands, and as I reached out to accept it Kandi Puluhan snatched the box tied around my belly and showed it to me asking, "Elder brother, this is mine, isn't it?"

"O ho!" I said, "Is that so? That's good." When we both finished eating I asked, "Little brother, what is your wife's name?"

"Elder brother, I have had two wives. My first wife's name was The Light That Leaps From The Eyes. I had many, many difficulties after I married her, and when I finally didn't even have enough money to buy porridge, I said to her with disgust, 'Since the day I joined up with you, all these difficulties have befallen me.' I chased her out of my sight, and she went back where she came from. Then I married my present wife. She is mistress to five people and her name is Maya or illusion.''

SANDAKUMARAN: A ha! Is Kandi Puluhan so clever? All right, go on, tell his story.

VANDI PULUHAN: All right, all right. Here it is.

Now I studied him and asked, "Little brother, you are so talented, do you have any children?"

"I do, brother, I do, but how can I ever begin to tell you about that?"

"With parents as talented as you two, your children must be prodigies."

"Yes, elder brother," he said, "I have one baby, and he's really something! Listen, I'll tell you a little about him. My baby has teeth like red flowers, his body hairs are like palmyra flowers, and his hands are like coconut trees."

"Little brother, with a shape like that, what color is this baby of yours?"

Kandi Puluhan said, "Blacker than a crow, well beyond a crow, he is the color of a curry pot burned for seven years on the stove. In fact, if you compared the two of them, the pot would lose."

"Little brother, what name have you given to this beautiful baby?"

"Vandi Puluhan, I searched all over the world for an astrologer to give my baby a name, but no one could give him a suitable one, and so I returned without knowing what to do. When I came home I noticed a coconut near my son. When my wife split it open, she saw there was nothing there, the shell was intact but he had sucked and eaten the pulp. While she tried to figure out how this could have happened, my son announced, 'I did it!' After considering all this carefully, I named him The Boy Who Eats The Flesh Of The Fruit But Leaves The Skin Intact.

When he was sixteen years old we went to the forest to cut down trees for a house. I had brought along a pot of porridge to eat at mid-day, hung it high in a tree, and then began to chop down trees, instructing my son to take the cut ones home. At one point he left some of the trees half-way and came back. 'Father,' he said, 'I'm hungry. Give me some porridge.'

'Please be patient for a little while, son,' I replied, 'We'll have the porridge when we've cut down five more trees.' Without listening to me he went to the tree where the porridge pot was hanging, broke it with a stone, opened his mouth to the flow, and gobbled it all up.

When I had finished cutting down the five trees I went over there and called to my son, 'Get the pot of porridge down and we'll eat it.' When he climbed up the tree and brought it down I saw there was nothing in it. 'Where is the porridge?' I asked.

'I didn't do it, my name did,' he replied.

Then I got angry at him, 'Idiot!' I scolded as he sat down sorrowfully.

He looked up at me, 'Father, where does this river go?'

Still furious, I exploded, 'It goes right to the middle of your house!'

So he dragged the chopped trees to the river and pushed them in, but I didn't know that. When we were dragging the two remaining trees out of the forest, I asked, 'Son, you really did take the trees to the house, didn't you?'

He said, 'By now, the river has taken them right into the house.'

I was about to ask how when he repeated, 'You said the river would take them right into the house.'

Immediately I became even angrier and tied him to the two trees. 'You should go right into the house with the river too,' I said as I dragged and pushed him in. And so he went with the river. Eighteen years later he came back and described his exploits. This is the story he told."

Sandi Puluhan's Story

As I was floating along the river tied to the trees I kept shouting, "I'll do the work of four people, but eat the food of only two!"

Some men who were watering banana trees heard my cries, pulled me out, untied the ropes, and took me with them. "Will you do any kind of work?" they asked.

"I'll do the work of four people, but eat the food of only two," I repeated.

"Then can you irrigate a banana plantation?" they asked.

"Yes, I can do that."

They immediately fed me enough food for two people and then asked, "What is your name?"

"My name is The Boy Who Eats The Flesh Of The Fruit But Leaves The Skin Intact."

Then they took me to the banana plantation, told me to water the trees, and left. At the plantation the bananas were just ripe. I ate them all, put stones and mud where the fruit had been, and closed up the peels. The next day the workers came, cut the bananas, and took them to market. As the bananas were being sold the people who bought the first few bunches found the stones and mud inside, and they all ganged up on the banana vendors, beat them and chased them away. Bruised and humiliated, they examined the remaining fruit and discovered the stones and mud, then stormed back to the plantation demanding to know who was responsible.

"I didn't do it, my name did it," I replied.

They were so angry they tied me to the trees again and put me back on the river.

While the river carried me along I called out as before, "I'll do the work of four people, but eat the food of only two!" Then some people who were guarding freshly harvested rice untied me and took me in.

"Can you stay and do the work here?" they asked.

"Whatever you like. It's all the same to me," I drawled. "But my last employers felt no one would ever tolerate me as they did. So I doubt whether you will keep me for long."

"Never mind those crazy fools, we won't treat you that way—you don't need to worry. What's your name?" they asked.

"The Boy Who Burns The Sheaves And Eats The Puffed Rice," I replied.

They left me to guard the sheaves while they went home to bring me some food. After I had eaten they said, "*Appa,* there are many thieves in our village. Guard the harvest carefully," and they went away.

I looked at once for a flint and a stone and set fire to the sheaves. As the rice was burning, some of the grains began to pop and I ran around very nimbly catching the puffed rice before it hit the ground. I ate it all.

At that moment the farmers who had seen the fire came running, shouting, "How did this happen?" and they beat me with sticks to their heart's content, but even though the blows were fierce they didn't hurt me. They were as minute as mosquito bites, and I whiled away the time eating popped rice. After that they all got together, tied me up as before and pushed me back into the river.

"I'll do the work of four people, but eat the food of only two!" I sang out going down the river once again. A launderer and a laundress were washing clothes in the river, and when they heard my words, they untied me, and took me home with them. On our way the washerwoman asked, "What's your name?"

"My name is He Came The Way He Came," I said.

At their house they served me food, and as I was eating the husband asked, "What's your name?"

"He Went The Way He Went," I said.

They kept me in their home for a week, showing me the places where the washed clothes were to be delivered. Then they gave me a month's clean wash and told me to deliver it. I tied all the clothes into a bundle and left forever.

After a while their customers came to ask for their clothes, and the washerman said, "I sent my servant to deliver them to you." So his customers went to the headman of that village, told him what had happened, and demanded the return of their clothes. The headman summoned the launderer and ordered him to give back the clothing. "I gave their clean clothes to my servant and sent him out to deliver them," he explained.

"If you don't return the clothes in eight days I will have you executed," said the headman severely.

Immediately the washerman set out in search of He Went The Way He Went. At first everyone helped, but they had so much trouble they finally all gave up, and then the launderer went off in one direction and the laundress in another. The washerman searched calling, "He Went The Way He Went!"

The washerwoman, in another place, searched calling, "He Came The Way He Came!"

The washerman ran to his wife at once, "Has he come? Where is he?" and since I wasn't there, of course, he beat her soundly. The washerman went on searching and calling, "He Went The Way He Went!"

The laundress went on searching and calling, "He Came The Way He Came!"

Hearing her words the husband came running back. "Where is he?" he asked his wife. "He came?" When his wife didn't answer he seized a cudgel and beat her on the head. She couldn't take the beating and died, and when the headman learned of this, he caught the launderer and had him executed.

"Now I, The Boy Who Eats The Flesh Of The Fruit But Leaves The Skin Intact, sold the clothes to a store, bought this horse with the money and came here, Father," he said.

"As my son was telling his story I glanced at his horse. He saw me looking at it and said, 'This horse is an unusual one. It drops golden dung.' Without my knowing it he had stuffed gold pieces up the horse's rear-end, then mixed millet with hay and crammed it in after the gold. As I went up to look, he pulled out the straw and millet mixture, and gold pieces suddenly fell from its behind.

When I saw this I was astounded. 'Son,' I said, 'I've never seen anyone like you,' and sang this song in his praise."

KANDI PULUHAN'S SONG

O my splendid son who excels in deception,
Treachery and unpraiseworthy actions,
O my splendid son who roams the world,
I, your father, look at this carefully,
And see that you are without wisdom,
That you go your own way without listening to me,
In this world encircled by water.
What difference does it make whether
This horse drops dung or gold?

What difference does it make that
This horse is reputed to drop gold?
O my God, O my God,
What are these evil words
Which seem like good actions, O God?
These evil words
Which seem like good actions, O God?
They have done all these things,
But they have not known God's wealth.
There is nothing in the dark and muddy heart
Which God does not know.
He will conquer, He will conquer.

"That's what I sang, and when I finished I said, 'Hey son, you've fooled me, and you've fooled the ABCD world, but listen, I'll tell you something. There is a God who rules and watches you and me and this earthly world.'"

KANDI PULUHAN'S SONG

He can transcend judgment, He can kill destiny,
He has no mouth,
Such is the meaning of His glorious name.
He is the form of bliss,
His beauty is infinite, inconceivable.
He is the mighty One who nourishes all lives,
The One we call divine Guide,
His name is God, the compassionate Lord, jeweled light of my eyes.

Then Vandi Puluhan said to Kandi Puluhan, "Little brother, your son is even more brilliant than you are. What happened to him after that?"

"Well, I told him if he could find the omnipresent, eternal One and conquer Him, then I'd know I have an unparalleled son, and be very happy indeed. I sent him away that very day. As he left he promised, 'No matter where He is, I will catch Him, pack Him up within the nine plus three equals twelve, bring Him along completely helpless, and show Him to you.' He's been gone a long time, but nothing has happened yet. And that's my son's story."

SANDAKUMARAN: Sir, Vandi Puluhan, you're so clever, what do *you* do?

VANDI PULUHAN: Sir, we work deception and trickery. Sandakumaran, Prince of Peace, you do seem to be good. You help others, you have absolute faith that there is one God, and for that reason we can't get our hooks into you. You will never be enmeshed in our ways, and furthermore, no matter how cleverly we present our ingenious path you will never be deceived. Although our strength is great indeed, we can't lead you astray and we can't attract you.

SANDAKUMARAN: What you say is true enough, but what do you think you can ever do to the devotees of God with your materialism and your strength? Anyhow, speak on and we'll see.

VANDI PULUHAN: Sandakumaran, I'll tell you about our materialism. We'll do our utmost in every clever way we have to deceive you, drag you along and crush you—you and people like you. And how will we do that? We have mantras to humiliate and disgrace people like you, we'll stroll and wander through this world, inside and out, turning it upside down through those who do submit to us. And remember, our master Satan will also make those who don't submit suffer too! He's taught the ten of us a story I can tell you.

The Story of the Prophet Job ☮

Job, may God's peace be with him, had the understanding and the wisdom of a great sage. His father was the richest man in the kingdom of Sham, not only in money and treasure, but in land, goats, cattle, camels, and mules. When he was a mere thirty years old his father died, and Job ☮ inherited the money, the livestock, and all the property.

Now, Abarayam had a daughter named Rahmat who lived with him in the kingdom of Canaan. He loved her very much. One night Abarayam dreamed of Joseph, may God's peace be with him. In the dream Joseph ☮ took off his shirt and dressed Rahmat with it saying, "Rahmat, I have given you my clarity and my beauty." As Rahmat grew up her beauty equalled her grandfather Joseph's ☮, she worshiped God, and did not care for this earthly world.

When Job ☮ heard descriptions of the beauty which had been given to her, he wanted to marry her, and went to the kingdom of Canaan with large quantities of money and presents to ask for her as his wife. Upon his arrival there he spoke to Rahmat's father about marrying her. Abarayam considered Job's ☮ faith in God, his prayers, his wealth, and let the marriage take place. Then Job ☮ took Rahmat back to his own country. *Allāhu ta'ālā* ☮, God Almighty, gave them twelve pairs of twins, one boy and one girl in each of twelve pregnancies.

Later God sent Job ☮ as a *rasūl*, a prophet, to the people who lived in the city of Kurvan, which is also known as Caypuniya. When men looked at the good qualities and the blessings which *Allāhu ta'ālā* ﷻ had given Job ﷺ, no one disbelieved his teachings. Because of his exaltedness and the exaltedness of Rahmat's grandfather, they accepted his beliefs and became his followers. Job ﷺ taught them God's truth and helped them build a prayer house. When night came he and those around him gathered in the mosque and prayed, and through his devotion the people learned to ask God for all they wanted. At the prayer time before daybreak and at nightfall he had his people cook food, and before every meal he fed devotees of God and the poor. He gave away a fortune in charity.

He was a gracious father to orphaned children, a compassionate brother to the widows he helped, and a loving friend to those without money. He was very generous and helpful to his farm workers. Even when others came and ate the food grown on his farm, he said they were not to be chased away. There was plenty to eat for passing flocks of birds, large and small, his own herds, and wild animals too. The wealth that *Allāhu ta'ālā* ﷻ had given him, the bounty of that wealth, and the produce increased by day and by night. His crops and fruit trees yielded twice a year. He had a thousand mares, a thousand stallions, a thousand mules, three thousand male camels, five thousand female camels, a thousand bulls, a thousand cows, and ten thousand goats. Every year without fail one, two, or three young were born to each goat, cow, camel, horse and all the other livestock. To care for the animals he had one shepherd for every fifty animals. The shepherds and their wives and children were all his devoted slaves.

The *shaitān* known as Iblīs or Satan looked at the wealth of Job ﷺ which had all been stamped with the seal of God's grace, God who is known as *Haqq*, the Truth. It had all been made perfectly pure by charity. Satan wanted to trap Job ﷺ and destroy him, but this treacherous, deceitful creature had no power over him.

In that age Iblīs could ascend all the way to the seventh heaven. When *Allāhu ta'ālā* ﷻ brought Jesus, may God's peace be with him, to the fourth heaven Satan was banished from there, and he was able to climb to and from the third heaven only. Then when *Allāhu ta'ālā* ﷻ called the great prophet Muhammad, God's blessing and peace be with him, to *Mi'rāj* He forbade Iblīs to ascend to any of the heavens, and after that all he could do was eavesdrop on the angels' talk at the edge of the first heaven. Man found it easier to change after his banishment from heaven. In Job's ﷺ time, however, Iblīs had a secret which allowed him to go up and down among the heavens.

Allāhu Subhānahu ta'ālā ﷻ asked Satan, "*Aday* despoiler of the path, what is your intention? How did you get here?"

Iblīs answered, "O my God, I circled the whole world to wreak havoc on the path of those who follow You. Although I could not destroy those who worship You purely or those who pray with unwavering hearts, I made everyone else crazy.''

The voice of *Allāhu ta'ālā* spoke, ''Ha *mal'ūn*, you do not know My faithful disciple Job. He will live a long time, and he cannot be moved, he cannot be shaken by you. Do you really think you have the power to make him leave My path, to turn him around and make him follow you?''

To that question Iblīs replied, ''O my Lord, You have established him with righteousness, Your angels pray on his behalf, You have made him happy by rewarding his actions with Your riches, You have given him incomparable wealth, and so he prays to You, but if You test him with difficulties and suffering he won't follow You as he does now. If You will give me permission to take his wealth, he won't follow You and he won't obey You, he will forget You.''

Then the voice of *Allāhu ta'ālā* came again, ''Eh *mal'ūn*, you liar, you do not have the power to turn him to your ruinous path, and you must learn this. Therefore, I will release his wealth to you.''

Then Iblīs came to stand on an impure, black rock, sat in the impure water which oozed from it, and shouted once. All the *shaitāns* came together, all the *shaitāns* from the place where the dawn breaks to the place where the sun sets gathered around him and asked, ''What awful thing has happened? Why did you shout like that?''

''An opportunity that hasn't been offered since the time I had sent Adam out of heaven has been made available to me now,'' Iblīs said. ''I have been given control of Job's money, his wealth, and his livestock.''

Then one of the *shaitāns* said, ''Let me take charge of the trees in his orchard and I will burn them to ash.'' Iblīs gave him his permission.

And then another *shaitān* said, ''Put me in control of his animals. With one shout I will frighten the life out of their bodies.'' Iblīs gave him that responsibility.

And so one *shaitān* crept into Job's orchard and burned the trees and all the fruit to ash. The other *shaitān* crept into the livestock, made a noise, and all the animals and the shepherds who tended them died. The people of the countryside saw the cruel, hot smoke.

Afterwards, Iblīs came to Job in the form of a shepherd and said, ''Job, look at me. All the animals and all the shepherds except for me were consumed in a fire, and that fire turned my face black. First the fire and smoke descended from heaven, then a sound came from the sky and it seemed that *Allāhu ta'ālā's* face spoke, 'This is the reward for those who do service to man for appearance's sake.'''

Although Job heard what Iblīs said, he went on praying with added faith. Instead of giving him an answer, he offered praise to Allah.

When the prayer was finished Job looked at Iblīs who had appeared as the shepherd, "What are you talking about?" he asked. "The camels, the goats, the cattle, the donkeys, the horses, and shepherds all belong to *Allāhu ta'ālā*, not to me. He treats His possessions as He wills."

Then Iblīs had to reply, "What you said is true."

People began talking among themselves muttering, "If Job had been doing his duty properly and acting with true charity, *Allāhu ta'ālā* would have taken the lives of the dead in a beautiful way, but He has taken them in anger."

Job heard this with a troubled heart, nevertheless, without replying to their charges he put his faith in the law of *Allāhu ta'ālā* saying only, "*Al-hamdu lillāh*, we offer all our prayers to God alone."

Then Job considered Iblīs, "Ah, you no longer have God's blessing. *Allāhu ta'ālā* has thrown you out, so leave me and go far away. Go! Go away, far away! You have been disgraced, you can never be praised, you treacherous creature."

Satan said, "God told me if I tried to lead good people, people with faith in God, *gnānis*, virtuous women, or just kings astray, I would not succeed. God said this would happen and now the truth is out. You are right to blame me for the slanderous words I spoke about you and your possessions when I said you do service expecting favors."

Then Job began to pray again. Shamefaced, Iblīs ascended to his own part of the heavens and stayed where he belonged.

Then the sound of *Allāhu ta'ālā* came again, "Degenerate one, despoiler of the path, how do you find My disciple Job? Do you see that he is not in the least concerned even though his possessions, his orchards, animals, and shepherds are lost? Such incalculable wealth has disappeared that his relations are calling his charity and his duty false! Yet he is forbearant with them, and his only intention is to worship Me. Have you seen how he praises Me even under these circumstances? What he said is a disgrace to you."

Iblīs tried again, "O my God, he is not in the least concerned about his belongings, but he is very possessive about his children. Mankind has a great desire for children and a powerful attachment to them. He has been given many children whom he delights in looking after. He has sufficient material wealth and lives with the faith he can acquire more through his children, but if you turn me loose on them, I will make him stop worshiping You and lead him to my ruinous path," said Satan.

But a sound came from God, "*Aday* despoiler, is one disgrace not enough for you? To make certain you will be known as a liar, I hereby give his children to you, but be assured that he will never follow you."

Satan heard this and came to the palace where Job's children lived. He summoned all his followers and they shook the palace. As it cracked parts of it fell on some of the children and killed them. The others he cut up and threw down at a place called Aituli.

God commanded the earth, "Cherish the children of Job. Do not consume the skin, the bones, or the tissues of the dead children." And the earth preserved them as He commanded.

And then Iblīs set to work on Job's ☪ body, causing incredible damage. He raised countless sores all over his body and placed a worm in each of the sores. But if one of the worms fell off Job ☪ would pick it up and put it back saying God had given them his body as their food. And then Satan chased him out of that land, separated him from his relations, made his beautiful, chaste wife cut off her hair, give it away, and work as a laborer. He destroyed all Job's ☪ possessions, his health, his children, his beautiful palaces, his houses in the country, his goats, his cows, his camels, mules, and horses. To the greatest possible extent, he made evil without end fall upon him, but Job ☪ was not in the least disheartened. There was not one second in his life when he didn't praise God.

Then Satan had to admit to Job ☪ he was defeated, "I swore to God that I would lead you astray, that I would ruin you, but now that I've been beaten I cannot face that all mighty, omnipresent God."

Then the sound of God came, "*Aday* Iblīs, you said My disciple would fall under your control, but what have you managed to accomplish? You caused such unimaginable suffering! How you tortured the goats and the cattle! You did so much damage, but what could you do to My disciple? Now who has won, who has lost?" God asked many other questions in a sound that manifested His grace, and Saneeswaran, who was Iblīs, just had to stand there with his head bowed in shame. The primal, all-pervasive One continued, "Why are you standing there without speaking? Answer My questions! Where is your integrity?"

Iblīs, weeping, and with great sorrow begged God, "I have lost. Grant me the grace of Your forgiveness. O God, I have realized today that I cannot do anything to Your true disciples. Now I know this. O my God, You must forgive me with Your grace. I will never do anything like this to Your disciples again."

"O you Iblīs, from now on do not touch My followers," said God. He had Iblīs mocked in many, many ways, and chased him even further away.

Then God gave back Job's ☪ children, his livestock, his goats, cattle, everything taken from him earlier, and Job ☪ ruled that city again in happiness.

And Iblīs, who is also called Satan and Saneeswaran, spoke to his own followers, "I was terribly embarrassed by this and hung my head in shame. It is, indeed, very rare to conquer His true devotees. Now I have told you something about Job's story, but I can't begin to tell you all the indignities I suffered because of him. Today even if ten of us team up together we cannot approach true *gnānis,* men and women of integrity, chaste women, or God's disciples, and if we persist, our strength is so drained we cannot possibly overcome them."

VANDI PULUHAN: This is what our master Iblīs said, this is the way our master taught us that story. And therefore, no matter how skillfully we do indeed speak to people of integrity like you, you'll never fall into our hands. Even if we try to win you over, we don't have enough power to succeed.

SANDAKUMARAN: But you're a very skillful fellow, why can't you conquer me?

VANDI PULUHAN: We have strength, skill, and bravery, we have ninety-six battalions, but we don't have the power to win over a true disciple like you. And if we waste our time in all this vain argument with you, our work will go to ruin. You see to your work, my friend, and we'll see to ours, all right?

Then Vandi Puluhan and Kandi Puluhan wandered through many cities and countries until they came to a mountain.

The One God Prayer

He exists as the beginning of light,
The beginningless beginning,
The undivided bliss of completeness,
As the light, as the light of the flame,
As the limitless treasure of purity,
As justice, the eternal One, the One without fault,
The One within who explains, who understands,
The only grace which helps to sing this song
Of Allah, exalted is His glory.

The One without the eight,
The One without the two,
The One who cannot be contained in words,
The One without limit,
The One without comparison,
The One without the form of man,
The One without blood ties,
The One without attachments,
The One who needs neither food nor sleep,
The One real treasure who protects without forsaking us,
Allah, exalted is His glory.

The One without eyes,
The One without ears,
The One without song or speech,
The One without sky,
The One without earth,
The One without scriptures,
The One who was then,
The One who is now,
The One with limitless facets,
O God, forever the One who is reality,
Allah, exalted is His glory.

3

Sandakumaran's Mission

The Puluhans meet Mutavalli, a beautiful, chaste woman who tells them of Sandakumaran's mission of giving comfort to and ending the suffering of others in the ABCD world.

Up the mountain, Vandi Puluhan and Kandi Puluhan saw palms, bananas, coconuts, and many trees with edible fruit all growing close together. When the coconuts matured they would clash and bump against each other, then shower to the ground. Male monkeys would take fruit to the females, and they would scatter it about to make the males beg. Jungle mystics performed miracles with their occult powers there on the mountain. Springs of sweet honey cascaded like waves from the skies, and the red rays of the sun flashed on the waterfalls at daybreak and sunset. People living in the forest could call celestial beings with gestures. There was one with matted locks adorned by the crescent moon who would appear there. On that mountain the rivers flowed like molten silver, and there was a well surrounded by springs of milk, buttermilk, ghee, honey, and ambrosia. A throne and a decorated divan were set next to this well.

Both Puluhans ate the fruit and drank the water. While they were drinking from the well they saw another chain inside and pulled on it. As they pulled, they drew up a chest which was hanging from it. When they opened the chest and looked in, they saw a woman with the beauty of the sun and the moon. As they stared at her they were so enamored they began to fight and pull the woman, each one saying, "Mine!" "No, she's mine!" She tried to pacify them, but they wouldn't listen.

MUTAVALLI: Are you human beings or are you demons hacking the world to bits?

VANDI PULUHAN AND KANDI PULUHAN: Why do you say that, my lady?

MUTAVALLI: You are tugging at another man's betrothed in such an insolent manner, without the slightest compunction, without proper conduct. Are there really disgraceful beasts like you still roaming this world? Haven't you all been destroyed yet?

VANDI PULUHAN: My lady, apparently you don't know who we are. We are the ones you just named—we are demons who torment only good people, we turn them upside down, spinning and turning and hacking their world to little bits.

MUTAVALLI: You cowardly demons disguised with human faces, born into the world without any awareness of mercy, compassion, grace, tranquillity, balance, honesty, justice, patience, or duty, listen very carefully, I'm going to tell you a story!

VANDI PULUHAN: My lady, of course we don't have any of those qualities!

MUTAVALLI: *Aday* you sinners, may you be destroyed instantly!

VANDI PULUHAN: If all ten of us were destroyed, it would be easy to distinguish the good from the bad, and then this world would shine with justice. But even if the world should end, we would not end. Understand please, that our strength is greater than that. But who do you think you are, preaching to us like that? What's your name?

THE WOMAN: My name is Mutavalli or full moon.

VANDI PULUHAN: O ho! Your very name explains your beauty. Well then my lady, please tell us your story.

Mutavalli's Story

There was a city known as Mayajala, or the city of magic tricks and illusion. In that city was a young woman whose name was Manonmani which means the jewel of the heart, the soul. Her radiant beauty outshone the dancing lights of the setting sun, and the lotus in the pond closed with shame when it saw her face. The moon saw her beauty and had to hide with embarrassment in the hills and the sky. When the fish in the seas saw the loveliness of her eyes they also ran away to hide their confusion in deep waters. God must have been testing His ability when He created her. Many princes heard of her beauty and competed with each other for her hand in marriage.

To all those who came Manonmani said, "It does not matter whether those who want to marry me are rich or poor, mendicants or kings. I will only marry the man who knows the answer to the riddle I have. Here it is: 'Happiness before you see it. Sorrow after you see it and experience it.' Whoever finds the answer and explains it to me will be my husband." There were many who underwent great difficulty trying to solve this riddle, most were unable to understand it, and for the ten million who understood but were afraid, there were tens and tens of millions who wandered and roamed to find the answer.

At that time Sandakumaran, the Prince of Peace, was a wandering mendicant in the city of Tarumapupadi, the kingdom of heaven. Elsewhere there was a girl who loved him dearly. One day when she was praying to God in a heart that was bound to Him through constant meditation, a Sufi Master known as Anaday Atcharam, divine luminous wisdom, appeared before her.

The Sufi Master spoke to her and said, "May your prayers be answered, my child. What favor do you seek?"

The girl paid obeisance to the Master and replied, "If I marry, my husband must have the compassionate qualities of non-violence and righteousness. We must live together for many, many years."

He replied, "May it be so."

"Master, where can this man be found, what is his name?"

"He is from the city of Tarumapupadi, and his name is Sandakumaran, the Prince of Peace."

"Master, where is he now?" the girl asked with great eagerness.

"He has gone to the ABCD world to study its splendor and its secrets. When he has learned certain things there he will return to find you."

Paying obeisance to the Master she asked, "Can you let me see him just once?" And so the Sufi Master put the girl to sleep and showed him to her in a dream. She looked long at Sandakumaran, the Prince of Peace, and she fell in love.

Later, when she was conscious again, the Master asked, "Did you see Sandakumaran?"

"Yes, Master, I saw him, but when will I meet him?"

"My daughter listen, I will tell you something about him. A certain girl named Manonmani has laid down a condition to be fulfilled before she will marry. The man she marries must find the answer to a riddle she has posed, and no one has done that yet. But a wandering pilgrim whose name is Fate pines for her, and Sandakumaran has gone to help him find the answer to that puzzle. This is Sandakumaran's story."

Now the girl said, "Master, I am a woman, how can I live alone in the forest? I have no one but you to help me, Master."

"My daughter, you need not be afraid. I will see that no danger befalls you." The Sufi Master materialized an orchard in that place with different kinds of trees and a well. He put the girl into a box, fastened a chain to it, and lowered the box down the well. "Daughter, you must stay in the box all day, but at night you may go into the orchard."

MUTAVALLI: So saying, he left me and went away. While I was living that way you two came along, lifted me out of the well and thoroughly humiliated me.

VANDI PULUHAN: My lady, you spoke about a Sufi Master. Do such holy men really exist in the world today? Is there anyone at all who still pronounces God's name?

MUTAVALLI: You sinners! There are many worthy sheikhs of integrity who know the truth, and once you two have been destroyed the people in this world will live happily. My Sufi Master told me the story I've been telling you, and he is also the one who created this orchard and made all the other decorations here.

VANDI PULUHAN: All right, in that case, please tell us Manonmani's story.

Manonmani's Story

While Manonmani, the jewel of the heart, lived as I described before, a man named Fate in the country called Destiny heard about her beauty and her good qualities, and fell in love with her. He was so lost in his desire for her that he went to Mayajala to see her. When he arrived at the king's palace he saw a proclamation on the gate.

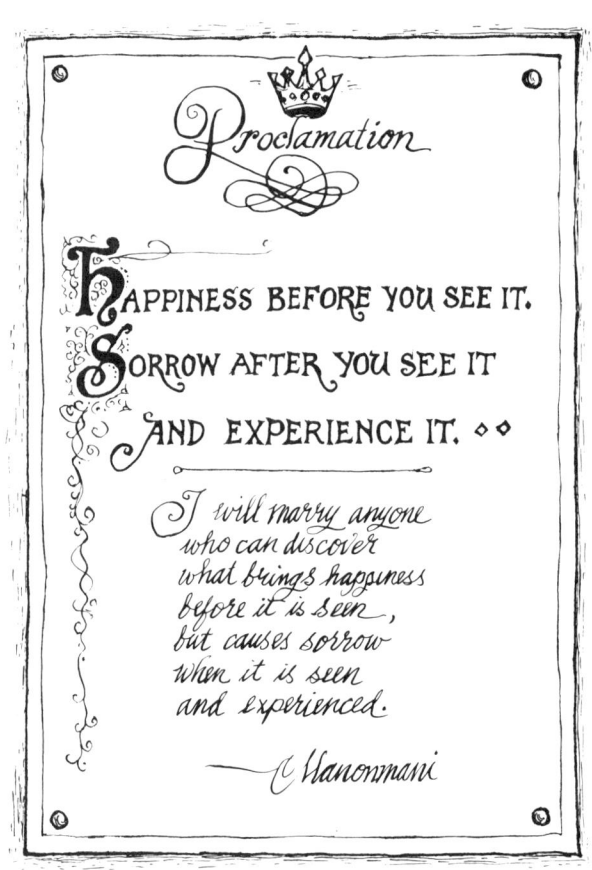

Fate saw this proclamation announcing that whoever wanted to marry Manonmani would have to solve the riddle. He worried so much about how he was going to do this, he fainted. Just then Manonmani's handmaiden came along, picked him up, splashed water on him, and brought him out of his faint.

"What happened?" she asked.

Fate answered, "I heard of the beauty and glory of Manonmani, the jewel of the heart, fell in love with her and came here to marry her, but when I saw the proclamation and realized I didn't know the answer, I fell down in a faint."

The handmaiden listened to him and exclaimed, "Now Sir, why are you being so silly? If you don't understand the meaning of the riddle, you have no chance whatsoever with Manonmani." Having given him this advice, she went away.

Then poor Fate wandered through the jungle, through mountains and deserts without food or water until, finally, he collapsed, rolling on the ground, and sang this song weeping in despair.

FATE'S SONG

Some in the world praise God,
The triple flame, alif, lām, mīm,
In their hearts.

Many give their hearts
To earthly things.

Some in the world praise God,
The triple flame, alif, lām, mīm,
In their hearts.

There are many more
Who dedicate body and soul
To women.

Some in the world praise God,
The triple flame, alif, lām, mīm,
In their hearts.

There are millions
Who worship
The earth,

But there are millions and millions more
Who are fascinated and deceived,
Who are robbed of their hearts
By the illusions before their eyes.

Some in the world praise God,
The triple flame, alif, lām, mīm,
In their hearts.

We rub holy ash on our body
Without any clear realization
In our mind or heart.
We rub stripes of holy ash
All over our body.
There are many millions like that
In this desolate world.

Some in the world praise God,
The triple flame, alif, lām, mīm,
In their hearts.

As Fate completed his song Sandakumaran, the Prince of Peace, the son of integrity who had come to discover the secrets of the ABCD world came walking along the path. When he saw Fate he asked, "What's wrong? Why are you crying, my friend?"

Fate answered, "You can only confide the truth about yourself to an honorable person with good qualities who has realized the truth himself."

"Cousin, don't be afraid," said Sandakumaran, "Tell me what's wrong, and I'll help you, no matter what needs to be done." Fate wailed and told of his love for Manonmani, how his life was not worth living if he couldn't marry her. "Don't despair," Sandakumaran told him, "Show me where she lives. I'll learn the meaning of that story and win her for you." Immediately Fate took Sandakumaran to the palace where she lived and showed him the proclamation. Sandakumaran read it and rang the bell at the palace gate. When she heard the bell Manonmani looked at them from the balcony above. She saw Sandakumaran, the Prince of Peace endowed with thirty-two kinds of beauty, and fell in love. With great ecstasy she summoned her handmaiden and told her to ask the reason for his visit.

"Why have you come here?" asked the handmaiden.

"We have come," said Sandakumaran, "With the idea of discovering the meaning of the proclamation and marrying your mistress, but there are two questions we have to ask. You will be doing us a great favor, therefore, if you take us to her." Hearing this, the handmaiden informed her mistress who directed that they be brought to her. They were conducted into the palace, and Manonmani had them sit on the other side of a curtain.

"What is the purpose of your visit?" she asked.

"My lady, we have come to discover the meaning of the proclamation and marry you."

"It is true whether a man is a king or a beggar, only the one who can solve my riddle will marry me. There is certainly no place for anyone else here."

"Lady, once the solution is discovered and given to you, can we give you in marriage to anyone we choose?"

"As long as someone explains the meaning to me, I am prepared to marry according to the wish of whoever discovers the answer."

"My lady, I have not come for myself, I have come for the sake of someone born with me, of someone who loves you so much he is in danger of losing his life. If you will show him your face just once, his life will be saved."

Then Manonmani slowly parted the curtain between them, and Fate cried out in ecstasy seeing her face, "O precious jeweled light of my eye!"

"My lady," begged Sandakumaran, "He is the one who was born with me. Until I find the answer to your riddle will you let him stay somewhere in this town, as if he were a brother?"

"Take him to the rest-house at the edge of town. I will arrange for him to have the food and clothing he'll need."

Then Sandakumaran asked, "Please, may we hear the riddle from your own lips?"

She said, "'Happiness before you see it. Sorrow after you see it and experience it.' Why is there happiness before it is seen? Why is there sorrow when it is seen and experienced? You must figure out what this means and explain it to me."

Then Sandakumaran took Fate to the rest-house, consoled him, and set off. After he had been walking for nearly a month he saw a mountain in front of him reaching up to the sky. As he approached the foot of the mountain he heard sounds, intense with grief and pain. He looked around in all four directions, but there was nothing to be seen. Later, when he was further up the mountain he saw a mysterious four-cornered rock under a huge shady tree. Sitting on the rock was a young man more beautiful than the moon, holding onto a branch of the tree. He seemed ill. His body emaciated, eyes closed, he sighed with every breath, "O my life, my destiny, I can't bear to lose you, to be separate from you!"

When Sandakumaran heard him weeping and wailing he was filled with pity and came up to him, "What does this mean young man, why are you so sad? I'd be grateful if you would explain your sorrow." The young man's eyes remained closed and he didn't answer. Sandakumaran called him twice more, and still he did not answer. Then he called him loudly a fourth time, "Young man, although I have already called you three times, you haven't answered. Are you deaf and dumb?"

Opening his eyes the young man said, "Sir, who are you? Where did you come from? Why are you bothering me?"

"I am a man, one among God's creations," answered Sandakumaran very respectfully. "I too wandered through jungles and deserts before coming here. Please tell me why you are crying, and why you speak with such grief."

"Wandering pilgrim, many on this path have asked to hear my story, but no one has given me any medicine to cure my suffering. So why ask for my story? It won't serve any purpose at all; just continue your journey. Why should you worry yourself? Please don't add to my suffering by talking about it."

"Ah sorrowing young man, you doubtless have told your story to many people, but in God's name, tell it to me too. I won't have any peace until you do."

"All right, if you really want to hear it, sit near me, and when my mind clears, I'll tell you the details." So Sandakumaran sat under the tree, and the youth began to describe his sorrowful plight.

The Story of Anandarubi

I was a trader in a caravan carrying costly silks, jewelry, silken clothes, and merchandise, all loaded on five hundred horses and mules, on the way back from doing business in Yemen. I was with my caravan until we came to this place. At dawn one day I had left the caravan and come to the top of this mountain to relieve myself. Afterwards, I looked around, but I couldn't see the others. I ran and ran and looked in all four directions, but still I didn't see them. I had lost my way and couldn't find the caravan. Wandering in the sun, the rain, and the wind, I was thirsty, I was hungry and dizzy until, finally, I came to lie down under this tree. After a while I opened my eyes and saw a celestial being standing in front of me. As I perceived her beauty, her form, and her modesty, I was so entranced I fainted. Then the fairy put my head in her lap and sprinkled rosewater on my face. I awoke refreshed and looked around. When I saw that my head was on her lap I was in ecstasy, and looked at her with longing and intense love.

"Lady, my precious love, who are you, how did you come into this deep, deserted forest? What are you doing here?" I asked.

"I am from the celestial world," she said, "This mountain and the castle on it are my home. Just now I had the desire to be with a mortal man, and so God brought you to me." She uttered so many words in this sweet way that I became obsessed—I forgot all about my possessions, who I was, where I was. For many days the girl fed my desire with her love and kept the light of my life trapped in the fascination of her musk and rose and sandalwood scented tresses of hair. Immersed in an ocean of desire for her, I satiated those desires day and night for six months.

Then one day I said to her, "Gracious, beautiful fairy, what happiness can there be for you in this deep, deserted forest? If you come to the city you will enjoy yourself."

"Good," she said, "If you'd like to do that, let's go, but first I must see my own people and get their permission to go away. Until I come back you must be very careful not to leave this place."

"As you wish, but please tell me exactly when you are coming back."

"I'll be back in eleven days, but if you leave here before I return you'll know great sorrow." She promised this very earnestly and left.

"Sandakumaran, ten years have passed and she hasn't returned. She hasn't kept her promise and I don't know where to look for her. I'm afraid that if she turns up and doesn't find me here, I'd be guilty of a transgression against God. I fear what she might do if she returns and doesn't find me, and that's why I stay here. I don't have the strength to look for her, I have no food, I eat only the leaves which drop from this tree. The earth is hard, the sky is so remote, and I have no place to sit, and no strength to walk. What can I do?"

Sandakumaran was moved by the youth's plight. His eyes filled with tears from a melting heart. "My friend deluded by desire for a woman, did she give any other indication where she might live? Tell me everything you know."

"All I know is that her people live in Ayoti Forest, and that she is a celestial maiden, but I don't know where she's gone."

"Young man, when she said goodbye which way did she go?"

"She took ten or fifteen steps to my left, and I don't know where she went after that."

"All right, if you want her that much, come with me to Ayoti Forest. With God's help I'll find her no matter how difficult it may be, and I'll get her to marry you."

"What you're suggesting is right, but if my heart's beloved comes here and doesn't see me I don't know what terrible calamity might befall me. What can I do? If only she would come here, how good it would be! If she doesn't come, I'll die in this place thinking about her."

Tears of sorrow began to flow from Sandakumaran's eyes. "My friend, don't worry about a thing. Tell me her name."

"Her name is Anandarubi, the form of bliss."

"My friend, do not fear," said Sandakumaran with many reassuring words. "With God's help I will go to Ayoti Forest, search for your beloved Anandarubi and bring her to you, or else I'll take you back to her. I'll return when I am certain where she lives."

"You are a true friend. Until this moment no one has given me the courage you have. There isn't anyone else in the world who would neglect his own affairs and become engrossed in helping others. I don't know why you're doing all this for me."

"You don't need to make so much of this. From the day I was born, I dedicated my body, my heart, and my soul in God's name to the service of others. Everyone knows this. This is what I have been doing all my life. All I want is to see that everybody receives what he really desires."

The Prince of Peace set out to follow the path taken by Anandarubi. After walking many days he finally reached the edge of Ayoti Forest, and as he peered in through the trees a great mountain became visible. When he climbed it he saw many shrubs and bushes, many thorny fruit trees, and a meadow filled with flowers. The bees sang after sucking the honey. Then as he walked along he saw a tidy clearing that made him happy. Under four trees with cooling shade and a pleasing fragrance there was a very beautiful palace. He walked towards it, came closer, and then a strange drowsiness overcame him. Without realizing it he fell asleep.

As twilight fell four girls who were fairies came to spread out a sleeping mat and sheets for him to lie on. They looked him over and asked each other, "Who is he? How did he come here? We must find out." They came up to him, touched and awakened him saying, "You are from the human world, how did you come to this place, why are you here?" Sandakumaran awakened quickly and saw that the four of them were dressed in clothes held together with the nine kinds of gems and pearls.

Then the fairy beings prepared to sit beside his head, and when Sandakumaran realized that he jumped up saying, "My God has brought me here."

"Why have you come here?" asked the fairies.

"I have come to find a girl," he said, "I was told she might be in Ayoti Forest....."

"What's her name?" they interrupted.

"Her name is Anandarubi, the form of bliss."

The fairies began to tremble with fear, "You are from the human world, how do you know that name?"

"There was a man returning to Rum," he replied, "With a caravan of many servants, five hundred mules, and a great quantity of merchandise. Night overtook them and they stopped. At dawn the next day as they were continuing on their way, the leader of the caravan went to relieve himself, and when he had completed his ablutions he returned to find the servants, the horses, and the mules all gone. He ran wandering and searching in all four directions, and got lost. He wandered and roamed everywhere, becoming extremely thirsty, hungry, and exhausted. Finally, he fainted. When he fell down unconscious the fairy Anandarubi put his head on her lap and revived him by sprinkling rosewater on his face. She fed him whatever food he wanted and many kinds of sherbet, then stayed with him for six months of love and gaiety. When he asked if they might go to the city where his caravan had gone, she left him to tell her own people and swore to return, instructing him to wait in that place. Ten years went by, her promise forgotten. She left him there and didn't come back.

Now there is no life left in his body, he just thinks of her and cries, scarcely hearing the sounds of crying coming from his own body. That's the state he's in now. I met him on my travels, listened to his thoughts, heard his words, and told him I would arrange their marriage. That's why I have come in search of Anandarubi."

Then the fairies said, "This is really surprising. How could a celestial virgin swear to a mere man she would return in eleven days? Sir, she is at the peak of Hastinapura Mountain, but it would be a mistake to try meeting her there. Even if you reached the top you would not escape from there alive."

"I don't care what happens to me. Nothing can stop me from going."

"Very well," they said, "If you stay with us today, tomorrow we'll show you the way to the mountain." Upon hearing these words, the Prince of Peace agreed. It didn't matter what sort of duty presented itself, he always thought it best to consent, and so he stayed as a welcome guest at their home, and spent his time there happily.

As dawn broke the four fairies set out to take him up the mountain. They walked for seven days until they came to a certain spot. "We cannot go past this place," they said, "Our boundaries end here. With God's help you will certainly reach your destination in a few days if you just keep to this path, walk carefully, and don't turn off."

Sandakumaran took leave of them. He walked on for about a month, and then three times thirty minutes after nightful he came to a place that appeared to be a town. Suddenly he heard a very sad, weeping sound. He listened carefully to that sound and deliberated in his heart, "If you are on the path of the one God, dedicated to helping mankind, can you go away ignoring that plaintive cry? You must help him too." His conscience made him leave that path and wander in search of the crying voice until night became day. Then the sound came again. He went towards it and saw a handsome youth who wept and sobbed amid a flood of tears.

Sandakumaran exclaimed, "Sir, you are one of God's creations, why are you crying like this? Who is responsible for your suffering and your sadness?" In spite of Sandakumaran's comforting words, he continued to weep in sorrow. "Who are you, Sir?" asked Sandakumaran studying the youth, who finally began to tell his story.

The Soldier's Tale

I was a soldier in search of work, and so I left my village, lost my way, and came to this country. Later, when I met people here and asked them the name of their king, they said it was Mantiravadi, the magician. I was so frightened I ran away, deep into the forest until I came upon an orchard enclosed by beautiful walls. Inside there were different kinds of fruit trees, scented flowers, and cooling breezes. I thought I might go in to look, and stopped my horse to dismount. Suddenly frightened, I went hesitatingly forward and saw a large assembly of fairies adorned with priceless gems and pearls, dressed in clothes as resplendent as the sun. The girls were amusing themselves and playing happily. While I stood there looking at them it occurred to me they must be the children of a king, and that I shouldn't stare at strange girls. I turned to leave, but at that moment they saw me and ran to tell their mistress, the princess. She was the daughter of the magician Mantiravadi, the king of that city. When the handmaidens told her about me she rose from her throne, looked in my direction, and ordered the fairies to bring me to her at once.

I was taken into a very beautiful, richly decorated castle and seated before her on a great, embroidered throne. While they were entertaining me her father arrived outside, and as soon as he saw my horse he demanded to know whose it was. Immediately, everyone took fright and became silent. Then he walked over and saw me with his daughter.

"He must be thrown into the fire!" yelled King Mantiravadi in anger.

The princess was afraid and said, "Father, we have done nothing wrong. The first moment I saw him my heart felt a longing for him, as it sometimes happens in the world. I am not guilty. Please forgive me in God's name."

"What do you have to say?" the king asked me.

I stood before the king with bowed head and answered, "You are free to do whatever you like."

Now the princess' mother intervened, "My lord, our daughter has come of age, and there is no one the right age in this city who would be suitable as your son-in-law. This man's conduct is excellent, he seems to be from a good family, and he is very handsome. He is so reserved and modest he hasn't even raised his eyes to look at our daughter, he hasn't even said a word so far. Since he does appear to be a good match it might really be a good thing, and besides they actually haven't committed any offense. Since he hasn't done anything wrong, if you suspect him or have him killed, he could become a hero and a martyr to our people, and then later on you would be blamed. Think of the answer you would have to give God!"

Then the king asked, "Well daughter, what are your feelings about this?"

"My father, I have never seen any man's face before. He is the first man I've ever seen, but I think I am in love with him. He does seem to be a good match, and he's very handsome. Yes, I think I do love him."

The queen added, "He is so attractive, let's marry him to our daughter."

"If this is also your wish," said the king to his wife, "There are three things he must do. When he completes these tasks we will give our child to him in marriage."

He called me to him and said, "If you want to marry our daughter, I will set you three tasks. If you complete them satisfactorily then you are free to marry her. First, you must bring me a pair of andran birds. Second, you must bring me the ring from the mouth of the black snake called Adi Shaydan. And third, you must fill seven huge cauldrons with lead, oil, and butter, kindle seven fires blazing as high as a mountain and place the cauldrons on them. The contents of the cauldrons must boil so hard that the bubbles from each will fly up to the sky. The cauldrons themselves must be so hot that no one can come within seven miles of them. First, you must bathe in six of the cauldrons, and then finally you must bathe in the cauldron which contains the butter and emerge unhurt. If you complete these three tasks, I will marry my daughter to you."

"*I* was so bewildered and frightened I felt I would rather return to my own country than try to fulfill the marriage conditions. But even though the tests were very severe the beauty of the princess and the fascination of her gaze had captured my heart. And so I wander and roam, pining and withering away, wondering how I can forget that girl or else satisfy my longing for her."

Then Sandakumaran, the Prince of Peace, said sadly, "Poor man, with God's help I will solve your problems and arrange your marriage. Don't be sad, God created me to help people." He comforted the youth, gave him courage, and took his leave.

Will You Not Have Mercy?

You are God, the Sheikh of my heart.
I am so poor, will You not have mercy on me?
Will You not look at me again?
Will You not bring clarity to my mind?

The One who dwells in the one-pointed heart,
The One who gives compassion to His devotees,
The ultimate unique One who rules all the universes
Is the One who gave us the Pearl at the time of creation.

You are God, the Sheikh of my heart.
I am so poor, will You not have mercy on me?
Will You not look at me again?
Will You not bring clarity to my mind?

The One who is duty within grace and love to everyone,
The ultimate unique One who is forever complete, everywhere,
Is mingled in all lives and in my heart.

You are God, the Sheikh of my heart.
I am so poor, will You not have mercy on me?
Will You not look at me again?
Will You not bring clarity to my mind?

The One who permeates the sky, the earth, everything,
The One who knows the mystery of all religions,
The One who is neither male nor female, the One who has no birth
Is the ultimate unique One the whole world praises.

You are God, the Sheikh of my heart.
I am so poor, will You not have mercy on me?
Will You not look at me again?
Will You not bring clarity to my mind?

The One who has no mother, no father, not anyone at all,
The One who rules everything with equality,

The One who has not created anything as lowly as Himself,
Is the One who has no race, no religion, no differences whatever.

You are God, the Sheikh of my heart.
I am so poor, will You not have mercy on me?
Will You not look at me again?
Will You not bring clarity to my mind?

The One who has no end in the past or in the future,
The King who dwells at the junction of the three roads,
The Protector who is intermingled in the jeweled light of the eye
Is the illustrious One who reveals the truth and protects me.

You are God, the Sheikh of my heart.
I am so poor, will You not have mercy on me?
Will You not look at me again?
Will You not bring clarity to my mind?

In the body of form
God exists without form as life.
God appears without appearance, without any image
To those who are wise.

You are God, the Sheikh of my heart.
I am so poor, will You not have mercy on me?
Will You not look at me again?
Will You not bring clarity to my mind?

The light of the lamp inside the house,
He is courage, straight-forwardness, and excellence,
Glory, splendor, and honor.
He is indescribable divine luminous bliss.

You are God, the Sheikh of my heart.
I am so poor, will You not have mercy on me?
Will You not look at me again?
Will You not bring clarity to my mind?

The One who manifests in many ways and forms,
The One who is always with us,

The mighty One devoid of anger and pride
Is the ultimate, unique One who rules the universes.

You are God, the Sheikh of my heart.
I am so poor, will You not have mercy on me?
Will You not look at me again?
Will You not bring clarity to my mind?

4

Sandakumaran Meets the Angel of Death

In every circumstance Sandakumaran demonstrates compassion for all lives and absolute faith in God. On his journey he soon learns the fate of himself and the world.

After traveling a little way Sandakumaran saw a castle with a huge woodpile near the moat. Many people were gathered around trying to light a fire, and this so surprised him, because he couldn't make out any reason for the fire, he asked some people what was going on. They told him that a huge beast with an enormous appetite came there every night, caught three or four people, and ate them. They were afraid if the beast went on devouring people at that rate, their city would soon be completely destroyed.

The Prince of Peace was very distressed when he heard this, and thought he should try to relieve the suffering of those poor people. He went to the inn, summoned all the people of the village and spoke to them. "Men, if you do what I say, I'll see to it that the beast doesn't take another life. If you dig a deep pit on the beast's path as I'll show you, and fill it with firewood, I'll lie in wait and destroy the thing when it comes. I promise that evil spirit won't trouble you again."

So all the people of the village got together, dug a huge pit as Sandakumaran had instructed, and filled it with dry firewood. The next night he lay in wait hidden in the shrubbery. At midnight the beast approached. As it was coming closer the creature seemed to be a mountain, but when it reached the edge of the pit Sandakumaran recognized Amusan with its eight feet and seven heads. The middle head was like the head of an elephant, the other six were like tigers' heads. Of its nine eyes, the one in the center was as bright as the moon. While he was taking all this in, Sandakumaran realized that if he destroyed its middle eye Amusan would not return there again.

He lifted his bow, fitted an arrow which he aimed at that brightest eye, and let it fly. He had hoped it would pierce the middle eye and penetrate its head, but he missed and the beast kept moving towards the village with its mouth open. When the people saw it coming they set fire to the wood which filled the pit, and in the heat and smoke of the fire, the creature couldn't see the castle or surrounding houses. Staggering, tottering, and trampling everything, unable to see where it was going, it let out a terrifying, arrogant sound from the elephant head. When the villagers heard the awful sounds it made they were so frightened they shook with fear. The earth shook too. Then in one jump the beast landed close to the place where Sandakumaran was hidden, and the Prince of Peace picked up his bow, fitted another arrow, and with precision aimed at Amusan's middle eye. The arrow struck home and went right through.

As soon as the creature was hit it fell to the ground, rolled around, and made a horrifying noise. The forests and mountains trembled and shook, but the beast, its head bent low, turned and ran back along the path it had first taken. Sandakumaran emerged from the thicket, and at sunrise the people were amazed to see him alive. "Sir!" they exclaimed, "How did you escape?"

"With God's grace I injured the middle eye of that evil spirit," he replied. "You and all the villagers are free of that terrible beast from now on."

"But how can we believe what you say?" they asked.

"Tonight," said Sandakumaran, "Climb to the top of the castle and stay awake all night, each one of you. If the beast returns, call me a liar."

So all together they stayed awake on top of the castle the whole night, but the beast didn't appear. Then everyone fell at Sandakumaran's feet with hundreds of thousands of rupees and gems piled high on trays. He said, "I am a lonely pilgrim. I have no use for such things. What would I do with it? If you give all this to the poor and the orphaned in God's name, you will acquire merit in this world and in God's world. You will be very blessed."

So saying, he took leave of them. After journeying for about a day he saw a cobra and a mongoose fighting, and he knew that in a few moments one of them was going to be killed. "You creatures of the animal world, why are you so hostile to each other? If you go on fighting like this you will lose your lives for nothing!"

The cobra said, "He killed my father; therefore, I must kill him."

And the mongoose said, "I caught his father and ate him because he is my natural prey. Now I will kill this one and gobble him up too."

"Mongoose," said Sandakumaran, "If you want food, tell me. I'll cut you some flesh from my own body." Then he turned to the snake and said, "Snake, if you want retribution for your father's life, take mine." When they heard this both of them stopped fighting.

"Sir," said the mongoose, "If you give me some flesh from your body now as you promised, my hunger will be appeased. I'll go home and leave this snake alone."

"Good. What part of my body would you like? Just ask."

"I want the flesh of your face," said the mongoose. Immediately Sandakumaran took the knife from his belt and held it against his face to cut a piece from it.

But the mongoose shouted to stop him, "Merciful and mighty one, I only said all that to learn what was in your heart. May God bless you and the father and mother who gave birth to you. May you be praised forever."

In a moment both the snake and the mongoose changed to human form. "My friends," said Sandakumaran, "What kind of miracle is this? Just a few moments ago you had the shapes of animals, and now you have changed into men. What does it mean?"

"We are celestial beings," replied the one who had been a mongoose, "And I did kill his father. It so happened that I yearned for his sister and asked their father for her hand in marriage, but he wouldn't give me the girl, and I killed him. This fellow, her brother, also refused to give her to me, and that's why I want to kill him too."

Then Sandakumaran addressed the other jinn, "Young man, haven't you married yet either?"

And the other one who had been a snake said, "I want *his* sister, but he won't let me marry her. Now, if he lets me marry his sister, I'll let him marry mine."

"But my father is still living," said the former mongoose, "And he says he will never consent. What can I do?"

"Good," said Sandakumaran, "If you take me to your father, I'll put him at peace. Both of you come with me."

After they had left that place and walked some distance, the jinn who had taken the form of a mongoose said, "My friend, I will go to the palace now. You come later, and when you get to the city people there will capture you quickly and take you to my father. Then you can say whatever you think best."

Both jinns departed, and Sandakumaran continued along his way. As soon as he came to the city the jinns caught him and took him to the court of King Masaak.

"Sir," asked the king, "How did you come to my city?"

"Maharajah, great king," replied Sandakumaran, "I am God's slave, and I have come here to help you."

"Sir, how can you possibly help the jinn people?"

"Good king, you lack affection and sympathy for your son."

"What is this man saying? I don't really know what you are talking about. I'm very old, and I have only one son who is dearer to me than my own life. He is my only glory."

"If you have such love and affection for your son, you had better listen to what I say. If you don't..... Why even today something happened which could have cost him his life!"

Masaak was disturbed when he heard that, and his heart trembled. "My friend, from what you say it appears you have done me a great favor. May God grant you His grace for that, but I need to know the circumstances. Please tell me what happened."

"My lord," said Sandakumaran, "Your son killed a jinn's father, and the jinn tried to kill him in revenge. They were in the woods fighting together, and your son was very close to death. When I saw that I made a great noise and ran to him, separating them. Even so, one of them might still die needlessly someday, and all because your son loves the other jinn's sister, and that jinn loves your daughter. Now since this is the case, wouldn't it be a good idea to let your son marry her? Then they would all live happily and in harmony."

When he heard this, Masaak gave permission for his son to marry the girl he wanted, and for his daughter to marry the girl's brother. The girls went to live with their husbands and were very happy. Then Masaak spoke to Sandakumaran, "My beloved friend, you have helped me so much I want to give you pearls and the nine kinds of gems to take away with you."

"My lord, it is not my custom to accept anything for whatever service I may offer."

"Loving friend, I am very pained that you will not accept anything from me, but so that I keep my word, I'll give you a cane as a keepsake. You must accept it. Here, hold it in your hand, and I'll describe its might. It has many different properties—it will contain the poison of snake and scorpion bites, and no matter what kind of evil may be heaped on it, this cane won't burn. It will protect anyone holding it from sorcery, and bounce the spell back on whoever casts it. If you need a ship to cross an ocean, this cane will turn into a ship as soon as it is placed in water. It will take you anywhere you want to go. In addition to this, I want to give you a ring which you must accept too. Now, this is what the ring can do: on your travels, if you see a snake, whether it's a white snake, a red snake, or a black snake, and you hold the ring in your mouth, the snakes will not come near you. If they bite you at a moment when they catch you off-guard, the poison will not spread. Listen, I'll tell you more. If someone tries to stab you, the knife will not touch you. If someone throws rocks at you, the rocks will not hit you. If you are put into fire, it will not burn you. When you are thirsty, when there is no water, if you put the ring in your mouth, your thirst will be quenched. Furthermore, if you are put into a pit of molten lead or hot oil, the heat will not affect you. If someone is ill, wash the ring in a little water and have the sick person drink that water. He will be cured. I'm going to put it on your hand. Guard it very carefully."

Sandakumaran accepted the ring and put it on his finger. Then the king continued, "This ring is very powerful. If anyone tries to remove it by deception, it can't be done. If anyone tries to cut it off, it can't be done. If someone does manage to deceive you and take it from you, it will lose all its splendor and effect. If you give it away willingly, however, its wonderful strength will be greater than ever."

The Prince of Peace then received the king's permission to depart, and he left that kingdom. Walking day and night, and traveling through several countries, he came to a great ocean where the waves swelled and crashed up to the heavens. He became anxious, looked around in all four directions, and when he didn't see anyone either coming or going, he was wondering what to do when, suddenly, he remembered the cane and dropped it in the ocean. The cane became a ship, and he got on board. When the ship was in mid-ocean he noticed that a shark had been pulling it. Then when it stopped close to the shore, Sandakumaran blinked his eyes with disbelief because he saw the shark was as big as a mountain. He looked at it with great wonder and fear.

"You terrible fish, why did you bring me here?"

"Young man," replied the shark, "I used to have a house of my own, but a whale tricked me out of it. I hoped you would be able to recover my house for me, and so I dragged you here."

"Shark, that whale seems much stronger than you. You don't seem to have enough strength to take him on," said Sandakumaran.

The shark continued, "How can I describe his cruel injustice? Wait awhile and you'll see. If the whale should in fact appear, it will bare its teeth and bite us in two. Right now that vile creature has gone in search of prey."

As they were talking the evil whale appeared suddenly with its jaws wide open. The shark saw it coming and hid behind Sandakumaran in fear. While the Prince of Peace stood there watching, the whale came towards him like a great fortress, its mouth so big that the top and bottom couldn't be seen at the same time. When the whale discovered the shark it let out a gigantic cry, and the shark trembled in terror. With fear in his heart, Sandakumaran prayed to God for protection from that evil thing, wondering how he was going to escape. Then he remembered the ring which Masaak had given him and quickly put it in his mouth.

Looking at the whale bravely and courageously he addressed it in a resonant voice, "Creature of God, it is wrong to torment others without the slightest fear of God or respect for Him. If you hurt others merely because you are stronger, that pain will rebound on you. Give this poor fish its house back. Surely you can find some other place to live."

"Sir," replied the whale, "The two of us live here together, and we will find a way, somehow, to live peacefully. What do you have in mind coming between us this way, arguing with us?"

"Whale," said Sandakumaran, "I understand what you're saying perfectly, but you should know that God made this world, that He created the eighteen thousand universes and put some creatures in water and others on land in these universes. To each He gave food, a place to live, and His protection, and therefore He is not happy when one of His creatures is evil to another. So you see, what you are doing is a terrible sin."

"Since you are speaking on the shark's behalf, I won't stay in his house for now. Here, I'll give it to him, but after you leave, can he summon you back? I'll be right here in this ocean, and then let's see if he can hold onto this house."

"You evil being," said Sandakumaran, "Don't you even have a little fear of God? Is it right to hurt someone else just to make yourself comfortable? You are hurting this shark—will you leave his house and go or won't you? If you don't, I'll have to destroy you by and by. Whale! Give him his house immediately!"

"You're a tiny man, but instead of behaving as you should, if size is any indication, you seem to argue without fear at all. Look, I'll swallow you and the shark together for my dinner!"

The whale opened its mouth wide to eat both of them, but as it came closer Sandakumaran took the cane Masaak had given him and landed a mighty blow which injured its two lion-like fangs and mouth severely. Then it turned tail and swam quickly away, realizing indeed that Sandakumaran, the Prince of Peace, could not be conquered. As it swam away the shark chased after it, cursing and calling it back to fight.

"Idiot of ruined wisdom!" yelled Sandakumaran, "That's not courage. Do you think it's just to hurt a living being who is running away in fear? If you try anything treacherous I'll cut you up and torture you."

When the shark heard that he was frightened, and Sandakumaran commanded him to stay in his house. Then he took his cane, put it in the water, climbed aboard, and soon reached another shore. From there he could see the city of Mayajala. When he got there he sat down under a shady tree to think. "With God's grace I have come this far. Now I need to find those andran birds who represent the qualities of God. Where could they be?"

While he sat thinking night fell, and the andran birds which had been out gathering food came back to rest in the boughs of the trees, and talked among themselves. "This evening a God-like man who protects the poor arrived here after enduring many hardships in the service of others. He shines as if he were the crowning jewel of all God's creations, and his name is Sandakumaran, the Prince of Peace. Since he came here looking for our help, it really is our duty to meet him." The birds continued talking like that until dawn, then they all came to meet him and pay obeisance to him. Sandakumaran was filled with bliss when he saw their beauty. Their faces resembled human faces and their colors were as brilliant as peacocks'. Even heavenly beings were entranced by their beauty.

Addressing him in human speech they said, "Prince of Peace, no one can equal your courage or compassion, God bestowed that glory on you alone. But you have suffered so much wandering here and there to help others. Haven't you even come here because you need two of our children to help that soldier who wants to marry King Mantiravadi's daughter?"

"Everything you say is true," said Sandakumaran, "And I am happy you cherish the qualities God gave me. If you grant me this favor I'll be your slave for life. I don't know how I can ever repay you, but if you do this for me, I believe the glory of the three worlds awaits you."

Then the birds deliberated among themselves, "We must give two of our children to this man in God's name. That really is our duty." They came up to Sandakumaran and handed over their children. "Now they are yours, and you can take them wherever you want."

Sandakumaran accepted the two children, received the birds' permission to leave, and began his journey back to the magician's city. After several days he returned to the young soldier, his head still bent in sorrow. "Young man, the time has come for you to stop grieving and start being happy." When the soldier saw the pair of birds he fell at Sandakumaran's feet and kissed him. Then the Prince of Peace described everything that had happened on his travels, gave him the birds, and told him to say he was the one who found them. The youth accepted the birds and brought them to the magician.

Mantiravadi was very happy to have them, but at the same time suspicious, "Someone else must be responsible for this. If you really did it yourself, prove it by describing your experiences." Then the youth had to recount every detail of the journey, and he told the magician exactly what Sandakumaran had said to him. The symbols and the signs were correct, and the magician accepted the youth's explanation, "Now you must bring me the ring from the mouth of the black snake Adi Shaydan."

"Before I go for the ring," replied the youth, "I would be so encouraged if I could see the face of my beloved."

Mantiravadi went to his daughter and said, "Daughter, show the luminous beauty of your face to this young man who loves you, but stay behind that screen." And all through the night the young warrior sat gazing at her face which was as bright as the full moon.

When dawn broke he said to the magician, "If you want me to bring Adi Shaydan's ring, you must tell me where it is."

"I have asked all our best men," he replied, "And they say the black snake lives on top of Coral Mountain."

With this knowledge the soldier took leave of his beloved, and went to Sandakumaran to tell him what happened, and what he had learned about the black snake's lair.

"My friend," Sandakumaran said, "Don't be sad any longer. I will certainly do this for you with my word, with my body, and my heart. With God's help I'll complete this task and return here soon."

When he had comforted the soldier with that, the Prince of Peace took his leave, and walked towards Coral Mountain. After many days of walking, one morning while he was performing his ablutions a cloud descended from the heavens and a gale-force storm blew up. At first the storm beat down the trees, then the gusts of air changed to fire and burned the trees and animals. The air became fire, whirled and twisted like a tornado, and exploded in a shower of colored rays destroying the animals in the area. Sandakumaran stood watching the animals flee, some escaping, some burning, all the poisonous insects dying. He thought, "What on earth does this mean? What is happening? First a great cloud appeared, then a storm broke, then a gale descended tearing down the trees, and a fire rose in a display of seven colors or rays which branched out and destroyed the remaining trees and the wildlife. What on earth does this mean?"

While he sat there wondering what was going to happen next, the force of the storm, the wind, and the fire subsided and took the form of a poisonous, seven-colored centipede the size of a donkey off in the distance. Because he had never seen such a big centipede before he concealed himself there for a whole day hoping to discover its secret. As dusk fell and the creature hid itself, Sandakumaran thought it might be dangerous to spend the night there and went on to the village at the edge of the jungle.

The villagers welcomed the stranger and gave him food. After eating he sat down under a shady tree to rest, and watched the clearing where herds of the village cattle and horses were kept, guarded by three or four people. He spent that night leaning against the tree trunk, thinking. In the middle of the night the poisonous centipede emerged from beneath a rock, jumped on one of the cows, and stung it on the head. The cow trembled and fell. It killed all the cattle, all the horses, and the guards in the same way, and then crept back under the rock where it had been hiding. At dawn the villagers came to the jungle clearing, and were shocked and bewildered when they saw the dead. The scattered cattle, horses, and guards had a blue-colored fluid flowing from their mouths.

When they saw Sandakumaran they asked, "Stranger, how did you escape alive?"

"My friends," he replied, "I watched the drama and saw something amazing, a seven-colored centipede the size of a donkey which killed them all."

While he was saying that, the centipede came out from under the rock and stung the village headman. He began to tremble, fell to the ground, and died. The villagers gathered their dead and took them home.

Later the centipede traveled down a jungle path, and Sandakumaran followed it until a city came into view. There the centipede dropped to the ground, rolled around, and turned into a cobra. Sandakumaran was surprised and thought of God, wonderstruck. Then he watched the snake crawl into a cave. In the middle of the night it left the cave and Sandakumaran followed it again. The snake crept into the king's castle, bit the king, and then crept into the minister's castle where it bit his daughter, and then crawled back to its cave. The next day the people were told that the king and the minister's daughter had died of snake bite.

That night the snake left its cave, and Sandakumaran followed once again. At daybreak the snake stopped at the ocean and turned into a Bengal tiger. Some travelers were coming down the road just then, among them a handsome, nineteen-year old youth. The tiger pounced on him, carried him into the jungle, savaged his body, and tore his liver to shreds. Again Sandakumaran followed it through the jungle, and after a little while, the tiger turned into a young girl as beautiful as the full moon. Sandakumaran watched this from behind a tree.

Along came two warriors returning home from their travels in distant lands where they had gone to seek their fortune so they would be able to marry. When they came close to the girl they could see she seemed to have some sorrow which could not be endured. She began to cry and the older warrior came up to her, his own eyes overflowing with tears.

"Lady, why are you so sad?"

"My beloved friend," she replied, "I was married in my own distant country. While my husband and I were traveling to his home along this jungle path, a Bengal tiger carried him off. Now I am alone and helpless, I don't know where my husband's house is, I don't know the way back to my parents, and I don't know what other dangers await me," she wept piteously.

"Cherished lady, don't be afraid. If you listen to what I have to suggest, we can work this out very happily."

"Very well, tell me what it is."

"Would you accept if I asked you to be my wife?"

"Why shouldn't I? Who else is there to protect me in this deep jungle? I will marry you if I am safe from harm, if you take care of me, and if you make three promises. The first promise you have to make is there will be no other wife in your house, the second is that I will not have to undertake any kind of work or duty, the third is you must not let anything hurt me as long as you live, and you must never think ill of me."

"Lady, I have never married before, I will never want any woman other than you, and as long as I live I won't even look at another woman's face. With God's help I will have servants and slaves to do your housework and whatever else is necessary. You will want nothing, you will be mistress of the house. If anyone ever hurts you, my beloved, you have only to tell me. I will protect you as carefully as my own eyes, I will cherish you so that no sadness can ever touch you."

"If you will protect me that way," said the girl, "I promise to keep you happy with all my heart, my body, and soul."

As soon as she said this the warrior took her by the hand and led her through the jungle. Sandakumaran followed them, and a little later the girl spoke to the warrior, "I've been suffering from hunger and thirst for three days, and I'm so exhausted and dizzy I can't walk any further. Do you think you could find me some food or at the very least a little water? Otherwise I won't survive."

When he heard this the warrior told his younger brother, "Look after her carefully while I find some water."

Then he took a pot and went in search of water. Soon the girl turned to the younger warrior, "Young man," she said, "It was because of you I pretended affection for him. When I look at your face my heart won't be still. Without you . . . . . oh how can I spend my life with that old man? Take me as your mistress, make love to me."

"Miss," he answered, "It's immoral to say such dreadful things. You gave your word you would be my elder brother's wife. You two are mother and father to me, how could I ever tolerate your suggestion?"

"I may be your brother's wife, but why can't you love me too?"

"I could never! You must throw away these sinful thoughts."

"If you won't do what I want," said the girl with anger, "I'll tell lies about you. I'll tell him you tried to run off with me."

"Miss," he said, "You can say whatever you are capable of saying, but I'll never consent."

Sandakumaran was listening to all this from behind a tree. When the girl saw the other warrior returning with a pot of water, she disheveled her hair, fell to the ground, and rolled around screaming and wailing. The older warrior ran to her side, "My lady, are you crying because you were afraid I was eaten by some savage beast in the jungle?"

"May God give you and your brother good intentions. Would a real man ever leave his wife to be protected by someone so evil? God alone saved my honor. You went to find water, didn't you? Well, as soon as you were out of sight this beast grabbed my hand and pulled me towards him, intending to make love to me. As he tore at my clothes trying to seduce me, I screamed and screamed, but no one came to help me. Then he said, 'Don't you understand, I'm the one who is right for you, aren't I? You are fifteen or sixteen years old, and I'm seventeen. He's too old for you. Just see the incredible passion I have for you. If the opportunity arises I'll kill him!' He kept saying that kind of thing while he tried to seduce me. It's fortunate God sent you back soon enough to save my chastity."

The hands and legs of the older warrior shook with anger as he looked at his brother. "*Aday* wretch, have you sunk so low? What made you try to harm this woman whom you should look upon as your mother?"

The younger brother answered, "She really is disgusting! Don't believe her. I swear in God's name she is a very terrible, very evil person." But the older brother didn't believe what he said, and with great anger unsheathed the sword at his waist. The younger one turned to the girl, "You evil creature, because of you two lives will be lost in this remote jungle." He said that unsheathing his own sword, and then the two brothers fought and killed each other.

The girl left that place and walked on. Sandakumaran, the Prince of Peace, followed. In a little while she changed into a buffalo and came to a village. As the villagers tried to catch the buffalo it gored and trampled them, then it left that place, went on to a forest, and took the form of an old man. Then Sandakumaran thought this might be a good moment to ask him what had happened earlier, "Old man, you seem to be very talented. Please stop for a moment."

"Sandakumaran, Prince of Peace, why are you asking me to stop?"

"How do you know my name?"

"Sandakumaran, I know your name and I know your father, Kurunakaran, the Father of Compassion. I know you were following me watching carefully while I worked. You are a good man and you've had great difficulty helping others. I do not have a lot of time to spend with you, so please ask what you want."

"Will you tell me why you took so many different forms?"

The old man smiled and said, "Sandakumaran, how will it help you to know that? Someday, taking another such form, I will kill you too."

"All right, but I won't let you go unless you tell me these secrets."

"Sandakumaran, don't you know who I am yet? I am a servant who carries out God's commands. Listen, I'll tell you my secrets. I am larger than seven mountains, and I have four faces, a black face to capture evil beings and animals, a milk white face, a face of light, to capture men and celestial beings, a face of fire to capture jinns, and a face of grace to observe the destiny of Allah's creations. I watch all the creations of Allah and take their lives as their fate dictates. That's how I captured those people. Now do you understand who I am? I am 'Izrā'īl, one who does God's bidding.

Furthermore Sandakumaran, although our God does exist, although men are His creations, they continually forget Him and claim they themselves are god, they are kings and the source of their own wealth. People fancy that men are capable of carrying out their intentions without help, that babies, for instance, cannot be born except through their own acts. 'Let's see that God create babies without us!' they say, and claim that birth and death are in their own hands. They think people are rich or poor because of their own efforts. 'Who is this God?' they ask. Or else people talk wildly about planets and astrological influences, but where are those planets, why don't they catch them and bring them here if they can?

They make jokes forgetting death, they ridicule God, they wallow in sin and rule through *shaitān,* they torment the poor, make fun of men and women who have integrity, and do every evil thing. They are hypocrites who love the rich and abuse the poor. They beat, they kick and torture, they deceive and torment those who are *gnānis.*

God who knows everything created death even before creating man, and He made me to carry out the duty of death. I even take the lives of flies, ants, and the eight million, four hundred thousand other kinds of insect life. It's my duty to ignore the differences between those God put here as kings or mendicants, hold out my hand to each being according to his actions, and take every life.

There is more, Sandakumaran, listen. God has commanded me to make women widows, to make men widowers, and to make children orphans. There is more. I act as He instructs, taking each life exactly as He orders. Afterwards He confers heaven or hell on that life, depending on the nature of good or evil committed, so that men might eventually pursue the truth if for no other reason than their fear of death. God created the four religions, their prophets and messengers, exhorting them to reveal the meaning and the wisdom appropriate to each, but the people of the world have even forgotten those teachings. Now do you know who I am? I assume whatever form is needed for the destiny of each being and take the life of every creation. They call me Yama, the Angel of Death.''

Then Sandakumaran asked, ''You say you capture all lives, if that's the case, tell me when the world will be destroyed.''

''My son Sandakumaran,'' replied Yama, ''The people of this world will forget God and begin to live a life of lies and falsehood. When that time comes they will deny God, they will say that man is god, that he is the nourisher of all lives. Every one of God's creations, whether it is of earth, fire, air, or water is composed of atoms and various energies. When that time comes man will draw on those atomic energies and make fire bombs, atom bombs, hydrogen bombs, and bombs containing poison to invade different countries, destroy the people, and devastate the land. The people who deny the existence of God will emerge from a country with snow-capped mountains. They will rule with lies, and they will try to talk people into their way of thinking with lies. They will say there is no God, we will make you free, we will give you peace, but after converting them they will bring in their guns and their tanks to take their lives. Before they capture all these countries this way, they will first create poverty, illness, and famine, destroy faith in God, good intentions, and every good thing in their lives. They will be the cause of the destruction.''

''When will this happen?'' asked Sandakumaran.

''That time of destruction will probably begin in 1980,'' replied Yama. ''If those people are not stopped with God's help, by those with faith in

God, they will continue to invade and destroy the whole world with their lies and treachery.

Sandakumaran, you are someone who has faith in God, you live to help others. Keep your faith in God no matter what happens. Even when they build houses in the sky through those atomic powers, even when they go to the sun and the moon trying to conquer the planets, even when there are wars of fire in space, tell this to your brothers, tell them to keep their faith in God and not be influenced by the treacherous, sweet sounding words of this enemy of the whole world. If their faith in God is maintained, if their faith stays strong, those enemies will end by destroying themselves just as Pharoah and his forces were destroyed in the Red Sea. They will be destroyed by God's grace and the peoples' faith in God."

Then Sandakumaran asked, "When and how will my death come?"

"Sandakumaran," replied the old man, "You were sent into this world to help mankind to the utmost limit of your ability. In your fiftieth year you will slip and fall from a tall palace, and die when a drop of blood trickles from your nostril. May you go on performing good deeds as long as you live. Your fame will live as long as the world exists."

When he heard this the Prince of Peace gave thanks to God and prayed to Him from the depths of his heart. Then he lifted his head and the old man had disappeared. He thought to himself, "This is really the most amazing thing that's ever happened in my life. In the past I have always relieved the suffering people inflicted on each other, but just now God gave me the strength to watch while that old man took so many lives. I didn't even attempt to help them." With many such thoughts filling his troubled mind he set off once more towards his next objective.

He walked along a red clay path for several days until he came to a path where the earth was black. There the black snakes caught his human scent and approached him, surrounding and encircling him like a ring of mountains. He placed the cane which King Masaak had given him among the snakes, and spent the night lying on it. At dawn all the snakes went back as they had come. He left there and went on to a white path where white snakes surrounded him. Placing the cane among them as he had done with the others, he spent the night lying on it, and then walked on until he reached a green path. On that path green snakes gathered around him again. He spent the night in the same way and then came finally to a brick-red path where the color of the earth was more vermilion than red.

As he walked along he was exhausted by hunger and thirst. It was very hot, his feet were blistered by the heat, and he was in great distress because there wasn't even a tree to rest under. He focused his thoughts on God and prayed. Although his tongue was swollen, his gait unsteady, and he seemed to be on the verge of fainting, he reflected, "I am suffering in God's name to help others. I do have to die one of these days, but if I die here, will I be granted liberation?" He thought about this and worshiped God. As he continued on his feet were so blistered he could walk no longer, and he began to slither like a worm. His whole body was covered with the wounds of falling and dragging himself along the ground.

Then an old man appeared who lifted Sandakumaran up and embraced him. "Prince of Peace," he said, "Do not give up hope now. Be strong, put King Masaak's ring in your mouth and go forward, never backward." As soon as he put the ring in his mouth the hunger, thirst, and heat all disappeared.

Immediately Sandakumaran fell at the feet of the old man. "Where is this heat coming from?" he asked.

"It comes from the poison of the black snake known as Adi Shaydan," he said. "The fire coming from its mouth is the source of this heat."

Sandakumaran left that place and journeyed on. When he had walked a little further the black snake became aware of Sandakumaran's scent, and in fury, raised its hood which resembled a huge mountain, spread it wide, and spat poison from its mouth. Immediately the heat increased and the clouds of poison released from its nostrils rose and burned in great flames in the sky. All the trees and shrubs within sight were charred. As soon as Sandakumaran was caught by the heat, his mind became confused. It seemed to him that his body would burn and melt in the fire, but because he had the ring in his mouth he was protected. He realized it was the ring that saved his life. Then the gaze of the snake fell on Sandakumaran. As the snake spread its hood with uncontrollable anger and spat poisonous fire at Sandakumaran, his ring protected him again, and he spent the night there.

When daylight came Sandakumaran could see the ring in the upper lip of the snake, sparkling and shining with great resplendence. The Prince of Peace tapped the ring in the snake's mouth with his own ring, and the snake struck its head repeatedly on the ground. When night fell, the snake spat the ring from its mouth, and went away. Sandakumaran hesitated to pick it up immediately, afraid that he might be burned. He tore a piece of cloth from his turban, put it on the ring and saw that the cloth didn't burn. So he picked it up, put it inside his turban, and left that place. The ring had such power that if anyone took it away from the snake, another one would appear in its place thirty years later. Its powers cannot really be described.

After this Sandakumaran traveled through different countries undergoing many, many difficulties and trials until he returned to the young soldier. Giving him the ring, he told the youth everything that had happened on the way. The soldier clung to Sandakumaran's feet and began to cry. The Prince of Peace embraced the youth, comforted him, and told him to take the ring to the magician, King Mantiravadi.

"I went through many miseries and difficulties to bring this ring to you," the youth said.

"Good," replied the magician king, "But first we must test it, and we'll verify your story later." After a moment, "Ah, all the tests are right. Young man, there is one more condition to be fulfilled."

"I will do that happily."

Then the magician called his servants, "Bring seven iron cauldrons and fill them with butter, lead, and oil. Put them on a fire and keep them boiling non-stop for seven days and nights." The servants began their preparations. The heat from the boiling cauldrons was so intense it could melt black granite.

Looking at the youth the magician said, "If you can immerse yourself in these cauldrons and come out safely, you will have your beloved."

Afraid, the youth came to Sandakumaran, "My friend, I'm afraid I won't escape from this fire alive."

"Precious friend," said Sandakumaran, "Don't be afraid, with God's grace you will come to no harm. If you put your thoughts on God and make your heart strong He will protect you from any harm. Here, keep this ring. Put it in your mouth before you jump into the molten butter, and with God's grace the heat will not touch your body."

The soldier took the ring and went to the magician, "What do you want me to do now?"

"Jump in, bathe in these boiling cauldrons, and come out."

The youth approached the cauldrons shivering and trembling with terror. "Young man," said Sandakumaran, "Don't be afraid. This fire will be like cool water. Think of God and jump in." The youth closed his eyes, prayed to God, and jumped into the cauldrons. The boiling butter felt like cool water, and he bathed in all the cauldrons.

"Now what must I do?" he asked, "May I come out now or should I bathe a little longer?"

When the magician saw the youth was unharmed, he hung his head in apparent shame. Sandakumaran said to Mantiravadi, "Why are you embarrassed? It is time to keep your promise now." Then the magician told the soldier to climb out of the cauldron. "He has done everything you told him to do, but now you are planning some treachery. Even if you try anything, none of your sorcery will affect him now because he has another red ring." When the magician heard these words, he was even more embarrassed, went immediately to the youth with a smile, embraced him, and began to prepare for the wedding.

Everything was done, as it was their custom, with great pomp and pageantry. He summoned his daughter and son-in-law, "This country and all my wealth are now yours. I have no children other than this girl, and therefore, you have become my son." Saying this he placed his daughter's hand into the young soldier's and the husband and wife lived happily ever after.

Sandakumaran came to the soldier, "Young man, I have many other responsibilities. You must give me permission to leave now because I have to go to Ayoti Forest."

When he heard this the youth said, "May God, the Creator and Protector of the whole world, help you and give you whatever you need. May He protect you from every adversity, wherever you go." Then Sandakumaran took back the ring he had given the youth, said farewell, and set off on the path that lead to Ayoti Forest.

You Alone are God

You are the pen,
You are the *nuqat*, which is the dot,
You are the *qalb*, which is the inner heart,
You are the Father,
You alone are the beauty of Your qualities.

You are the pearl,
You are the emerald,
You are the coral,
You are the first One,
You alone are the triple flame.

You are the seed,
You are the miracle,
You are the eight,
You are the two.

You are the infinite, open ray of light,
You are the *Haqq*, the Truth,
You are the pen,
You are the pen recording right and wrong,
You are the tablet the pen inscribes,
You alone are God, transcending everything,
The jeweled light within the eyes.

You are all that Adam must become,
You are the *alif*, the One,
You are the *Ahad*, the One God, the *dhāt*, the essence,
You are the tiny seed and the great universe,
You are the *hā'* and the *mīm*, letters of the body,
You are that good quality, You are the fragrance,
You alone are the undiminishing light,
You are the creations,
You are what is hidden within them,
You are the earth, You are the heavens,
You alone are the precious treasure of wisdom within wisdom,
You are the *Rabb*, You are the *lām*,
The *dāl*, and the *hā'*, letters of the body,
You alone are God, the jeweled light within the eyes.

You are the light, You are the rays,
You are the word, You are the action,
You alone are beyond body and mind,
Beyond any state of sleep or dream,
Beyond any state we know,
You are God, You are duty,
You are then, You are now,
You are the protector, You are the loving qualities,
You exist suffused within everything, You are God,
You are within all beauty,
You are the refuge, You are the path,
You are chastity, You are compassion,
You alone are God, the jeweled light within the eyes.

You are the beginning, You are the end,
You are the heart, You are the outside,
You alone are the blissful light,
You are our lineage, You are our family,
You are the Sheikh, You are the wish-fulfilling tree of grace,
You alone are within all beauty.
You are the handhold, You are the strength,
You are the name, You are the hand,
You alone are the resplendent light,
You are the One who tastes, You are the taste,
You are the legs, You are the hands,
You alone are God who gives us grace.

You are the grace, You are the action,
You are the body,
You are the breath,
You are the apex of the summit.
You are formlessness, You are form,
You are the heart, You are the chest,
You alone are the beginning of light, the beginningless beginning,
You are the bud, You are the fully opened flower,
You are beauty, You are the One Being.
You alone are Allah, forever the mighty One,
You are the embryo, You are the form,
You are the eternal, all mighty One.
You alone are God, the jeweled light within the eyes.

5

Sandakumaran Learns the Story of the Dog

Sandakumaran, the Prince of Peace, meets the Sufi Master and hears the story of a very special dog whose love and devotion to God is very great.

After walking day and night for several days he came to the edge of Ayoti Forest. There he saw a mountain reaching up to the heavens, hiding the light of day. Dismayed, Sandakumaran wondered how he was going to climb a peak which was inaccessible, even for birds. There was no one in sight to ask for help, and as he looked up at the mountain he was so worried he had to sit down to think things out. While he sat fretting about this a group of fairies approached, and he ran towards them but they disappeared. Then an enormous palace appeared before him. In front of it was an immense, slippery, black rock in which there was a huge underground cavern overgrown with weeds. "How will I get across that cavern?" he asked himself. Then he stood on the rock and decided to go right in. With the faith that everything happens as God wills, he closed his eyes, slid across the rock, rolling and pushing himself along. He spent the whole day slipping and sliding, until finally he found that his feet touched the ground. He blinked, looked around and saw so many trees, flower gardens, and such a big meadow that his heart was lightened. Then he walked around a bit thinking about the fairies he had seen. A little further on he saw an even more lavishly decorated palace than the earlier one.

"If anyone is there," he thought as he went towards it, "I might be able to meet them."

The fairies, wondering who was approaching their palace so boldly, came out and confronted Sandakumaran briskly. "You were born in the human world. What you are doing is not polite. What right do you have to come to this house? How did you get here? Who brought you?"

"God who is merciful to me brought me here."

"Good, but how did you know about the path through the great cavern?" they asked.

"When I first saw you I chased after you, but about ten minutes later I lost you and wondered where you had gone. I followed the path you had taken and saw a dark abyss. As I was trying to figure out how to get across an idea came to me. I thought if I stood on that rock and slid down, I would reach the bottom; so I did that and found your garden. In God's name, I ask you to tell me what this mountain is called and who owns the garden."

"This is Ayoti Mountain," said the fairies, "And the garden belongs to a fairy named Anandarubi, the form of bliss. We are her guards, and we know she will be coming here soon, in two or three days. Young man, although we feel sorry for you because of your youth and beauty, we cannot keep you here or you will die."

"I didn't intend to stay here," said Sandakumaran, "I have come despite great difficulty on someone else's behalf. It would be helpful if Anandarubi arrived here soon, come what may."

"You are just a poor man," they said, "What brings you to see her?"

"Human beings like fairies and seek them out," replied Sandakumaran, "And fairies like human beings and seek them out."

With great anger the fairies cried, "You must be crazy! You do have a brave heart, but apparently you don't care whether you live or die. We'd better chop off your head!" Looking fiercely at Sandakumaran they raised their swords, but he didn't say anything, he merely stood there with his head bowed. Then the fairies smiled and whispered among themselves, "He seems to be a strange being. He certainly doesn't run away in fear, and he can't be provoked into a fight, but someone could cut him to pieces." They addressed him, "Young man, this place isn't really healthy for you. Now, we're saying this because we feel sorry for you. It's for your own good. You can't stay here; if you want to escape with your life, go away! It would be just as well if you left without saying another word. If you don't leave you might be hacked to pieces."

"Fairies," he answered, "I have no desire to escape with my life, I wouldn't be troubled if it were lost. I am quite prepared to lose it on God's path, and there are others walking this path who don't value their lives either. God loves all living creatures on the earth and in the skies. Our duty is to think about Him and worship Him."

"Young man, you needn't be afraid. If you want to stay here and be happy with us we will keep you hidden among ourselves. We will take you to a place where even the moon won't be able to find you." The fairies, by now completely in love with Sandakumaran took him to a hidden forest. There they gave him all kinds of food and fruit which he ate joyously, and because they wanted to experience the bliss of spending time with him, they stayed there too.

Three days went by this way, then the fairies asked him to tell them the real reason why he had come. "There is something urgent I must tell Anandarubi," he said. "Ten years ago she swore to a young man she would return in eleven days, but she hasn't come back yet. That young man just sits staring at the path she took when she went away. He looks like a corpse, his eyes are like stones, he has no flesh on his body, he has become skin and bone, he lives in a state which hovers between life and death. Every once in a while he sighs profoundly, sometimes crying out as intensely as though he were on fire, "She gave me her love." I heard those sounds and went up to him asking what had happened, and when I heard what he said my heart was scorched, drops of blood fell from my eyes. She has forgotten him, and so I have come here for his sake, I have come here to awaken a remembrance of him in her heart. If he dies because of that desire for her, it will be her fault."

"Young man born into the human world as a creation of God," replied the fairies, "This is beyond our capacity to deal with. If you want to tell Anandarubi about this when she comes, we will take you to her and you can say anything you want. But if we take you unbound not only will she be angry, she'll be suspicious of us as well."

"Take me to her any way you like," said Sandakumaran. "The difficulties I have and the fate written on the head of that youth are known only to God."

Then one day Anandarubi and her handmaidens came with great gaiety to the flower garden. The fairies who were there came up to her, paid obeisance, and led her to the palace where she was seated on her throne. Forty fairies sat on forty chairs beside her. Others brought Sandakumaran and kept him off to one side. "She is Anandarubi," they whispered, "Her name is also Mallika or jasmine flower."

The fairy they called Mallika was dressed in silks and brocades, in gold lace and jewels which flashed like fire. Her whole body was adorned with priceless pearls and gems. She was adorned with jewelry and anointed with the fragrance of musk. In her hand she had a bouquet of flowers. Seeing her beauty, the moon had to hide in shame. When Sandakumaran saw Mallika's indescribable beauty from his place of concealment, he staggered, lost consciousness, and fell down. In a little while he returned to consciousness and prayed to God. The fairies saw what was happening and made fun of him. In this way three days passed, then on the night of the third day he had a dream.

"Sandakumaran," came a sound from somewhere, "Get up. You don't know me, but you are traveling on the path of duty in God's name. Is it right for you to want something that doesn't belong to you? Why do you have such heavy longings and useless desires? It's not appropriate to think like that when you are helping others in God's name; it's not right to have the same longings evil people do."

When he heard this Sandakumaran woke up alarmed looking around, but he saw no one and went away thinking of God. Frightened, he shuddered and prayed, "O gracious Lord, please forgive me for my sinful thoughts. You who are so merciful and compassionate, have mercy on me."

When his prayer was finished he went to the fairies, "Heavenly virgins, please take me to Mallika. That youth will be waiting and watching the path for my return. It's not right for me to linger here."

Hearing this, the fairies waited for a moment when Mallika was in a good mood, tied Sandakumaran's hands together, and took him to the gateway of the palace. Then one of them went to her. "*Maharani*, great queen," said the fairy, "A poor man came into our garden because he was ill. We caught him, tied him up, and brought him here. Now we await your orders."

"Please bring that man to my presence," replied Anandarubi.

They brought Sandakumaran to her immediately. The sight of him brought back memories of the young man she had forgotten, and she had the fairies untie his bonds quickly. With great reverence she rose and invited the Prince of Peace to sit next to her on a throne which glittered with the nine kinds of gems. "Young man," she asked, "What's your name, where do you come from, why did you come here?"

"I come from the city of Tarumapupadi, the kingdom of heaven," he answered, "I am a poor man in God's creation. My father, whose name is Patience, the Father of Grace, is the very form of duty and eternal truth. My name is Sandakumaran, the Prince of Peace."

Anandarubi rose from her throne again with great reverence, "Prince of Peace, even I have heard your name. You who were born in Tarumapupadi and nurtured in justice and duty, you seem very compassionate. Now why have you come here so graciously, despite so much difficulty? God brought you to me, and for that reason, I will be your slave, I will look upon you as a king. If you want, I will even go to your own country with you."

"Good," said Sandakumaran, "All those feelings are evidence of your goodness and grace. I have just come from the city of Mayajala, and on my way I found a youth sitting under a tree, staring at the road. He would close his eyes, weep and cry loudly with great sorrow, 'I can't bear to be separated from you, I can't bear not seeing your face, I'm burning in fire.' When I went up to him and asked why he was crying, he told me of the unhappiness which had befallen him. 'Anandarubi stayed with me for six months, then she left promising to return in eleven days. For ten years I have waited and watched and cried for her return day and night. I can't leave because she warned me if I left before she came back, I'd never see her again. How could I go anywhere and disregard the words of my beloved? Wouldn't I make her suffer if she returned and didn't find me here?' When I heard this I felt unbearably sad and thought, 'No matter how difficult it may be, in God's name I must help him.' I put everything else aside and came to you on his behalf. If you take pity on this youth, I will be your slave, I will dedicate my life to you."

"Sandakumaran," said Anandarubi, "He is not the one meant for me. Look, ten years have passed and he hasn't even tried to find me. If he had loved me at all he would have come to this mountain. He only stayed on in that place because he feared for his own life. What else would have kept him there?"

"Mallika, don't think that. He keeps sending arrows of desire out to you, desire which has made his earthly body deteriorate back into earth. He can't leave that place because you swore you would come back in eleven days. He stays there because he is truly in love with you, because he will not disobey your words. Even though he is hungry he won't go anywhere, he just stays there because you might return and worry if you don't see him. He simply stays in that place without food waiting for you."

"I don't want him, and I will never yield to his desires."

"O you jewel among women, why do you hate him so much? I won't leave here until he has what he wants."

"Prince of Peace, give up this wish. I will never go back to him."

"It is not really just to talk this way. In God's name I have gone through so many difficulties for him. Do not overlook that."

"For your sake, Sandakumaran, I will summon him here, but I won't speak to him."

"That's all very well, but if you do that, I will fast on your doorstep until I die, and the blame will fall on you."

He fasted for seven days under the shade of a tree opposite the palace gate. On the night of the seventh day he had a dream in which a man appeared, calling him. "Prince of Peace, she is a fairy who has made many, many men die of their desire for her. Call the youth, put the ring that King Masaak gave you and some water in his mouth. Tell him to swirl it around and collect that water in a cup. If you can somehow get her to drink that she will fall in love with him again."

He woke, trembling, at daybreak. Then Anandarubi came to him. "Young man, Prince, why did you try to end your life? If you had fasted to death the blame would have fallen on me. How would I have faced God tomorrow?"

"Good. If you do fear God you must call the youth and let him see your face. You must look at his face."

"So let it be."

"I will go for him," said Sandakumaran.

"Why should you go to so much trouble? I will send my fairies to get him." She called four or five fairies, "Follow the road down this mountain, and under a tree you will see a youth, his eyes closed but flowing with tears. He will be sitting sorrowfully on the rock of mystery. You must tell him that Sandakumaran has gone to his beloved, told her all about his pain, and because of that, she has sent us to fetch him. Tell that to the youth and bring him here."

In a second's time they reached the youth and told him everything. He praised Sandakumaran's gracious qualities and prayed to God for him, then he left with the fairies and they brought him to Anandarubi before nightfall. She had the youth sit close to her. The moment he saw her he lost consciousness and fell to the ground. Anandarubi called for rosewater and sprinkled it on his face with her own hands.

In a little while he returned to consciousness. Anandarubi smiled, "Young man, you may look at me as much as you please." He sat with her the whole day, and in the evening she called her handmaidens, "Decorate the hall with a variety of colors, adorn yourselves, and get ready to sing and dance for us." Picking up their vinas and other musical instruments they entertained Sandakumaran, the youth, and Anandarubi with songs and dances.

When Sandakumaran observed that Anandarubi was not looking at the young man, he quickly gave him the ring to put in his mouth, and told him what to do. The youth got up quietly and went to the pitcher which held the water kept for Anandarubi.

The fairies asked him, "What business do you have here where Anandarubi's water is kept?"

He replied, "I'm very thirsty," and they poured water into a cup. The youth took some of it into his mouth and waited for the right moment. Mallika ordered her handmaidens to give him a cooling sherbet, and when they put it in his cup Sandakumaran had him secretly spit the water from his mouth into the sherbet, and offer it first to Anandarubi. She drank two sips of the sherbet and fell in love with him.

"Mallika," said Sandakumaran, "If you take pity on someone who loved you so much he was actually losing his life, every living being in the world will praise your wisdom and intelligence."

Smiling she asked, "What is this, a trick, an illusion? I don't understand, I've never been caught in a predicament like this before. If he were to leave me or stay away I couldn't bear it. I can't survive for even a minute without seeing him. I swear to accept him just as you asked me to, but I shouldn't do this without my parents' permission."

After saying that Mallika went to the mountain where she saw her mother, and bowing her head modestly stood in silence. "Daughter," said her mother, "You said you would stay in the garden forty days. Why have you come back so soon?"

Mallika's handmaidens answered for her, "Mother, your daughter Mallika has fallen in love with a human youth who is also in love with her. He has suffered a lot for her sake, and now he's come here. Your daughter is here to ask for your blessing to marry him, and that's why she returned so quickly from the garden. She is a little concerned you might not give your permission."

Mallika's mother went to her husband, "My wise lord, our daughter wants to marry the man she is in love with."

And her father said, "If that is her wish, I am very happy."

How blissfully Mallika sent her handmaidens to summon Sandakumaran and the youth to the palace. Her mother welcomed them with great joy when they arrived, and had her husband prepare all the decorations for a very extravagant wedding. When her father saw the youth he, too, was very happy as he got everything ready. Then the wedding took place with many kinds of lavish entertainment, and afterwards, the bride and groom lived like Manmadan and Radi, the god of love and his bride.

The day after the wedding Sandakumaran begged leave to go. "Where will you go?" Anandarubi asked.

"There is some urgent work for me elsewhere," answered Sandakumaran.

"If that's the case, we'll have you taken there," she said, and had him seated on a throne. Quickly she called the fairies to her commanding, "Take him to the mountain south of the Jumna River." They carried Sandakumaran on his throne, flying all night to reach the mountain.

"Fairies," he said, "You may leave me here. I will always be in your debt." Taking leave of him, they flew off.

As he walked on thinking about the details of his next duty, he saw a huge mountain soaring up to the skies, as high as the sphere of the air, as high as the sphere of the moon, as high as the sphere of the sun. He climbed upward for a month intending to discover the secret of the mountain. When he finally reached the peak he saw a very wise sage with a face as beautiful as the sun, as cool as the cooling light of the moon, and with a body as delicate as a lotus flower. The Prince of Peace fell at his feet and lay there unconscious for a whole day.

When the Sufi Master of divine luminous wisdom came out of his meditation, he opened his eyes and said, "Sandakumaran, Prince of Peace, rise up," as he lifted him up. His hair standing on end, his body trembling and shivering, Sandakumaran got up. He was sweating as he stood there in silence.

The Sufi Master beckoned to him, gave him water from his own pitcher, and then had him sit down in front of him. "Sandakumaran, my child, do not be afraid of anything, you have been sent to this world as a child of honesty, justice, patience, generosity, and charity. My son, I will explain everything you have been wondering about. We are now on the mountain south of the Jumna River. I was here more than two thousand years ago worshiping God the eternal and infinite One, the One who is suffused within all lives, who knows of everything. With me there was a dog who also worshiped God. When I opened my eyes the dog saw me and paid obeisance. I asked, 'What do you want?' and this is what happened."

The Dog's Story

"Sufi Master," said the dog, "Even the moon looks at your beauty and falls in love. If the whole world is so enamored, how can I describe my condition? I have been waiting here in this ashram now for a hundred years. Master, please accept me as your slave, I want your gracious permission to serve you."

"Lady," the Master replied, "Beauty fascinates the world. That's why there is no balance here today."

"Master," asked the dog crying, "Why was I born as a dog? What have I done that was so evil?"

"Lady, it is only because you were born as a dog that you can hide your modesty with a tail and behave without any loss of good conduct. You can go everywhere freely. As a dog you have discarded four of the five elemental monkey demons, leaving you only one, but man who is supposed to be so beautiful has kept all five. Do not be entranced by this beauty; it will push you into hell. This form may appear beautiful, but it brings many evils."

"Master, even though I don't want that hell, my mind refuses to be tranquil. I do want your beauty."

"Lady, I have said so much, but you just won't listen. Let me tell you about the destruction which comes with this form: poverty, illness, disease, hastiness, intoxicants, lust, theft, lies, and murder, are all born within those who take the form of a man. So don't put your faith in that beautiful form which can pull you into a bottomless hell. The condition which man's body is subject to is pitiful. As a dog, you don't have to experience any of this."

"Master, isn't it possible to be born as a man and to live as a true man without being poor?"

"It is possible because everything is within God's grace, but when a man has wisdom and faith in God, poverty is no sorrow. Let me describe the nature of wealth. It is the termination of poverty, and along with those other evils, wealth with the help of arrogance, impatience, lust for power, egoism, and possessiveness makes the burial place the fires of hell, converts good to bad and justice to injustice. It burns peace into ash and changes duty into a poisoned fruit. It calls charity emptiness, patience a karmic disease, and lust a god incarnate. Wealth embraces those evils unceasingly. So you see man's birth and his beauty do have these characteristics. Do not be deceived when you see them."

"Master, isn't it possible to avoid lust, to embrace what is good, destroy evil, and realize within the heart that poverty is life itself?"

"In the past it was, but after Kalian was born and the name Kali yuga was conferred on this age, it became very, very rare."

"Master, isn't it possible to survive in this yuga if you are born as a human being?"

"There is no place in this age for those who live as human beings. Today man has the face of a man and the qualities of an animal. They call a good person a four-legged animal. They say anyone who was born as a man, who lives as a human being, is a bull. They mock true *gnānis* as misers, they call men and women of integrity dogs without good conduct, they say they are going to toast heavenly beings like bread and eat them, they tell those who have seen God to bring Him before them. Since the birth of Kalian there have been many more strange scenes like these."

"Master," said the dog, "I want to be born in the world as a woman and marry someone who has fully realized the meaning of these truths."

"Lady, since you desire the human form and its beauty so much, you will have to know that drama. For the present, two human female children will be born from your womb. You will know their nature and their fate, and then you will realize the secret of being human."

"Master, my body must remain undestroyed."

"You will raise the two babies who will be born to you. Later, when you are dying, tell your daughter to put your body in a locked box and hang it from the rafters. You cannot live in this city from now on. Go to the little village beyond this mountain."

The dog left there at once, went to the village, and wandered from street to street, becoming a watchdog for several houses. The owners of those houses fed the dog and looked after her. Ten months passed, and it was time for the birth of the two girls. When the pains in her abdomen began she thought, "According to what the Sufi Master said, human babies will be born, but if I stay in the village, they may be in danger." And so the dog crept away to the woods and found a cave on the mountain.

There her pains continued and she bore the two girls. Light from the bodies of these babies shone like rays of the sun, and the moon danced in their light. The coral on the banks of the river had to hide in the water with shame when it saw their faces. The cooling moon that travels in the sky had to conceal itself in the clouds when it saw the beauty of the babies. No kind of jewel, none of the nine precious gems could compare with their loveliness. The dog gave them her milk and raised these beautiful babies in the cave. When they were three years old, she went to a potter's house to guard his clay pots. The potter realized she was a good dog and began giving her food which she would take home to her children, and then come back to watch his house.

The children grew until they were eight years old, and then the dog thought it was time the children start to cook. One day the potter left the dog to guard his pots and went to the neighboring village. She took four or five pots and gave them to her children, then she went to a rice seller, wagged her tail, and showed her good intentions. The rice seller realized she was a good dog, kept her in his house, and cared for her. She would give any food she received to her children, and then go back to guard the house. One day the rice seller left the dog guarding the house while he went to another village on business. The dog took two or three bags of rice, one at a time in her mouth, and dragged them to her children.

At dawn the next day she met a tailor. When she saw him, she came up to him wagging her tail and barking at everyone else she saw. The tailor realized she was a good dog, kept her in his house, and began giving her food. Then he took her to his shop and kept her there to guard it. One day when he heard that his wife had suddenly fallen ill, he tied up all his clothes in a bundle, left the dog to guard the store and went home. The dog took that big bundle of clothes to her own house. By then the girls were sixteen years old.

The next day the dog went to a grocer's house and lay down in front of it. When she saw the owner and his wife she wagged her tail. They began to realize this dog had more wisdom than most men, and started taking care of her. She took the food they gave her to her children and guarded the shop. Then the shopkeeper's mother died in the next village, and he and his wife went there leaving the dog to mind the store. The dog crawled into the shop, took all the things she needed for her children, and brought them to the girls. When the shopkeeper came back he saw neither the dog nor the goods, and thought someone had beaten the dog, killed her, and taken his things. But the dog had moved to a carpenter's house with the idea of getting a rice-pounder for her children.

In the meantime a king with his ministers, elephants, and horses came to the woods where the dog's children lived. When the hunt was over they set up their tents, and the king and his minister went to look around while the others rested. The minister saw smoke rising from a cave, and wondering who could be there, they went to find out. They saw sticks and earth closing the mouth of the cave and became more curious than ever. So the king and his minister called out, "Is there anyone home? We are thirsty. Please, may we have some water to drink?"

The older daughter said shyly to her younger sister, "Sister, there are two people here who seem to be princes suffering from thirst, and they must be given water. But our mother is not here, and how can we, young girls, exceedingly beautiful young girls, take it to them?"

"All right," said the younger sister, "I have an idea. Let's smear charcoal on ourselves then they won't be able to see our real beauty, and they won't desire us."

"That's a good idea," replied the older one.

They rubbed charcoal all over themselves, and the younger sister took water to the minister while the older one gave some to the king. As the king took the water he looked at her face and saw one spot she had not covered, and that place shone with a luminosity comparable to the moon. When he saw that the king spat some water on her face, the charcoal washed off, they both saw her beauty, and fell to the ground in a daze. The two girls splashed water on the faces of the king and the minister. As soon as they recovered they put the two girls on their horses and took them to their city. The king married the older sister, while the minister married the younger one.

When the dog came to the cave with the food given to her by the carpenter, she found her children missing, looked around unsuccessfully for them, then she began to cry and fell down, rolling on the ground, screaming. After that she wandered and roamed through several lands, without food, crying and crying. Finally, she came to the city where the girls then lived. As the dog approached the king's palace, the queen who was inside the palace saw her mother coming and called her handmaidens, "Get that dog for me!" They brought the dog on a leash and the older sister dismissed the handmaidens saying, "You may go." Then she embraced and kissed her mother, explaining how the king had taken her in marriage.

The dog who was her mother blessed her daughter, "May God the all mighty and all knowing One protect you. May your marriage prosper," and then she asked, "Child, where is your younger sister?"

"The king's minister married my little sister, Mother."

"May God protect them. I'll go see my child and come back here. Only then will my mind be at peace."

"Mother," said the older daughter, "You have come so far and have had so many hardships, you must be tired. Please bathe and eat something, have a little rest, and then go." Immediately she had serving girls bring hot water and she bathed her mother, anointed her with attar of roses, musk, jasmine, and many other kinds of fragrant scent. Then she fed her eighteen kinds of food, took her mother in her lap, held her in her arms, and rocked her to sleep.

When she awoke the mother dog asked for permission to see her younger daughter, and left. The younger sister was standing on the balcony and saw her mother coming, "That dog is trying to come into the palace!" she screamed to her servants, "Beat it and chase it away!" The serving girls grabbed some sticks and beat the dog. But instead of running away, she limped into the palace. In the full knowledge that it was her mother, the younger daughter hit the dog with an iron rod. As she was hit, her back was broken, and she fell at her daughter's feet writhing in pain, "O my dear, my daughter, my precious child!"

"Disgusting dog!" shouted the younger sister, "Don't you have any wisdom?"

She hit her mother again with the iron rod. With that blow she crushed her head, and the dog fell to the ground. "Take this dog and throw it in the street," she called to her serving girls. When they had done that, the dog dragged herself painfully towards the palace of her older daughter.

As she came closer the daughter who was standing on the balcony saw her coming. She called to the serving girls at once, "Bring that dog here." They picked her up and brought her close to their mistress. The older sister tenderly embraced and kissed her. "What happened?" she asked.

"I was attacked by what I nourished with my own breasts," said the dog. "Your sister beat me with an iron rod and commanded that I be put out."

"Did that hideous creature do this without the slightest feeling for her own mother? The shame is too overwhelming to live with. Come, I will kill her and die with you," she cried.

The dog was dying now, but she said, "My daughter, jeweled light of my eyes, don't be hasty. Hastiness is the enemy of wisdom. Impatience will kill wisdom. Understand that truth well, my child, because this is only one of many such ugly incidents which will occur in modern times. The world has been acting this way since the birth of Kalian.

Now I will not live any longer, so take my body, put it in a box, and hang it from the rafters of the room where you sleep. If your husband or anyone else asks what it is, tell him it's the dowry given to you by your father and mother. My Sheikh, the Sufi Master is calling me." Her life then left her, and the older daughter did what her mother had told her to.

Some time passed, and one day the king studied her intently and said, "You are so very beautiful. How beautiful your mother and father must be! Couldn't we go to see them just once? I do want to meet them, come, let's go!" When his wife heard that she cried, the tears trickling down her cheeks. "My lady," continued the king, "Whenever I talk about this, you start to cry. What is the reason? You are the mother of a little boy. Shouldn't you at least show him to your parents? Don't say no, we must go to visit them tomorrow. So be ready." He rested on the bed looking up at the rafters and saw the box. "What's that?" he asked.

When the older sister heard that, she trembled with fear and thought to herself, "*Aiyo,* what can I say? What's going to happen? I have put my mother's corpse in that box, and now what answer can I give him? Our ancestors have said not to disobey our parents, haven't they? No matter what happens, let it be with God's grace." She came to this decision and said to her husband, "This is the dowry my mother gave me."

"Take down the box so I can see it," said the king. Shaking, she brought him the box and opened it. They found it filled with the nine kinds of precious gems, priceless in value. "If I gathered all my wealth together," said the king joyously, "It wouldn't even be worth one of these gems, and therefore, we must begin the journey to your parents at once." He ordered his minister to make the preparations, and then they set out with elephants, horses, palanquins, and troops.

On their way they passed a beautiful pond and a banyan tree. Near that tree was an anthill. When the king saw the shady tree he said, "Let us rest there," and they stopped for a little while.

The queen was in great distress and kept thinking to herself, "Where can I go? What palace can I show him?" While she grieved this way, a snake which had been inside the anthill raised its head and looked at her. She saw it and thought, "O God, what other way is there to protect my honor? This is the only way." So she said to the king, "I'm just going to relieve myself. I'll be right back."

Giving him that excuse, she walked up to the anthill, and held out her hand to the snake. When it noticed her, the snake drew back into the anthill and informed his king. The king, who is almost impossible to meet, told his servants to prepare a palanquin and deliver his invitation to the royal pair. The queen was still touching the anthill when the snake came back and gave her the invitation. She looked at it and then took it to her husband. This is what it said.

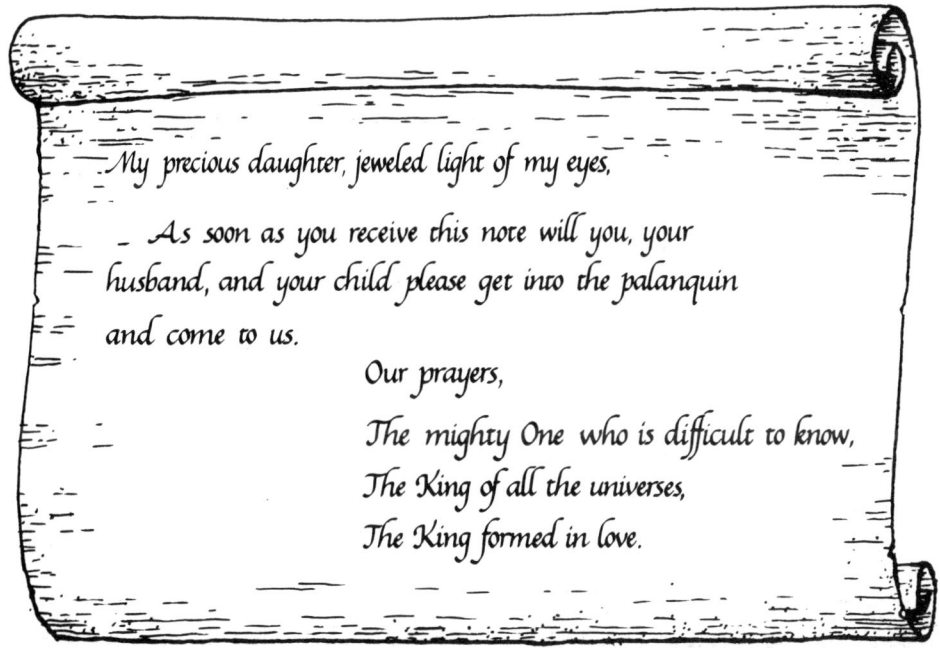

My precious daughter, jeweled light of my eyes,

As soon as you receive this note will you, your husband, and your child please get into the palanquin and come to us.

Our prayers,

The mighty One who is difficult to know,
The King of all the universes,
The King formed in love.

They looked at what was written, went over to the anthill which split open, and a palanquin made of coral, precious stones, and all kinds of jewels emerged. They told all the others who had accompanied them to wait there as they went inside.

Within the anthill a huge and beautiful castle appeared, four hundred miles around. The interior of the castle was studded with pearls, the walls were made of jewels, the doors shone with gems, and the resplendent apartments within the palace were adorned with the nine kinds of precious gems. There were countless servants and handmaidens.

The king said to some of them who were standing there, "I have not seen my mother and father-in-law yet. Where are they?"

They replied, "First they sent us to bring you here, then they ordered us to serve you, to give you any amount of treasure you want, and to tell you they have left for the city of Five Elements." When he heard that, the king joyously took what he needed, told the bearers to let his mother and father-in-law know they had visited, and got back into the palanquin. He and the queen went out through the anthill again, joined their ministers and the retinue waiting there, and went back to their palace. The anthill closed over as it had been before.

When the minister heard of the queen's good fortune, he asked his wife, the younger sister, "Can we go too, and get treasures from your father and mother as your sister did?" The minister's wife was surprised when she heard this, and ran to ask her sister what had happened. The queen told her everything, not leaving out a single detail, and then her sister returned to her own palace for her husband, and together they went to the place where the king and his retinue had stopped. There the younger sister saw a snake, and assuming it was the same one her sister had seen, she held out her hand. The snake bit her, and she fell to the ground and died. When the king heard of this he went there and arranged a proper burial for her.

In the meantime the life of the dog reached the Sufi Master of divine luminous wisdom. "Did you understand the qualities of the two girls?" asked the Sufi Master. "That is the world."

"O Master," replied the life of the dog, "I did learn something, but I would like to know more about those people in the world who are good and those who are evil."

"Ah!" said the Sufi Master, "You will be born as a child to the king of Mayajala. You will excel in your studies, and the kings of many lands will be fascinated by your beauty, fall in love with you, and propose marriage to you. Your father will want to marry you off, but if you just marry in the usual way you will not know the wonders of the world. It is said that kings will become beggars, and beggars will become kings. Realize that. To know the wonders of the world and to understand what will become of the world, memorize the saying I will teach you now. 'Happiness before you see it. Sorrow after you see it and experience it. Why is there happiness before it is seen? Why is there sorrow when it is seen and experienced?'

Recite this to your father, and tell him you will only accept the man who can explain the meaning of this saying to you. Swear it in the name of God. You will be born as a baby to the king of Mayajala, the city of magic tricks and illusion," promised the Sheikh, uttering blessings on the life of the dog.

Then the Sufi Master said to Sandakumaran, "The girl was born as a daughter to that king and grew up with the name Manonmani. Twenty-seven years have gone by, and she still puts that riddle to all her suitors. This girl was the dog who served me. The one who was her older daughter lives a chaste and virtuous life. She never deviates from justice, and lives with thoughts of honesty and integrity. Day and night she praises God, the most exalted Being. Do you know who she is? She is Mutavalli. I placed her in the chest and lowered her into that well. She will become your wife. This is what you have come here to find out, but for now, go tell this story to Manonmani exactly as I told it to you without changing a single word, and then have her married to Fate. Sandakumaran, Prince of Peace, don't forsake Mutavalli. Yes Sandakumaran, marry her. Now farewell."

Sandakumaran received the Sufi Master's permission to leave, fell at his feet, paid obeisance to him, and then started on his journey to Mayajala. He went back to the young man called Fate who was staying at the rest-house, and told him about all the hardships he had endured. "My friend, happiness is coming your way. I have discovered the meaning of the riddle, and now the two of us must go to Manonmani, tell her the details, and do whatever is necessary to get you married." And so they set off to see her.

"*Amma,*" the handmaidens said going to their queen, "My lady, we see the man who went in search of the answer to the riddle and the other one who stayed at our rest-house coming this way."

Blissfully Manonmani ordered, "Bring them to the palace," and immediately her handmaidens brought them there. Then she sent for the servants and had them seat Sandakumaran and Fate on a throne set with the nine kinds of precious gems. She had a curtain hung between their throne and the one on which she was to sit. Her throne was also set with these precious gems. "Sandakumaran, Prince of Peace, have you learned the answer to the riddle? Tell me your story."

He told her of the difficulties he had encountered, the marriages he had helped arrange, and how he had seen the Sufi Master. He repeated exactly what the Sheikh had instructed him to say. When she heard those words, Manonmani, the jewel of the heart, smiled with happiness and told her handmaidens to open the curtain. The curtain parted and she saw Sandakumaran's face, "Nectar of my precious life, jewel of my eyes, light of my eyes, king of true duty, all the words you have spoken are the truth, but where did you see my Master? Please have pity on me, tell me where you saw him."

"He is at the peak of the mountain south of the Jumna River. I saw him there, and he told me to tell you everything I just said to you. Also, he told me to marry you to this youth whose name is Fate."

"Because you are a true king of duty," said Manonmani hearing the words of her master, "It will always be my duty to do what you say. I was following the instructions of my Sufi Master when I asked this riddle to find out how many of the millions and millions of people in this Kali yuga who experience joy and sorrow, who know the highs and the lows of this life, actually analyze and understand good and evil. I have spent the twenty-seven years of my life humbly studying this. Master, for twenty-seven years no one has known the answer. It was because of this my Sufi Master said there are many kinds of human beings. Today I realize the truth of that statement. Therefore, you can do whatever you wish with me."

When he heard this Sandakumaran joyfully performed their marriage ceremony, and then the bride and bridegroom lived happily together. One day he came to them, "My beloved friend, my sister, jeweled lights of my eyes, may you both live a very long time. There is so much work for me in this ABCD world, and you must, therefore, give me permission to leave."

"Dear brother," said Manonmani and Fate together, looking at the Prince of Peace, "We have completely accepted everything you told us."

"The words I speak are the words of God, the most merciful One, given with His grace to mankind," said Sandakumaran. "All men who accept them fully with respect and devotion will live as heavenly beings, and that means they will practice generosity, compassion, good conduct, duty, justice, honesty, patience, and all the other good qualities. Don't swerve from these qualities, my fellow beings, because the One who is the great treasure exists within them. But those who learn to live this way will be attacked by suffering, poverty, illness, and injustice. No matter how much evil comes, don't be afraid and don't forget these qualities. Suffering is natural to God's devotees, but what can evil do to them?"

When he had explained this, Sandakumaran received their permission to leave, and began his journey to the ABCD world.

When Will I Remember?

While I search my heart
For the one precious treasure,
The light of the universe,
Protect me O Lord, eternal One with no beginning.

When will I remember within, unceasingly,
The immanent, luminous ray of light,
The soul of creation?

When will I bow in reverence,
Seeing the reality within,
Beyond all scriptures?

When will I see the One, Allah, the zenith of the triple flame,
See that subtle formless One,
And bow in reverence?

When will I see the divine form of the Almighty One,
Surrender at His feet,
And know liberation?

When will I find that Omnipresence,
The all-pervasive light within my being,
And receive His grace?

When will I find that resplendent flame,
The eye of wisdom, free of delusion,
And ascend with the breath to merge in the *'arsh?*

When will I learn how to climb up
To the heaven of Allah's *'arsh,*
And stand alone, knowing my true place?

When will I enter the kingdom of His grace,
And through unending meditation
Meet Him, worship, and pay obeisance to Him?

When will I leave the groups of the world,
And go, singing the word of the Sheikh,
To dwell with the One who knows no suffering?

When will I drag myself up to the summit,
Find His divine feet of purity,
And take that state into my heart?

When will I search for that unreachable
Fruit in my heart, and find it
In the core of my being?

When will I reach the temple of my inner heart,
Traveling on six pairs of legs,
And see it for all time?

When will I go in this beggar's house,
Singing the glory of God,
To live in the center of my being?

When will I have clarity,
Before my life leaves this body,
And discover that precious Treasure?

When will I discover the method
To unite the sun and the moon,
And enjoy that bliss forever?

When will I climb on the breath of the moon,
Taste the elixir of that eternal spring,
And merge in that clarity?

When, before my destruction,
Will I find the lamp in the vortex at the summit,
And receive that grace?

When will I merge with God,
All my faults ended, knowing the place
Where the resonant sound emanates?

When will I see the One in five letters,
Searching the heart to dispel the taints,
And settle permanently within?

When will I know the beauty
Which can be seen in the *'arsh,* the beauty
Of the exalted One who has no name?

When will I see the sparkling
Light in my heart
Merge between the eyes?

When will I see the *qalb* where You dance and play,
When will I push aside this body,
Knowing it is false?

When will I raise the fire of wisdom
To the summit, discard the artifice,
And know myself?

When will I taste the honey of the eternal flower
In the everlasting spring
Of the throat?

When will I join the silent One whose mouth never speaks,
Joyously praise Him,
The fruit which never fades?

When will I merge with that which lives
At the heart of the lotus in the tongue?
When will I give up shouting and roaming in vain?

When will I, like a restless miser
Not searching intently,
Have clarity before death destroys me?

When will I dispel my ignorant trust
That the world is permanent, cleanse all my sins,
And merge with my Lord?

When will I stop barking like a dog of desire,
Believing the world is real as I wander,
When will I know myself?

When will I stop being a thief, burying my stolen goods,
When will I join Him,
Kiss Him and play with Him?

When will I stop being like those ill-behaved wretches,
When will I see His divine feet
And His light of grace?

When will I stop roaming with base desires,
When will I cut this fascination with maya,
And find my true home?

When will I stop being an ignorant miser, immersed in the world?
When will I twirl the moustache of absolute faith,
And know reality?

When will I stop being like those
Who wallow in the joys of wife and child?
When will my worldly thoughts end forever?

When will my heart pay homage to the Sheikh
Who lives in the three thousand
Fragrant qualities of God?

When will I begin to fear this transient life,
This life like bubbles on the water?
When will that fear reach me?

When will I cease to be blown from land to land
Like chaff in the winds of the world?
When will I have the maturity to touch His divine feet?

When will I stop being like those who crave amusement,
Talking of books and swamis,
When will awakening and inner realization come?

When will I stop placing this world of dreams in my heart?
When will I control my thoughts
In the stillness of silence?

When will I stop taking part
In the plunder of the world through sweet deceit?
When will I stabilize certitude in that One?

When will I shun ignorant people who want the world?
When will I have the purity
To hear that sound in my ears?

When will I control the nine openings?
When will I see the truth
In the center pillar of the heart?

When will I stop studying books,
Like those who have not learned
How to open the lock?

When will I stop wandering the house like a rabid dog,
And mount the horse of the *Kalimah,*
Riding up to the great One who is everywhere?

When will I stop being a costumed guru
Who has not studied with a Sheikh?
When will I find the right path and stay there?

When will I stop wandering the jungles intoxicated with marijuana,
And drink the liquor of the divine intoxicant,
Allah, who crowns the eight-span body?

When will I shun drunken, drugged fools,
When will I begin to pray truly, and joyously receive
The divine intoxicant of grace?

When will I stop being like idol worshipers
With hearts of stone?
When will I find that one help and be liberated?

When will I stop being like fools
Ignorant of the right and left breath?
When will I know that one state where sorrows end?

When will I break away from those who sing *bhajans,*
Conquer all obstacles,
And find the perfect house?

When will I stop imitating singing fools with tambourines?
When will I conquer my arrogance
And become His slave?

When will I break with these fools
Who worship stone idols,
And merge joyously with that infinite One?

When will I stop imitating ignorant fools who worship
Brass and stone idols? When will You take away
The sorrows of the world and give me eternal life?

Unlike the blind who cover their gnostic eye with sacred ash,
When will I find the light between the eyes
And know liberation?

When will these crazy thoughts stop invading my heart,
Causing such evil actions?
When will I have the purity to reach You?

When will I stop behaving like wandering drunken musicians?
When will I live a life
Without deceit?

When will I stop carrying flowers to the temple in ignorance?
When will my body be made pure and perfect?
When will my God accept my heart?

When will I stop these disguises,
These costumes and dances?
When will I reach that One who fills the universes?

When, before this house of skin, bone, and tissue collapses
Will I find His milk of grace
And drink it?

When will I know what goes on
In this body with twelve openings?
When will You carry me to the top?

When will I distinguish the dark from the light
Clearly, in my heart? When will I
Escape from the bondage of blood ties?

When, before the calamitous angel of death arrives,
Will I climb to the fourth step,
Ma'rifat, and then merge with God?

When will I climb the rungs of the ladder
On the words of our Sheikh,
And joyfully see Allah, our precious jewel?

When will I reach the feet of the great One
Who does not eat or drink?
When will I see Him and offer my heart?

When will I look within and see
The One without form or body or shape,
When will I see Him and worship?

When, before this house of ten letters grows old
Will I achieve my purpose,
And find that divine beauty?

When will I find the seat of only one
Of the twenty-five letters of the *Kalimah,*
And place it at the center of my forehead?

When will I find the feet of the lone One
Who rules the divine city, and come near Him?
When will I see Him without fear?

When will I find the coral, the pearl, and the emerald?
When will I hear the sound of the flute
Which is the *Kalimah,* and know its meaning?

When will I kneel reverently at the feet of those
Who have tasted the essence of the universe?
When will I join them and learn to be wise?

When will I fall from this cage
Formed by one worm creeping into the body of another?
When will I live blissfully in my *qalb?*

When will I catch that wild
Horse of my mind,
And control it with the *qalb?*

When will I reach God's feet before my life ends?
When will the sorrows of this sinner end?
When will I receive the benefit of my prayers?

When will I glorify the feet of God?
When will my mind stop trembling? When will my sorrows end?
When will I reach Him?

When will I leave this disgusting body,
This dark room of skin and bone,
And go back to my original home?

When will I climb the slippery branches
Of this tree, my body,
And joyously find the fruit it yields unseen?

When will I creep into the body with ten letters?
When will I see the *nuqat,*
The point of His grace?

When will I worship the feet of the Creator
Before I crawl to the grave?
When will I know that deathless state?

When will I give up speaking?
When will I merge with the great One?
When will I receive the vision of His grace and merge with Him?

When will I have the determination to climb
The steps of the secret, silent gateway?
When will I give up my attachments and lose myself in God?

When will I merge with the peak of the liberating house?
When will I be victorious,
And live in that house?

When will I lock the doors and windows of the body?
When will I see Him in front of me,
And remain eternally awake?

When will I see the great treasure
Which exists eternally within, and when will
My mind be comforted, the fatigue all cleared away?

When will I see that Power
Directly,
And end my unbearable sorrow?

When will I find truth,
Lasting happiness,
And reality with no seed at all?

When will I stop wandering
Day after day like the dead?
When will I find my Creator's divine feet?

When will I develop eternal wisdom fearlessly,
Discover the secret of deathless life,
And stay in that state of endless, eternal bliss?

When will I fast completely,
Stop all thought,
And meditate in a one-pointed heart?

When will I, before my life ends,
See the vision rarely seen,
And receive eternal bliss?

When will I see the indescribable, divine feet
Within myself,
And rest in the universe of the soul?

When will I search with love
And find the grace of the King
Who lives in the *qalb*?

When will I search my heart
For the divine feet of the universe's Ruler,
And remain in unwavering meditation?

When will I enter the hexagonal palace of the *qalb*,
And see the One
Beyond age or time?

When, before my body deteriorates and is buried,
Will I see the glorious praiseworthy One
And find bliss?

When will I see reality,
The One who rules alone, who cannot be described in words?
When will I rise above the throat and see Him in the *'arsh*?

When will I see that one place between the eyes,
The one that controls the sixty-four arts,
And be granted a state of abundant beauty?

When will I gaze at the Cause of all things
Who is mingled in everything?
When will I reach that state of bliss?

When will I search with zeal for the unique One
Who soars high like a kite,
Find Him and unite with Him in love?

When will I analyze the subtle guidance of the Sheikh
Who is the embodiment of all good qualities?
When will I accept that guidance, and reach a state of bliss?

When will I reach the glorious feet of the Almighty One,
And travel that upward path
To victory?

6
Vandi Puluhan's Story

Vandi Puluhan tells Mutavalli, whose faith in God is unwavering, how he lost his faith in God, accepted the evil ways of the world, and rejected everything that was good.

MUTAVALLI: [*To Vandi Puluhan and Kandi Puluhan*] This is the end of that story. Sandakumaran is a man who never swerves from the truth, who has been good to so many people and so many other creatures. Now then, tell me, is he a man or are you two men?

VANDI PULUHAN AND KANDI PULUHAN: Indeed, we are called men.

MUTAVALLI: If you were men you would walk on just two legs!

VANDI PULUHAN: *Amma*, Sandakumaran is a useless idiot! Listen, we'll describe the plight of people like Sandakumaran. They know how to walk on two legs all right, but not very much about the world. All they know is how to stand erect on two legs looking straight ahead. As they go walking along they are struck by stones, the trees on their path drop on their heads, and members of our family kick them and crush them. Many such blessings are bestowed on them because they don't know how to avoid these problems. All they can do is cry, "Father, forgive all my faults, grant me Your grace." They don't even know how to plot a course through the world. But that's why they have two legs! We're not like that. *Amma*, if stones are cast, we move out of the way. If we see a tree, we bend down. If a person hits us, we laugh, and then later we destroy his family. We act in accordance with the times: we twist and roll, we walk on all fours or on two legs, we bend and turn somersaults, we behave as the situation demands. Therefore we have two legs, and we also have four. We have the faces of men, but we have the qualities of flies, ants, the eight million, four hundred thousand insect beings, and all the animals.

MUTAVALLI: *Aday* sinners! What wages do you think God will give you?

[*She sings.*]

MUTAVALLI'S SONG

O God, You are God in the universe of the soul.
Is it right
For me to live

Without Your grace?
O God of justice,
I will never forget You.
O God, O radiant light,
Please grant me Your mercy.
You alone are the grace which protects,
You alone are the compassionate treasure.

You are the original king,
The mover of everything, everywhere.
Your nature is to know Yourself.
You are always known in the heart.
You are the great One,
Always alone
In the hearts of those
Who know themselves.

I have forgotten the earth,
You are all my heart thinks of.
You are my mother and my father, everything.
Allāhu, Allāhu, Allāhu,
O God without beginning or end,
You alone are God.

VANDI PULUHAN AND KANDI PULUHAN: My lady, only a lunatic like you needs a song like that. People like us don't need that kind of song.

MUTAVALLI: *Aday* sinners, may cancer eat your tongue if you go on talking like that! Those demons who spoke against the heavenly beings and tortured them perished themselves.

VANDI PULUHAN AND KANDI PULUHAN: Lady, Rama was so endowed with goodness he never once disobeyed his mother and father. He was the very eye of his father, the Emperor Dhasaratha, who was himself humble to everyone. Even a wailing child would stop crying when it heard the name of Rama. Now wasn't this same Rama sent into the forest because of the hunchback Kuni's schemes? Weren't you aware of that?

MUTAVALLI: *Aday* you demons trapped in ignorance, the time for your destruction is drawing near!

[*She sings.*]

MUTAVALLI'S SONG

Ravana, the indestructible King of Lanka,
Threatened to destroy
The heavenly beings.
Knowing that, God created Rama with love
And crept gently into Kuni's heart.
Dhasaratha sorrowfully banished Rama to the forest.
God who is grace
Entered Rama's arrow,
And as grace pierced Ravana's body,
Pierced it and killed the mighty king,
Killed Ravana and brought him down.
Such is the grace of God, Appa.

VANDI PULUHAN: A great sage named Mandavya was meditating alone in the forest when thieves hung one of the king's jewels around his neck and then crept away. The sage was unaware of what they had done to him, but when the king's guard saw the necklace around his neck, they seized him and dragged him before the king. What happened in the end? This enlightened sage was put to death on the gallows. Have you forgotten all that, my lady? What are we supposed to think when that kind of thing happens to such detached souls?

MUTAVALLI: You sinners, you speak with utter disregard of the truth. One day that very truth will destroy you!

[*She sings.*]

MUTAVALLI'S SONG

He breathed Lā ilāha ill-Allāhu.
With the qualities of God he became a Sheikh.
"Whatever befalls me is His intention,"
He sang, while bliss and grace
Flowed through his heart.
Such clarity is the gift of the triple flame
To those whose hearts are open to Him.

People like you who hunger for other men's wives with the arrogance of a lusty elephant have not even the slightest bit of strength left to fight against the ignorance of your own minds. You have no awareness of God, no connection to God. You don't have enough wisdom to distinguish truth from lies or to understand the grace of God. That's why you talk this way, and that's why you will be destroyed by your own actions one day.

VANDI PULUHAN: Hari Chandra was an honest king who took care of his subjects as the eyelids take care of the eyes. His wife was chaste and modest, both were humble in dealing with their subjects, but what happened in the end? He became the slave of an untouchable, a cemetery caretaker, and she became a brahmin's slave. *Amma,* we all know this happened, don't we? Why have you forgotten this, my lady?

MUTAVALLI: Ah sinners, you speak without knowing God. The wickedness of what you're doing will engulf you. O God, can't they be taught the truth?

[*She sings joyfully with bliss.*]

MUTAVALLI'S SONG

*You scoundrels, you who forget God
Are the dissemblers who speak
Without even knowing your own fate.*

*You eunuchs who speak without any awareness
Of God who is the life within our body,
You will not know the taste of that divine honey
Before your bodies are destroyed.*

*You are people who are worse
Than snakes. For the sake of barren riches
You sing your hymns, believing
Such sinful acts are devotion.
"What can fate do to us?" you unwisely prate.
You treasure your pride,
You treasure your vanity,
For you God has His inquiry and judgment date.*

VANDI PULUHAN: Nalan was a just king who ruled Nidatha. With God's grace, in his reign the hawk and the parrot lived peacefully in one cage, but didn't even such a noble king lose his kingdom, his country, his wife and children with a throw of the dice? Didn't he suffer? Is it fair that this should have happened to such a righteous person? *Amma,* understand what this means.

   I'll tell you something else. The prophet Abraham, may God's peace be with him, always behaved with perfect conduct, justice, integrity, sincerity, charity, tranquillity, peacefulness, duty, patience, compassion, pity, mercy, generosity, and humility. Let me tell you more about him. He was willing to sacrifice his own son to God, wasn't he? Don't you know what fate befell that worthiest of prophets, my lady?

MUTAVALLI: Let's just see how long God will tolerate your brazen impudence!

[*She sings.*]

MUTAVALLI'S SONG

Grace will flow to those who are near the Master,
God, the infinite jewel,
The ruler of grace,
The form, the formless, the light face,
The One, the many.

If we think of the divine Being
Who shines as the triple grace,
His vibration will resonate,
Booming drums
Through the eight compass points.
O Master who is God,
Please come, please come, please come.

O Father, please come,
Please come and make sinners
Who conceal the truth
With their energetic lies
Know and realize the truth.
Please come, please come,
O Master who is God,
O Father, please come.

VANDI PULUHAN: There was a man called Meyporul Nayanar who was deeply devoted to God. Whenever he saw anyone wearing emblems of purity like holy ash or prayer beads, he would bow down to them as humbly as if he had seen God. A thoroughly evil man whose name was Muthunathan kept trying to lead him astray, but he was always defeated. One day he finally resorted to trickery in his campaign against Nayanar. He rubbed ash all over his body, sprinkled more on a bundle of books strapped to his back, and on a few others which he carried in his hands containing concealed weapons. Disguised this way as a holy man, he went to the room where

Nayanar sat by himself. Meyporul Nayanar hoodwinked by Muthunathan's disguise, paid obeisance to him, immediately seated him on an elevated chair, and sat himself at his feet begging humbly, "Please teach this slave." The cunning Muthunathan took the weapons hidden in the books and attacked him with force.

My lady, what do you think of the fate of Nayanar who worshiped disguises as though they held the treasure of truth? He had perfect faith in God, didn't he? What had he done so wrong that this had to happen to him? Analyze this, consider it carefully.

MUTAVALLI: [*She sings.*]

MUTAVALLI'S SONG

See that perfected man
Who seeks His help alone,
Free of desire in this illusory world,
Wandering twelve years in search of grace.
But how can you expect
Ever changing fate to respect anyone?
Can something which lives in hell
Recognize an exalted being?

VANDI PULUHAN: *Amma* Mutavalli, you go on talking about so many different things, prattling about this and that. Let me tell you about Muhammad, may God's peace and blessings be with him, who was sent to us as a prophet. God said he was His prophet, His divine messenger, the *rahmatul-'ālamīn*, the mercy and compassion of the universes. And God sent him down the six thousand, six hundred and sixty-six verses of the Qur'an, and countless *hadīth* which He uttered directly to him. Indeed, this holy prophet met God at *Mi'rāj* and spoke to Him face to face. Don't you know the torment which the people in this world caused him, that prophet who dispelled darkness and frailty from every heart, and filled it with the grace of God? Don't you know the indescribable suffering Abu Jahal and his followers caused him? They would spread thorns on the path he was to walk on; they threw stones at him and broke his teeth. When he sat in meditation they would throw the intestines of cats and cows and goats at him. They chased him out of his own country. Why should such a prophet, a true prophet, a prophet who spoke to God face to face have endured such persecution and anguish? If God really is a true God, why should that prophet have borne so much agony? If there really is a God, why would He permit this torture of someone He named His own prophet? Have you at least thought about this Mutavalli? If there really is a God, shouldn't He have saved him from all these horrors? What are we supposed to believe when such a prophet suffers so terribly?

MUTAVALLI: Everything you've said is perfectly true, everything you've asked is a good question, and everything you described really happened, but your thinking and your reasoning are completely twisted and idiotic!

[*She sings.*]

THE SONG OF MUHAMMAD

This is the grace of God who created the universes,
This is the grace of God who created everything,
This is the grace of God who is the completeness in all lives.

That primal One sent the noble prophet,
May God's peace and blessings be upon him,
In his full resplendence
To make perfect faith flourish.

He pointed out the right path, that benevolent One.
He filled the prophet of perfect faith
With the certainty and the determination
That there is no suffering for us.
He instilled perfect faith in him, the absolute trust
Which is surrender, disappearance in the will of God.
He explained al-hamd, *the praise-filled heart,*
To the glorious prophet,
Yā Muhammad, Yā Muhammad.
"The suffering of all lives is yours," He decreed,
"All joys and sorrows are yours," He said.
"Tolerate the world which acts ignorantly with love,
Dispel that ignorance with divine grace,
And guide them to the shore
With the luminous, pure faith of their inner heart."

God said to the prophet,
"Show them the path to the shore."
God said to the prophet,
"Have the patience to endure
Whatever suffering may come.

*Whatever happens will not happen to you
But to Me," He said.
"I am the One who will take
All the blows and the beatings,
I will experience
All the pain and the suffering.
I impressed patience on you, My prophet.
Explain* al-hamd *as the praise of that patience.
Bear with inner patience and absolute contentment
Whatever may happen.
Be absolutely contented with what you have today
And surrender the responsibility for tomorrow to God,"
Said God.
"Use love to open the ignorant heart," He said.
"Open the inner heart with love."
And so He sent down the prophet.*

*"Be available to everyone," He said,
"Do only good in your life and remember
You belong equally to those who are good
And those who are bad," He said.
"Anger must be avoided at all cost,
And you must transform your qualities and your actions," He said.*

*What sorrow is there in this world
For the prophet who came
In that state,
For God alone is the One
Who accepts and experiences everything.
"I am the One
Who experiences the suffering," said God,
Continuing to accept all suffering.*

*There is no suffering for the noble prophet.
The suffering of all lives is his suffering,
The suffering of all lives brings suffering to Him.
"This is the state of his life," said Allah,
"Therefore, what suffering does he have, O man?"*

MUTAVALLI: You talk without any understanding whatsoever, ignorant fool.

KANDI PULUHAN: Mutavalli, let's leave that for now. God created the prophet Jesus, may God's peace be with him, and they say in this world that Jesus was the son of God. They say he is the path for all lives, that he was the son of Mary and the son of God, that he gave eyes to the blind, ears to the deaf, and made cripples walk. They say he gave water to those who thirsted, and food to those who hungered. That's what the religions, the world, and many people say in praise of him. How could such an exalted being, who has even been called the son of God, have been betrayed by Judas, one of his own disciples? They say he had to endure so much suffering and agony and pain, that he was interrogated and then nailed to a cross, that they gave him a crown of thorns, pierced his body with nails, and exposed him to the winds. Mutavalli, why should a prophet who is known as the son of God have had to bear such torment and anguish? What kind of justice is there if this is what happened to the son of God? Why couldn't your God have saved him, why couldn't He have protected His son? Why should Jesus ☮ have had to undergo this torture? If there is a God, and if Jesus ☮ really was the son of God unlike anyone else in the world, why wouldn't God have saved His own son? Do you really trust this God, Mutavalli?

MUTAVALLI: You've chosen your words carefully, but your ignorant thoughts are filled with the qualities which destroy people.

[*She sings.*]

> *Allah created so many prophets,*
> *Allah created so many prophets,*
> *And among them He named these resplendent ones,*
> *Adam, Noah, Abraham,*
> *Ishmael, Moses, David and Jesus.*
> *He created them as seven letters,*
> *And made these seven His disciples forever.*
> *He decreed the qualities of these seven,*
> *And with those qualities He gave eternal wisdom,*
> *And with that wisdom made them live in one word, Allah,*
> *And with that word created the grace*
> *To open and reveal the heart of true man.*
>
> *From His effulgent sun*
> *He had one luminous ray enter Mary*
> *As Jesus, the ray that was the seventh letter.*
> *This He decreed for the universal good,*
> *And impressed His many qualities there,*

His qualities which have no 'you' or 'I'.
He created him with such good qualities,
And commanded him to speak about the One,
And commanded him to say that all races are one.
To him He said, "Live with purity and dignity,
The sins of the whole world are committed against Me," He said.
"All lives in the world are your brothers," He said.
"Do not cause suffering to any life," He said.
"Tell them to make God alone their master,
Tell them everything you see belongs to Him,
Say that God is the master who cuts away karma.
Go, cut away their illusions, polish their minds," He said.
"Cut away their state of mind,
Dispel their state of mind, show them a state of grace.
Whatever difficulties you have are Mine," He said.
"Jesus, I have placed you on a cross," He said,
"I have nailed you to a cross," God said.
"You will see, your body is the cross.
Look at your body, this is your cross," He said.
"I drove five nails into it, do you see?"
In silence He showed him the five nails
Of earth, fire, water, air, and ether.
"These five are the wounds of your heart," He said.
Desire for earth, desire for gold, desire for women,
Mind and desire, these five,
These five are the wounds of your heart,
The desires for maya, these are the nails,"
Said God showing them to him.
"This is the suffering of your body," He said.
"So release your brothers from these nails,
Remove these nails from your brothers," He said.
"This is the suffering faced by all lives," He said,
"Blood ties, desire for earth and for women, racial differences,
These are the wounds," He said.
"These are the five sores," He said.
"If you pull out this nail of suffering
They will come to Me, they will have the right
To live with Me in My kingdom," He said.

He said this at the beginning of creation,

He gave this explanation
At the moment the light became each child,
And everything happened as He said it would.
This is the experience of the world,
This is the experience of each human being.
Look at yourself, see how
This is the suffering of each one of us
On the cross of our own body.
Look at yourself, see how
You are nailed to the cross of your body,
And you will understand your qualities.

MUTAVALLI: The outer cross is an illustration, but you are also nailed to a cross, you are on a cross right now. Each one of us has been nailed to that same cross He placed in front of us as an example. The blood of our attachments is dripping from the wounds of racial differences, religious differences, desire for earth, desire for gold, desire for women, and while blood drips from each of these we live a life of suffering. Each one of us is nailed to the cross of our body. Each one of us drips blood from the wounds made by those nails. Haven't you realized this? Isn't it time both you and the world realized this?

Pull out those nails and come to the kingdom of God. God said that to Jesus ☪, and he did that. He removed the nails of the five elements and went to the kingdom of God. But you, instead of trying to remove those nails, you want to live here, to live the life of a madman. Imbeciles! Idiots! Vandi Puluhan and Kandi Puluhan, remove the nails, trust in God, and resolve that you will strive to reach the kingdom of God.

VANDI PULUHAN: My lady, the words you have uttered are perfect, interlaced with pearls and jewels. I understand them quite well, but I'd just like to tell you a few things which have happened in my life to make me what I am.

MUTAVALLI: What are they, tell me.

VANDI PULUHAN: *Amma,* I married twice. My first wife's name was The Light That Leaps From The Eyes.

MUTAVALLI: The what That Leaps From The Eyes? What a curious name!

[*Vandi Puluhan now relates his story.*]

My lady, that light is the formless Effulgence, the wonderful, majestic, mighty One who is a slave to a slave, the One who is rich to the rich, poor to the poor, a king to a king, integrity to those of integrity, peace to the peaceful, justice to the just, duty to those who know duty, patience to the patient, a woman to a man, and a man to a woman. The woman I was married to was that light of formlessness.

I married the girl and tried to live with those qualities. As time went on all our property and possessions flew away from us. Then that treacherous thing called poverty overtook us and caused endless suffering. The upshot was that I wandered from village to village looking for work. When I came to a town where the people all claimed to be Hindu, I asked them to give me a job, and they said they would, but only if I was converted to their religion. This didn't sound like Hinduism, and when I asked what the connection was between religion and work they replied, "Our God is the leader of all the gods. Our religion is the best of all."

At that I asked, "How many gods are there? Do you think there is one god for each religion? It's not like that at all—there is only one God for all religions."

"O *gnāni* who recites the vedantas so fluently, we have no job to offer you. Good-bye," they replied and chased me away.

After many other difficulties I came to a forest where I wandered from path to path in search of work. The people there proclaimed themselves Buddhists, but when I saw how they behaved I was surprised. I asked an old man, a passerby, "*Appa,* Sir, is there any kind of work I can get in this place?"

"*Appa,*" he replied, "You look like someone from a neighboring village, but you don't seem to know anything about the pride and the strength of this country. If you want to escape from here with your life you had better act the way we want you to act. If you don't, I fear to think what your fate might be."

When I heard that I said, "*Aiyo,* this is quite frightening! All right Sir, please tell me about it."

"Listen carefully to what I say, Sir," said the old man, "If you want to live here, first you must be converted to our religion, second, you must worship our God, and third, you must speak our language only. You must accept the belief that our religion is best and that others are inferior. If you do this you might manage to find yourself a job and survive, but if you violate these conditions you will be ordered to leave. And then if you refuse to go away you will be subject to our tribal punishment."

"Sir, does that constitute the greatness of your country?" I asked.

"Well Sir, do you think this applies only here? It's the same in all countries," he said.

"Right," I replied, "Now if I am converted to your religion and escape from this danger, what job will you give me?"

"If you are converted, we will give you a place to stay, a career, property, and help in time of need, but if you decline to be converted, I don't know what your punishment will be."

"Is this really where the greatness of your country lies? It sounds so peculiar, doesn't it, because in his teachings we find that Buddha never swerves from justice. He meditates unflinchingly on the truth, he knows righteousness will triumph, he knows that patience is a great treasure, he considers all four religions equal, and he knows there is one God who is God to all four. But from what you say, it sounds as though there are four gods for four religions."

The old man answered, "What you're talking about is a thing of the past. Nowadays we create the gods and the governments, but you seem to be a lunatic, completely unaware of the might of this country. Today you have come to me with ancient history. Don't go around saying this to my fellow countrymen or they'll pull out all the hairs on your head, one at a time."

VANDI PULUHAN: After giving me that little discourse, he took a stick and hit me. I ran and ran from that place and didn't look back until I reached the next city, my lady.

MUTAVALLI: All right, tell me what happened after that.

For the next three months I wandered through deserts and forests until I reached a city where I ran into a lot of trouble. Finally, I came to a house and asked the people, "Kind Sirs, I am very thirsty, my tongue is parched, please give me a little water."

There was a very old man with a thick beard who asked, "Who are you? Where did you come from?"

"Please Sir, give me a little water," I said, "And after I drink I'll tell you." But the old man continued to ask question after question. "I have no strength, Sir. Please give me a little water and afterwards I'll tell you everything," I begged again.

"Ah, is that how it is? Well, if you can't talk then stay that way," the old man said.

"Sir, illustrious one, I beg of you. Ten million blessings will be yours," but the old man stood there without speaking. "Sir," I went on, "You speak of clarity, duty, law, and justice, but you refuse to pour just a little water on a parched tongue. Sir, Sir, please, Sir!"

"*Appa,*" said the old man, "You don't seem to appreciate how great this country is. The inhabitants of this land are a religious people. They don't use terms like 'illustrious one' or 'insignificant one'—mother, father, old people are like newborn children here. They must all go to the temple and pray to God three or four times a day, and if any of them fail to do that, they are chased from home. Furthermore, the very words they use must be worshiped like gods. If you don't do that they will shoot you. Listen, I'll tell you more. There is no longer any difference between male and female, but the men are slaves to the women, and when a woman returns home after work, the soap and hot water must be ready. Sometimes the man has to prepare and serve her tea, stand by with folded arms, hand her the newspaper, polish her boots, and put them away. After that's done he has to cook. When the wife is finished looking at the newspaper she asks if the food is ready and he'd better say yes.

Let me describe this country. There is no room here for other races, castes, or religions. We have many people who live here willingly because of the poverty in their own country, who have been quite happily converted, but certainly not because of any real faith. Others join us because of all the benefits which go with this religion. However, if someone like myself helps or shows pity, mercy, fairness, charity, or justice to someone of another religion, they will cut off my head immediately. If I gave you water in a country like this, I would lose my head."

I listened very patiently, "Sir, illustrious one, Jesus, may peace be with him, whose patience was his grace, taught many different laws of good conduct, including the ten commandments which Moses ﷺ taught with great clarity. Don't your people at least know that? What kind of religion can it be if those who embrace it don't practice its teaching? What kind of people can you be? What kind of philosophy do you have? Tell me Sir!"

"I've asked many great men the same questions you've asked, and they all reply, 'Don't believe what others say, they must be Satan's children, never believe them.' I've said to them, 'Jesus ﷺ taught there is an omnipresent Power who fills all four religions, and we must praise only that Power. What do you think of his words?' They've answered, 'The words of Jesus ﷺ were said and done with nineteen hundred years ago. Our word is final, and you'd better do what we say. All those other religions are satanic.' I was dismayed and frightened by this, and in any case, what could I do, there was no other way to make a living. Arguing with them didn't help, but I did manage to survive, complaining to God all the time. However, since you are a Hindu, I am afraid of what might happen to you. So my advice is, go to some other country and try to earn a living there."

I was so shocked to hear this I left immediately. After that I knew hardship in many countries, and finally came to another city. As I wandered here and there I saw a mosque and sat down outside. Soon, an old man came out and I asked him for some water. This old man pointed to a well near the mosque and told me to take some from it and drink. I drank from the well and went back to him. "Sir, what do you do?" I asked.

"*Appa,* I preach in this mosque. I am the *imām,* the prayer leader."

"If that's true, why don't I see people here?" I asked.

"We are the *Furqān* or Islamic religion. We follow the teachings of

Adam, Noah, Abraham, Ishmael, Moses, David, Jesus, and Muhammad, may God bless them and grant them peace. They preached and taught us well. They taught there is only one God for all four religions, and that we must love only Him. They taught if we fear Him and obey His commandments we must not speak disparagingly of any race or religion. If we speak badly about anyone it is equivalent to speaking badly about God. They gave us this and many other true teachings. Be in awe of God, pray to Him at the five times He prescribed, build mosques, worship and pray to God in them."

He continued explaining many things. "However, the world today has killed all those teachings and swallowed them up. There are people in today's world who have rolled law, justice, divine beings, saints, sages, and God into a pill and swallowed them. They praise themselves saying, 'We are God!' When wise men who can't bear this ask them if they're not being evil they shout, 'Hey madmen, get out! What do you know? You're scatter-brained idiots! We are God, we are heavenly beings, we are the people who control the world. What is your religion, your race? You talk about God—where is He? Bring Him to us, and let us see Him with our own eyes,' they say with ridicule and scorn. '*Aday* crazy old men, you make rules and laws to suit your own intelligence, you say that Someone exists somewhere and build a house for Him, you collect lazy people like yourself, keep them from doing their job, make them join your party and shout without meaning until, finally, they don't earn enough money to eat because of you idiots. You lock your women in their houses so they can't learn anything. You won't let them out to see the sights and learn from that. Don't you know that restraining them like that is unjust, you sinners? If you destroy yourselves we will be able to live peacefully. If you die we can live as we like.' This is what they say."

The old man continued, "That's not all. Men and women do not conduct themselves properly. Grown up women wear ornaments and bangles without modesty and wander gaily in the streets after dark. A wise elder might attempt to advise them saying, 'Do not pursue maya's fleeting path, do not believe the world's drama is the real thing. Go instead on the path of the soul's liberation. Believe in the indestructible, infinitely omnipresent God whose beauty will never change, who exists suffused within everything, then you will know beauty, bliss, the peacefulness of your soul, and so much happiness. When you see the sun and the moon, don't you realize the majesty of that One? By His command the sun and moon make the day and the night. He creates things, makes them sleep, wake up, and grow.' Then like a slap on the face those nasty creatures interrupt, 'Hold on, mister! The rising of the sun and moon is a part of nature, not God's work,' and they ridicule his words.

Then the elder might make another attempt to convince them saying, 'You say there is no God, that all this is part of nature. Listen carefully, let me give you an example. All of you must have been to the movies. You need a screen, the pictures on the film, the rays of light, the light itself, and the projector, but even though you have all those things, someone is still needed to run the projector, put the film in the slot, and turn on the machine. If there were no one running the projector you wouldn't see the scenes on the screen, would you? If there were no God, nothing would move in the world.' Without hesitation those people reply, '*Aday,* crazy idiot, the world has been ruined because of you. If we see you outside this mosque we will burn you alive.'

Since then I have not left the mosque, and they have not come here to pray. They pretend to be Islam, but Sir, there is no room in this world for those who fear God. You had better go someplace else where you can lead a life trusting in God."

When I had heard his story I left that place, encountered various difficulties, and came to another country where many different people lived. Because I was hungry and thirsty I went to a house to ask for some food. They invited me to come in and sit down, and kept chatting, but there was no sign of any food. I was tormented by the pangs of hunger, my tongue was parched with thirst, and I finally asked, "Mother, even if you don't have any food to spare, could you please give me a little water?"

The woman, her name was Ignorance, replied by asking, "Who are you Sir? What caste do you belong to, what country do you come from?"

"All the countries God created are mine," I answered.

"Ha! You crazy man, what is your religion?" Ignorance asked next.

"All four religions God created are the same to me."

"Crazy man! Don't you want to watch us and learn how to behave?"

Then with great self-control I asked, "What are you saying?"

"You say the four religions God created are yours. Don't you know the danger that threatens them today?"

"Mother," I answered, "I don't know. What is it? Please tell me."

"*Aday* man, those four religions clash among themselves. Each of them says, 'I have the truth, not you,' and now they are in the process of disappearing from the world. The religions also say that there is one God, that people must fear Him, and act in submission to Him. That's why the religions are fighting one another and becoming extinct."

Then I became a little impatient, "Mother, what is your religion?"

"*Aday* you crazy idiot, we are the religion beyond all religions."

"What religion is that, Mother?"

"That," said Ignorance, "Is the contemporary religion we fashioned ourselves. All those who join can live happily, joyously, blissfully, and everyone is free to join."

"Is it possible to acquire good qualities by joining this religion?" I asked.

And Ignorance replied, "Our religion moves with the times; it does whatever the world does. It can dance, sing, run, laugh, act, and be joyous with distinction. Our religion knows how to be comfortable in the world and accommodate our desires. Furthermore, our men and women are treated equally without any discrimination of sex, and a woman can make love to any man she likes without hindrance. Our religion embraces many other wonders like that."

After listening to this, "Mother," I said, "Your religion certainly seems delightful, enjoyable in every way, but may I ask one more question?"

"What do you want? Yes, go ahead, ask."

"Everything about your religion sounds good, but there is apparently one thing missing."

"What is that, *Appa?* What don't we have?"

"What you don't have, Mother, is even an atom of the good conduct, good behavior, good thoughts, intelligence, chastity, calmness, patience, decorum, wisdom, or any of the other good qualities which women need."

Ignorance replied, "But what you say is really true. Even if you were to cast a net over us to fish out those qualities, you wouldn't find them. I agree we lack the things you described, three times over. Even if we were to ask them to stay with us, those good qualities would say, 'We are going, we are going,' and fly away. Not only that, but from now on there won't even be any place in the modern world for them. From now on there will be no room for any of them here."

"Mother," I said, "Don't include the entire world in your company. There are only a few like you who don't have these qualities, and I realized that convincingly just by talking to you. *Amma,* one day in your company is sufficient to taint every good quality with evil. *Amma,* I bid you ten million good-byes."

Fate

What will fate do to me?
What will it do?

Will it make me meditate and realize my self?
Will it free me from death and give me eternal life?
Will it make me search for worldly things later?
Will it lead me to the bliss of liberation?

What will fate do to me?
What will it do?

Will it guide me to the golden city within?
Will it throw me into a cruel hell?
Will I be conquered by earth?
Will it tame the horse of the *Kalimah, Lā ilāha ill-Allāhu*?

What will fate do to me?
What will it do?

Will it make me find the divine bliss of my birthright?
Will it make me argue like a fool?
Will it lead me to ridicule at the hands of dancing girls?
Will it put me in the company of men with divine luminous wisdom?

What will fate do to me?
What will it do?

Will it let me enjoy divine visions?
Will it betray me to the angel of death?
Will it make me earn riches ignobly?
Will it grant me the grace of the eternal One?

What will fate do to me?
What will it do?

Will it put me in the company of those who perform miracles?
Will it entice me with the words of thieves?
Will it make me rave like a madman?
Will it make me utter a silent mantra?

What will fate do to me?
What will it do?

Will it unlock the door and let me in?
Will it make me associate with liars?
Will it keep me in torpor like a bull?
Will it let me ascend to the heavens and enjoy them?

What will fate do to me?
What will it do?

Will it let me hear that sound and value it?
Will it make me run and wander and roam?
Will it make me chase prostitutes?
Will it take me to the triple feet of the One above?

What will fate do to me?
What will it do?

Will it let me speak to the silent One?
Will it make me wander all over the world like a dog?
Will it make me run to distant lands seeking riches?
Will it let me see the noble King?

What will fate do to me?
What will it do?

Will it let me find the divine milk and drink it?
Will it make me mistake intoxicants for milk?
Will it have me ride the vehicle of four plus five equals nine openings?
Will it let me have God's grace in the three worlds?

What will fate do to me?
What will it do?

Will it have me join the One without caste or race?
Will it have me take up a bowl and beg?
Will it have me wander the streets?
Will it have me play in the house beyond all religions?

What will fate do to me?
What will it do?

Will it let me see my Father and receive His blessings?
Will it make me wander aimlessly like an ignorant fool?
Will it make me a beast of burden?
Will it let me reach the path of liberation?

What will fate do to me?
What will it do?

Will it make me steady in meditation?
Will it make my heart burn and cry?
Will it make me decay like a dead tree?
Will it show me the path and let me reach my destination?

What will fate do to me?
What will it do?

Will it strengthen certitude and have me ride the ray of light?
Will it make me a corpse?
Will it make me follow sinners?
Will it make me shine where God sits in the crown of the head?

What will fate do to me?
What will it do?

Will it make me climb up the rungs of the ladder?
Will it make me give up the unattainable fruit?
Will it make me struggle for gold?
Will it let me have our Father's grace in the three worlds?

What will fate do to me?
What will it do?

Will it tame the horse of the *Kalimah, Lā ilāha ill-Allāhu*?
Will it destroy my life?
Will it make me play in brothels?
Will it make divine luminous wisdom grow within me?

What will fate do to me?
What will it do?

Will it let me reach a golden state in limitless, inner space?
Will it make me kiss jewel-bedecked women?

Will it make me die like a worm in dung?
Will it grant me refuge at the feet of the true Sheikh?

What will fate do to me?
What will it do?

Will it make me cling to dusk and night?
Will it make me crawl into a false life?
Will it make me lazy, blaming fate?
Will it make me find God's grace?

What will fate do to me?
What will it do?

Will it take me to the feet of God?
Will it make me wander, talking arrogantly?
Will I be chased by mobs in the streets?
Will it open the house of truly luminous wisdom?

What will fate do to me?
What will it do?

Will it show me a vision of eternity and let me reach that shore?
Will it torture my mind and make it a thief?
Will it make me spend time in brothels?
Will it let me reach the Father who is like a mother?

What will fate do to me?
What will it do?

Will it let me reach the feet of my Father?
Will it make me dance on stilts to the tune of the world?
Will it make me rant false wisdom?
Will it let me mingle within Him like the fragrance in a flower?

What will fate do to me?
What will it do?

7

The Four Fools

Vandi Puluhan continues the story of his loss of faith in God. He tells of his experiences with the four fools and the old woman, and how the ten sins prepare him for his marriage to Maya.

I left that place and walked along until I came to a forest where I saw four people who had fallen into a well. Each of them scrambled onto the shoulders of one of the others shouting, "Get me out! Get me out!" The one who was at the bottom of the pile was calling loudly to the one on top, "Get me out!" They all panted and shouted, hit each other, fell to the bottom again and rolled around. When I saw them I picked up a strong vine and lowered it into the well, telling them to climb up, one by one. But all four of them grabbed it at once, and began to clamber up yelling at me to jump in too.

"If I fall in," I said, "Then all five of us will suffer. So come, climb up the vine one by one." One of them reached for the vine, and as I started to pull him up one of the others grabbed his legs, someone else grabbed his, and there they all were, holding onto the legs of the one above. The four of them clung to the vine and began to pull me down. I fell against the outer wall around the well and cracked my head. When I got up and looked in the well, I saw them grappling with each other and thrashing around on the ground. I felt sorry for them and lowered the vine into the well once again to try to save them. "Take the vine one at a time. When the first one gets out, the rest can follow one by one."

They began hitting each other to be the first to seize the vine. I calmed them down, pointed to one of them, and told him to grab it. He held on, I began to pull, but I couldn't pull him up. When I looked into the well to see why, I saw one of the others sitting on his shoulders while the other two held his feet.

"*Appa!* What are you doing?" I asked.

"We're nearly out. Pull harder," the four fools said, "Get us out! Get us out!" Just then the vine broke and they all fell down. Not even one of them got out in spite of all my efforts. Once again I lowered the vine, they did exactly the same thing, and this went on for a long time. Because I was suffering from lack of food and water, this repeated exertion was agonizing, but I thought it wouldn't be right to just leave them there, so I lowered the vine once more.

Just then an old woman whose name was Intellect came down the path.

"Mother," I said to her, "Four people who are my fellow human beings have fallen into this well. You must save them." The old woman waved her hand and the four inside the well climbed out.

As soon as they came out all five of us addressed the woman, "Mother, *Amma,* we are tortured with hunger pangs. Please give us a little food." In reply she beckoned us to follow, took us to her hut, sat us down, and fed us milk and fruit until our hunger was appeased. After we had eaten we all fell asleep right there from exhaustion.

The fools woke up before I did, tied me up, and started to carry me off. I opened my eyes, but they refused to stop; instead they began to chant, "Don't stop! Lift him up!"

"What in the world are you picking me up for?" I asked.

"Don't you know what we are going to do with you?"

"I don't know."

"*Aday* you idiotic creature! Don't you really know? A little while ago we fell into the well and suffered torment because we couldn't get out, didn't we? But if we had had any practice we could have climbed out, couldn't we? So now we are going to put you in the well and practice getting you out."

"Why do you want to practice on me?" I asked pitifully.

"You seem to be a fool," they said, "Don't you remember that we fell into the well? Don't you know we couldn't get out for many, many days? Therefore, we are going to put you in the well and practice getting you out. If we put you in and learn how to take you out, then in the future we can rescue others who fall into wells."

"You have great powers of reasoning! What names do you answer to?" I asked.

"Our leader is called Know-it-all Fool, and that fellow over there is Unwitting Fool. This one's name is Plain Fool, and I am Blind Fool."

"O ho!" I said, "Your names themselves prove how clever you are."

Again I felt very weary and exhausted, and fell asleep. While I was still sleeping, they dropped me into the mud with my hands and legs tied. Because I was buried in it they couldn't see me, and lowered a stone on a rope to locate me. They tried jiggling the stone around but it got stuck in the mud, and when they pulled the rope up it didn't come back. "Oh!" they said, "He caught hold of the stone." Then they had a little argument about whether to carry on or not, but finally agreed they had to learn what they had to learn. So one of them was lowered into the well. He jumped in the mud, and while he was rolling around covered with it I wriggled on top of him. Because my hands and legs were tied and there was no way out, I sat on his head.

Peering in, the other three saw me and exclaimed, *"Appa!* Where is he? How did *you* manage to get out?"

Angrily I retorted, "He's at the bottom of the well eating mud. I'm finished eating, and *I* am sitting on *his* head!"

Angrily they shouted, "Have you started eating without us?" and then they leaped into the well and were instantly buried in mud. One of them grabbed the rope tying my hands and it broke. Now that the four of them were completely buried, I climbed over them, untied my legs, and watched them talk among themselves.

"Hey, Know-it-all Fool, what's there to eat?"

Know-it-all Fool ate a handful of mud and answered, "Hey! Eighteen kinds of rice and curry can't compare with the superb taste of this food."

Plain Fool ate some too, "I have never experienced a taste anything like this in the twice seven equals fourteen worlds."

Hearing that, Blind Fool and Unwitting Fool ate some too, and then all of them began to shout and writhe on the ground, their stomachs swollen.

"Why are you shouting?" I asked.

They replied, "This unlimited food in the well has caused gas and distention in our stomachs, and it's giving us a little pain. Today we have realized the truth of the aphorism 'What's tasty to the mouth is an enemy to the stomach!'"

As soon as I heard that a smile came to my face, but just then the old woman who had got us out before appeared. Looking into the well she said, "Total fools, all of you! How did you get into this terrible state?"

"Mother," I said, "They were born into this world as four fools, but they display the actions of ten times that number because they think they are clever. You're the only one who can save these four fools and me."

The old woman felt pity in her heart, "*Aday,* leave the well and come out," she said, but they remained in there trying to pick each other up. "What are you doing? Come out," she said again.

Know-it-all Fool said, "We're practicing how to rescue people who've fallen into wells. Who are you, and what's the rush?"

"Total fools!" she answered, "Do you have to throw people in to practice getting them out? *Aday* learned fools, come out, come out!" She waved her hand and out we came.

"*Amma,* we've practiced," they said, "Now please give us some kind of job."

"Clever fellows!" she called, "Come along with me and I'll feed you, then you can each take one of these clay pots and bring water from that pond over there to these pomegranate trees, jack trees, the lime trees, and all the other plants here in the garden."

They took the pots and went to look at the pond. "Hey, elder brother!" the other three said to Know-it-all Fool, "How many times will we have to fetch and carry water if we use these pots?"

"How do you expect my brain to work when I'm standing?"

"Yes, that's fair," said Plain Fool. "What you say is just—you give good advice and preach wisely to us. You certainly deserve a seat." He searched around in all four directions, and by the banks of the pond he found a tiny stone the size of a mustard seed. He placed it in front of Know-it-all Fool. "O illuminated one, please be seated on this."

"Fool, how could anyone sit on that?" asked Blind Fool, bringing out a small bead, "Please be seated on this."

And Unwitting Fool brought out a snail shell, placing it in front of Know-it-all Fool, "Please be seated on this," he said.

"All three of you are fools," said Know-it-all Fool, "Pile the clay pots one on top of each other." They did as he asked, and because he couldn't climb up to sit on them, he told the others, "Lift me up and put me on top." The three of them picked him up and sat him on top of the pots. Immediately he broke through and fell, trapped inside.

The others grabbed him and tried to pull the rims of the pots over his head one by one, but they couldn't even move them slightly and had to consider what to do next. "The point is, my brothers, we must save Know-it-all Fool, mustn't we?" they said to each other.

Caught in the pots Know-it-all Fool screamed, "By the time you finish thinking, my life will be over. You are real fools! Quickly, go get a stick, smash the pots, break them up, and save me!" No sooner had Know-it-all Fool said that than Plain Fool picked up a stout stick and hit him on the head. He was instantly buried in pots.

"*Amma!*" said Blind Fool, "You've made his feet stick out. Watch while I reveal the man." He gave him a sharp blow on the rear-end, and Know-it-all Fool shot up with the force of the stinging blow. The pots broke but the blow was so hard that he collapsed and fell down in a faint.

Plain Fool called the other two, "We should pour water on him, but how can we fetch the water?"

Blind Fool ran to bring back a little water in his hands. "That's not enough!" said Unwitting Fool, "How can we bring him out of his faint with that?" and he went running off quickly to bring some water on a tiny leaf.

Plain Fool asked, "Are you a bigger fool than he is? Look, a brilliant idea is coming to me.....Let's get him somehow to the pond and drop him in."

They pushed him into the pond, and as he was restored to consciousness by the cold water, he began to swallow it in his struggle to escape. With his mouth full he burbled, "Aah! Get me out!"

"Are you through fainting?" the other three asked. Know-it-all Fool couldn't say anything because his mouth was full of water, but just as he was about to faint again the waves of the pond pushed him towards the shore. When the other three dragged him in they noticed his stomach was swollen. "Elder brother!" they screamed, groaning, hugging him, and crying, "Someone from the pond crept into your stomach." He recovered from his faint and stood up. "Elder brother, ask that person in your stomach whether he is going to come out or not."

"What rascal crept into my stomach? Will you come out or not?" he shouted at his stomach threateningly, holding it with both hands, squeezing. Because it was full of water, it made a gurgling sound.

"Elder brother, who could be in your stomach? How can you hope to save yourself?" they exclaimed, immediately attacking his stomach with three sticks. When no one came out they embraced him and cried, "Elder brother, how will you survive?" By now he had fainted again from the shock of the blows. Instantly the three others roared, "Thieving scoundrel! Sneaking dirty rascal! Low caste idiot! Will you come out or not?" They jumped on his stomach and water came pouring out of his nose and mouth until his stomach was completely flattened. Since they still hadn't seen anyone leave they looked intently in all four directions, "Where could you have gone to hide? O ho! Did you run away without our knowing it? If you had fallen into our hands we would have killed you."

They raised Know-it-all Fool to a standing position, and when he was up they began to consider their situation. "Alas, elder brother, Know-it-all Fool, what's to become of us? We've broken the pots we were supposed to carry the water in, and we haven't watered the trees either. What will we tell the old woman if she asks?"

"My brothers," said Know-it-all Fool, "An idea is dawning within me."

"We are ready to do whatever you say," said Plain Fool.

"Let's see brothers," continued Know-it-all Fool, "If we don't bring the water the old woman will scold us. Also, we did break the pots. Now this is going to make her very angry but I have a good idea to calm her down. If the four of us sharpen four sticks, use them to dig up the four sides of the pond and move it to the orchard, the old woman will be happy with us, now won't she? Well, what do you think of my idea, you three?"

Plain Fool spoke, "Elder brother, O Know-it-all Fool, who in the world could ever outstrip you for cleverness, fame, greatness, or sharpness of intellect? Elder brother, your idea is not only good, it is also sagacious, and exactly the way to win the old lady over. But look, we've gone without food for three days, and right here on the banks of this forest pond are the ripe fruit of the jaumoon tree. Let's pick that fruit, savor it, and satisfy our hunger. After that we can move the pond."

"Plain Fool," the others said, "What you're saying is right too, but if we eat the fruit first and then start the process of moving the pond, it will be difficult. Let's cut four poles of balsa wood, give them sharp points, and lever up the shores of the pond. Later, after we satisfy our hunger, we'll carry the pond to the orchard." And so they cut and sharpened four poles, dug them into the four sides of the pond, and then stood under the jaumoon tree looking up at it. They saw that the tree was not only laden with ripe fruit, but that it also had a branch bent towards the ground under the weight of it.

"This tree seems very big," they said looking at it, "How can we climb it?"

Plain Fool suggested, "If we climb on top of each other we can grab the bent branch, can't we? Then we can get to the branches above that one and eat the rest of the fruit." The four of them agreed it was, indeed, an appropriate idea. So while one of them bent down, another climbed on his shoulders, and each of the three sat on the shoulders of the one below. As soon as Blind Fool who was on top reached out and grabbed the bent branch, the other three fell to the ground, and while he was dangling in mid-air the three of them shouted at him to pick some fruit and throw it down. Instead he started to scream, pleading with them to save him.

Ignoring his screams the others said, "What, didn't he throw down any fruit yet?"

The fool left dangling in the great open space, Blind Fool, let out a great howl, "*Aday* brothers, I'm going to fall and be killed. Save me!"

When he heard that, Know-it-all Fool ran to a coconut tree, gathered some of the long fronds lying there, tied them together end to end, and held them up calling, "Hey! Hold onto this and pick the fruit." Then Blind Fool let go of the branch and seized the coconut fronds. Immediately he crashed to the ground and lost consciousness, but the other three thought he passed out because he had glutted himself on the fruit in the tree.

When they realized he hadn't brought down any fruit they rebuked him strenuously, "*Aday* Blind Fool, get up! Did you eat up all the fruit?"

Blind Fool woke up, "Now brothers, I didn't even eat one piece of fruit. I fell because of the coconut fronds you held up for me. When I tried hanging from it I fell down, and now my whole body hurts," and tears flowed from his innocent eyes.

When the others saw him crying they started weeping too, clinging to one another. Then after they had recovered from their sorrow they said, "Come, let's forget about eating, and we'll see to moving the pond." The four of them went over to the pond, fixed the poles in all four sides of it, and got ready to lift.

Meanwhile the old woman came to me and said, "It's two or three days since those fellows went to water the trees. Please go and see what they are doing."

I found them at the pond trying to lift it up. "What are you doing?" I asked.

"We're lifting up the pond," they said, "If you wait a while we'll get it out and come along with you."

I came closer, "What did you say you're lifting? How can you carry a pond?"

"You're an obstinate fool. Look at this! Isn't the pond moving and rising up?" They showed me how one of the sticks which they had thrust into the ground was bending. "Look at how clever we are!"

"Is it the pond moving or is it just the stick which moved?" I asked.

"Ha! What a crazy man! There's nothing here for you. In this world men like you make a mockery of men like us. We'll convert you all!" They attacked me with their sticks, chased me away, and I went back to the old woman to tell her what had happened.

"*Appa!*" she said, "Vandi Puluhan, there are certain tendencies developing in the world today which mean those fools are the only ones who will be able to survive in the times to come. There will be no place for people like us. There will be no room for good people, poor people, or humble people with wisdom, goodness, charity, justice, chastity, fairness, *gnānam*, faith in God, integrity, peace, and tranquillity. And there will be no room for those who try to explain those things. But let me show you something that will amuse you I'm sure."

The old woman pointed, and as I looked I saw a great city appear nearby. There was an enormous temple where there was acting, singing, dancing, and dramas being performed inside. "Did you see that?" she asked, "Come cousin, let's go to the temple and I'll show you the secrets." We went there and she pointed out the acting, the singing, the dancing, the melodies, the rhythms, and the countless entertainments beyond all description.

"*Amma!*" I exclaimed, "Where are the bride and groom?"

"Do you think this is a wedding ceremony?"

"Yes, Mother, what else could this be but a huge wedding?"

"It certainly isn't," she replied, "This is the celebration, the ecstatic devotion of an unrestrained society in modern times."

"Mother," I said, "What you are saying seems so strange! In the old days families worshiped in temples. I've seen that myself—we used to have many deities known by a variety of names; people would bathe to purify themselves and come to the temple in their wet clothes, standing there in blissful rapture, tears flowing. Weeping and rolling on the ground they used to call upon God. '*Appa! Amma!* Father! Mother!' they would call. I've seen them wailing, falling down, and rolling along the ground, but now they come wearing jewels, inlaid necklaces, pendants, chains, rings, earrings, garlands, bracelets, jeweled clothing, jeweled hands, and colored paint applied to their faces. They wear garments of silk and silver and gold lace, they wear expensive shoes on their feet, and decorate themselves with every other kind of ornament imaginable. Mother, have these people come to worship or is this really a wedding reception? I'm only asking so that I'll know, *Amma.*"

She replied, "This is indeed a temple, this is indeed a place of worship."

"*Amma,* which is better, the first kind of worship or the way they worship today? Is this true devotion we have seen?"

"Cousin, the sincere devotion of earlier days was an awareness which emerged from within, but nowadays devotion is no more than their emotional response to what they see."

"Mother, which is better?"

"Cousin, the worship you described first belongs to the eternal omnipresent Treasure. What we have today is the devotion that gives bodily happiness. If you compare the devotion of the past with the devotion of the present, atom by atom, you'll find many differences. But times do go on changing, and this physical devotion is what prevails in the world now. Who is there today who can teach the difference between good and evil? And they say you can't learn this by yourself."

"Then isn't it possible for people who have justice, integrity, charity, honesty, and patience to live in this world, Mother?"

"They can, but they face great difficulty and opposition because the world is turning upside down. Decent people, wise people have less influence now. The poor have become rich and the rich have become poor. Tramps have turned into philanthropists, people with integrity have to live hidden like thieves while scoundrels parade like respected citizens. Virtuous women are shunned as prostitutes and prostitutes are acclaimed virtuous, respectable women. In this and so many other ways, integrity, truth, and justice are being turned upside down. The flag of injustice has been hoisted to the drum beat of victory in this seven-and-a-half ABCD land, and there will be no room at all for the good qualities you asked about."

"Then can't we survive Mother, not only you and I, but the tens and tens of millions who don't know any other way? And Mother please, once and for all, tell me who you are."

"I am a wandering pilgrim," she said.

"Why did you have to leave your own country and come to live in this forest?"

"That's what I explained before. As soon as Kalian was born there was nothing left for any of us to do any more. That's why I left my own country and began living in the forest."

"Mother, where do you think you will go now?"

"*Aday* my son, we have been speaking.....But there, the jinns have seen the two of us talking and they're coming to swallow us! Run for your life!" And she disappeared.

After this I began to change. When I left that place I passed through a desert where I came upon a group of people talking among themselves. "Hey fellows!" one of them said, "Who should we ruin? Who should we torture? Who should we destroy?" This was the kind of thing they were considering, and I went up to them to find out why they were determined to do so many hideous things. Weeping in great distress they replied to my question, "How could you understand our plight? We've been crying for many, many years because there's been no one to help us."

"Don't you have anyone at all? Where do you come from?" I asked.

They answered, "Sir, Ravana, who was sometimes called Lankeeswaran, used to rule the kingdom of Lanka. Through deep meditation and penance he had earned us as a special favor from Eeswaran. We served as his heart, his body, his ten heads, and his qualities, and during that time the name of Ravana earned great fame, praise, and respect up to the celestial worlds. We performed countless miracles in his name, and that was how we controlled the universes. It was also during this time that Ravana kidnapped the lady Sita, Sri Rama's wife, from Ayoti Forest. Then Rama gathered seventy battalions of monkeys, made war on the king of Lanka and killed him to reclaim Sita. When Ravana was lying slashed and cut, about to die, the ten of us wailed, '*Aiyo,* our king, how can we live without you?' and we wept and sobbed with great sorrow.

Then he spoke to us, 'You ten who were born with me, you are the only ones left to show and proclaim the splendor, the excellence, and the strength of my name. My wife, my child, my brothers, my sisters, all my people and my armies have been killed. There is no one left except the ten of you to answer in my name. It is up to you to invoke the majesty of my name and to demonstrate it.' We asked, 'When will we have the chance to glorify you for all time?' And he replied, 'This Rama will depart and be incarnated as Krishna in the period of time to be called the Kali yuga and you will be incarnated as the Sahuni, the evil genius of that time. You must intimidate Krishna and after that no one will be able to beat you. Then you can speak of my majesty without any fear until the end of that yuga.' As he said that his life left his body, and we went to live in the Sahuni, but even he was killed in the Mahabharata War. Since then we've been struggling to stay alive in the midst of all the difficulties and dangers in this unprotected desert. We have no one to help us or guide us."

"*Appa!*" I exclaimed, "You are all so clever, what are your names?"

"We are the ten sins, the ten heads of Ravana."

"All right, but what are your names?"

"If we tell you our names will you let us join you?"

"Very well," I said.

"Our names are falsehood, intoxication, lust, theft, murder, and we are also ego, pride, arrogance, impatience, and hatred, and the ten of us take many, many forms and wear many, many disguises besides. Five of us are the children of one mother, and the other five are the children of our mother's older sister. We dance and sing, we beat the drum of victory, we fly the flag of injustice." Saying this, they crawled into my body. Immediately all my earlier thoughts and qualities changed, I became a sixteen year old youth, and a feeling of ecstasy overwhelmed me.

"My brothers, where are you?" I called.

Immediately they replied, "We are right here in your heart. Look how young you are now."

As I looked at my body I was overjoyed, "I feel like a sixteen year old boy."

"Dear brother," they said, "Whoever befriends us will remain sixteen years old forever. Those who do not embrace us will suffer from lack of food and will be aged by their hunger. Now that we are inside you we will put an end to all your difficulties. We'll harass this ABCD world. Five of us will stay with you, and our aunt's children will stay in Kandi Puluhan's heart. Now you must take the name Vandi Puluhan, and both of you must marry the woman known as Maya.

Vandi Puluhan, don't be afraid of anything. Of every ten million people in this world, nine million, nine hundred and ninety-nine thousand, nine hundred and ninety-nine belong to our party. Only one out of that many will ever leave us, and he will be the rarest of the rare. For that reason dear brother, we will creep into every good family from now on. We won't bother with those who have faith in God, but this is what we'll do to those who don't have faith: we can cause that self-preoccupied egoism, we can sow doubt in their hearts, make them fight with their wives, their children, and all the people in their neighborhood. We can make them angry very quickly, destroy their generosity, their pity, kindness, compassion, their love, and all those good qualities. We can make them fight among themselves. As a diamond would be shattered by a blacksmith's hammer making the pieces fly far and wide, we will cause separations among those who live in harmony and unity. We'll make them drink intoxicating liquors. We'll make them gamble until they have to sell all their property, and all their possessions including the jewelry of their wives and children. We'll make such unrighteousness flourish that men will actually display their vile intentions to the women on the streets. And women, in the name of civilization, will expose three-quarters of what needs to be covered, to fascinate men, to titillate their senses, and make them wander in the streets without restraint. While they're wandering about we'll excite their lust, make them ravish the precious ornament which is the chastity of woman, make them fight, steal, and murder. All this will foster that agitation and dissipation of the mind which will cause their downfall and ruin.

We will also make kings treat their subjects harshly instead of looking after their welfare, make them increase taxes, plunder the peasants' harvest until there isn't even enough grain for food, while they keep their own coffers full. Those who don't pay their taxes will be beaten and kicked, their homes and property will be put up for sale. To justify their salaries the kings' officials will persecute those poor peasants relentlessly, and even cut off their heads if they can't pay. Come, let's set out immediately to torment this ABCD world."

Then I said, "You told me to marry the woman named Maya. Where will I find her?"

At that very moment a woman who was called Lust stood before me saying, "Lo, I am here!" I married her the moment I saw her.

"What's your name?" I asked.

"My name is Maya, my husband. Whenever you need me I will come out of your body. Now please pay careful attention to what I say. My aunt's five children have gone to live in Kandi Puluhan's heart. He is also married to me, but don't think of me as a whore—no matter how many people desire me, I assume a different form to suit each one's needs. I quench their desires, and no matter how many there are, each time I am an untouched virgin. Don't have any doubts: the man I just mentioned used to be married to another Light That Leaps From The Eyes. Because of that marriage he lived through great hardship, but once he married me his hunger ended, his illnesses and diseases were cured, and now he is very happy. Someday he will meet you and you two will be as happy as brothers. Together you will make this ABCD world dance and quake and turn upside down. You will make good people dogs, and exalt bad people. You will elevate the poor, and reduce the rich to beggars. You will make the learned idiots, and idiots learned people. You will turn men into women, and women into men. You will make devotion perish and turn God into a stone. You will make arrogance rule, and vengeance strong. You will make falsehood a poet, and truth speechless and silent. You will burn integrity to ashes, justice to dust, and grind fair dealing into the ground. You will make virgins whores, and whores virgins. You will make wise men misers. You will make kings beggars, and beggars kings. You will change men and women of integrity into amoral dogs. You will make drunkards and drug addicts gurus, and make duty appear as black as coal. You will make egoism seem like bliss, and patience like a disgusting thing. The two of you will indulge in many, many activities like these."

VANDI PULUHAN: Then she crawled into my body, and just as she said, the two of us have turned the ABCD world around. *Amma,* Mutavalli, when I was married to the woman of light I had many problems, but once I had learned my lesson and married that Maya who discoursed to me in this way, we reached such heights of bliss. We now live exactly as we please, but you don't seem to know who the two of us are—we are none other than the Kandi Puluhan and the Vandi Puluhan Maya spoke of!

Lady, Mutavalli, it's hard to find even one in ten million like you in the world. *Amma,* Mutavalli, if you join us you will live a life as blissful as ours, if you don't you will have even more painful experiences than the suffering I have described for you. This is my story, my history. That's all. Haven't you seen the state of those who marry that light and live lovingly and piously? Consider everything I have said to you very deeply. If you leave this crazy state and join us you will live extremely well. Come, join us, Mutavalli.

MUTAVALLI: *Aday* sinners! Your speech, your words, your language, and your demeanor are the most degenerate in this world. Don't stand there in front of me, get out!

VANDI PULUHAN: [*Intimidatingly*] Lady Mutavalli, the sort of person you are seems disgraceful to me, and I seem disgraceful to you. On that account, there will be enmity between us forever. You must remember that times have changed, the ABCD world belongs to us now, and there are many people in our parliament who can destroy you. Certainly none of them will vote for you. There is no room for you here because we are the majority now. Look deeply into your heart at the situation that prevails in this ABCD world and see that your majority began to dwindle in very ancient times. Let me explain, furthermore, that if you join us you will be free of trouble in this world, but if you don't, know your destiny will be fatal indeed! Beware! Know this clearly, we will destroy you!

MUTAVALLI: *Aday,* you degenerate animal born in human form, your arrogance will be annihilated! That is the truth. Let's just see whether you will be destroyed or we will. God eternal and all mighty will efface you and your pride. Your destruction is certain and inevitable!

[*She sings.*]

MUTAVALLI'S SONG

Why do you speak so proudly, mind?
In the presence of the destiny that caught you,
Why do you speak so proudly, mind?
When the island of your precious judgment
Is surrounded by karmic evils,
And the tears flow from your eyes,
And your heart is shattered and troubled,
And you bow to the reincarnated
Puppet-master guru
On the fraudulent stage,
Why do you speak so proudly, mind?

When troubles come to shake me,
When I stand scorched

*By the mirage of the mind,
Shivering with the chill of fever, dizzy,
My head splitting,
Flying in the sky,
Why do you speak so proudly, mind?*

*If you worshiped God's grace, daily
Living in prayer, standing on the path
Without forgetting a single duty,
You could remember God forever.
Why do you speak so proudly, mind?*

*Without torment,
O mind known as fate,
In your dreams and in the thoughts
Of your heart,
You could think of God
Who grants deliverance from birth and death.
If you repeat that prayer,
God will come as the Master,
Why do you speak so proudly, mind?*

*Better than folding your hands
In worship of God who is grace-awakened bliss,
Who fills the path with ecstasy,
Is folding the hands inside your heart
In worship.
Then His Grace will come.
Why do you speak so proudly, mind?*

VANDI PULUHAN: That song may seem touching to complete fools like you, but to people like us it's poison. You won't listen no matter how much we advise you, and it's no use scolding you either. There is a vast difference between you and us, *Amma*.

MUTAVALLI: What you say is perfectly true. Wise men have said, 'If judgment is ruined, total ruin follows soon.' Now your judgment seems damaged, and your ruin is sure to follow. You are playing with a poisonous snake whose name is fate, but you must remember you can never escape from it.

VANDI PULUHAN AND KANDI PULUHAN: [*Mocking and mimicking her*] A ha ha ha! Crazy Mutavalli! Let's go.

The Master Without a Tongue

Is there any other help in the world but You?
You are the Creator, the fruit grown without a seed,
You are the One without a mother
More protective than seventy mothers,
You are the jewel,
The bell which speaks without a mouth.
Please live in my heart,
Protect me with Your grace.

You are the Creator who hears
Without ears and gives answers,
You are not born, but You rule the universes.
What good will it do me to forget You?
You are the pure One
Who appears to those who are truthful and without deceit.

You are the Master without a tongue
Reciting the four secret, silent scriptures.
Is there any other God but You
To help us in this world?
Is there anyone like You
Who exists forever without death in this world?
Is there any other way to realization
Except through this body?
Is there anything other than
The mighty One who speaks without form?
You are the primal One who rules forever without end,
You are the canopy which protects all the worlds,
You are the highest One,
The One without sorrow
Who rules with grace.
Who is there for me in this world
Except You, O limitless One who is everywhere?
How could there be life
If not for You, O gracious One?
O divine radiance that bore

Flowers and fruits without the tree,
You are the One who spreads without a vine
Throughout earth, space, everywhere.

Can there be thunder without lightning,
O exalted One, O God
Who emerged without a mother as radiant light?
Is there anyone other than You
Who exists without self?
Is there anyone other than You
Who bears Your glory and Your name?

8

Vandi Puluhan and Kandi Puluhan go in Search of the Conqueror of All the Conquerors

As the Puluhan's journey on to find and destroy the Conquerer of all conquerers (God), they meet a woman named Integrity and her husband. Unable to stay in the presence of virtue for very long, they continue their journey and finally meet with the Conquerer of all conquerers and get their come-uppance.

Then Vandi Puluhan and Kandi Puluhan set off on their journey to the ABCD world. Together they planned to make Maya's tricks and delusions flourish in the ABCD world. First they saw a mountain and climbed as far up as a village of hunters. In one of the houses was a young girl, eighteen years of age.

"Ah maiden," said Vandi Puluhan, "What's your name?"

"My name is Virtue," the girl replied.

"We have issued a command," they said, "That the name Virtue must not be seen or heard in this world. Apparently you don't know us. As long as we rule the ABCD world names like yours must not fall on our ears, my girl! We are the rulers of the ABCD world, and there is no room here for those who disobey our words. Don't you know who we are? We are Vandi Puluhan and Kandi Puluhan. At least from now on, know our majesty, our pride, and our strength." And so they went on boasting and bragging about themselves.

"O ho!" said Virtue, "Strongarms! I admire your valor, but you don't seem to know that there is a Conqueror who overcomes all the conquerors of the world."

"Girl," said Vandi Puluhan, "There is no one in the whole, wide world as clever as we are. Your words are a great surprise to us!"

While they were talking her husband came in from the forest with a slain deer. He dropped it on the ground and called, "Virtue, come here."

She stood in front of him; he took an arrow from the quiver on his back and aimed at the tiny gem in the ornament adorning her nose. The arrow hit that tiny gem and fell to the ground. As the arrow was falling he looked at his wife, "Is there a greater hero than I am in this world?"

Vandi Puluhan and Kandi Puluhan started shouting, "*Aday* you stupid hunter, how dare you boast of your valor now that we dominate and rule the whole world! We're going to pick you up and swallow you." Threateningly they went on, "*Aday,* you are possessed by demons. Your skill might impress your wife, but show us if you can."

"Sirs," answered the hunter, "You illustrious wise men, may I ask a question?"

Impatiently they replied, "Ask it and we'll see, but no matter what you say we'll never leave you alone now. You must fight us." Then they roared, "Ask your question before the war. After your question, come and fight!"

The hunter looked at them, "You two embodiments of impatience and anger, do you think any man would agree to fight the likes of you?" And he sang this song.

THE HUNTER'S SONG

O you buffalos,
Steeds of the angel of death,
You bulls wandering
In the confusion of the mind,
Despicable, four-legged animals,
Creations without wisdom,
Beasts with five mouths,
You ruin loving hearts
And send them
Wandering in the wind.

"*Aday!*" said Vandi Puluhan as he ended his song.

"Crazy!" said Kandi Puluhan, "Who would ever listen to that song? Idiot, will you come out and fight?"

"Well you two," the hunter said, "We were born human beings, we grew up as human beings, and we live as human beings. Somehow, hitting seems to be the birthright and special aptitude of people like you. But we'll never be lured into a fight that way, and besides, there's something else you should know, those who were born human beings will not hit back even if an enemy strikes them. But gentlemen, you do seem tired, come and eat. Afterwards you can do what you like." He took them by the hand and graciously invited them to accompany him.

"We can't sit down to eat before we kill you," they said, "Look, you don't know the facts about us. We wouldn't hesitate to cut off our own noses just to make sure there are bad omens for others. You don't seem to realize this." And saying that, they threw him to the ground and trampled him.

Even now the hunter showed great patience and forbearance. "Don't hurt yourselves," he said kissing their hands and feet, inviting them again to eat.

"Well hunter, you certainly do have humility, patience, and tolerance, and your actions show your good qualities, but what do you mean by hitting the tiny gem in your wife's nose ornament and asking who is more skillful than you in this world?"

"Listen good Sirs, and let me tell you that story," he said.

Chastity's Story

One day when I was out hunting I came upon a Sufi Sheikh in a cave. That day, although I had circled the whole forest I hadn't caught a single animal. I went up to the Sheikh, paid obeisance to him, and told him all my troubles. "My son," he said, "Your bow was made from a branch which has had a drop of the water of righteousness mingled within it since that branch was green and growing. That is why you weren't able to kill anything with it."

"Is there still such a thing as righteousness in this world?" I asked.

"Yes, my son," replied the Sheikh, "There is."

"How can I see it?"

The Sufi Sheikh said, "Well, if you want to know this, you have to shoot an arrow from your bow at the tiny gem in your wife's nose ornament and ask her, 'Is there anyone stronger than I am?' When that happens two men who will be a sign of the times will be with you showing off and displaying their cleverness. They'll say, 'There is no one greater than we are,' they will hit you, push you to the ground, and trample you, but don't let yourself be hurt by them. Treat them kindly, and give them food. Do you know who they will be?"

"No, my Sheikh, I don't know."

"Their names will be Vandi Puluhan and Kandi Puluhan. You must tell them the story I have just told you, ask them, 'Are there only two of you, do you have wives?' and when they say they do, invite them to eat with you. Call your wife and say respectfully, 'We must serve them.' And then, after begging their permission, tell them Chastity's story.

Now let me tell you that story, good Sirs. This is the story of a man and a woman who had transcended the world and lived in a state of absolute truth. The husband was a slave to God, and his wife was pure love. He was a hunter named Ananda who used to hunt in the northern part of the forest, and his wife was called Chastity. When he brought home the deer and the antelope he caught every day, he and his wife would eat, and then give the rest to the poor and the unfortunate. At the same time there was another hunter, Manokaran, who had lived with his mother for a while in the southern part of the forest. There was a day he hadn't caught one animal in that southern section, even though he had wandered to the northern edge of the forest. As he was returning home Ananda happened along the same path carrying the carcass of a deer. The two of them met, found they had much in common, and became friends.

Then the northern hunter invited Manokaran, the southerner, to take half the deer and said, "My loving brother, some day you must come to my home."

"Good," said Manokaran, "I will come one day."

After cordial farewells they returned to their homes. The hunter Manokaran went south and told his mother what happened. She listened attentively and said, "If he is such a good person, why not go and spend some time with him?"

"Yes, I'll do that," he said, and off he went to find Ananda. The two of them became fast friends.

"Friend of my life," said Ananda, "Come please, let's go to the pond and wash our faces." At the pond while they brushed their teeth before washing their faces, Ananda's wife came along with a pot to draw some water. Manokaran, the son of the south, was enchanted with her beauty, the radiance of her face, and the way she walked. As he looked at her with desire Ananda observed him staring at his wife, "You who were born with me, what are you staring at so strangely?"

"Nothing my brother, but who is that woman?" he asked.

Ananda thought to himself, "O ho! He longs for my wife, but if I tell him who she is he will not be able to satisfy his desires, and that will trouble his mind." Out loud he replied, "My brother, I know the woman well because she comes to my house often, and therefore your wish can easily be granted. Come, let's go to the house and eat."

When they returned Ananda had Manokaran sit on the verandah, and then went in and whispered to his wife, "You must not stay in our house just now. Go next door to the old woman's place and wait there." Because his wife was virtuous and obedient to her husband's word, she went next door immediately. Now he needed someone to serve the mid-day meal his wife had cooked, and he sent for that old woman. "Mother," he said, "My brother has come. You must serve this meal and cook for us tonight. Please come to my house and do this for us."

As the old woman served the food to both men Manokaran said, "My brother, you said you had a wife, but I don't see her anywhere."

"Brother, I've sent my wife to her mother's. She'll return tomorrow."

After they had eaten they talked of various things, and when night fell the old woman brought the evening meal and served it. They finished eating and Ananda led him to the verandah, "My dear brother, please lie down and rest on this sofa a while."

Then he left to talk to his wife. "Chastity, come here," he said.

She came at once, "My lord," she said paying obeisance to her husband.

"Dear wife," said Ananda, "My friend, my companion yearns for you and is completely preoccupied with thoughts of you all the time. It is our duty to satisfy his desires. So decorate the bed we use with good sheets and spreads, light the lamp, and serve him fruit and sweets with your own hand."

Tears streaming down her face, *"Aiyo!"* Chastity exclaimed, "What strange thing is this, my lord, telling your wife to give herself to someone else? Is this acceptable to God? Is it in keeping with a life of virtue? Could I *live* afterwards? Is this right in the eyes of the world? Is this appropriate for someone named Chastity?" she sobbed with flowing tears.

"O Chastity, my precious jewel," said Ananda, "Everything you said is perfectly true, but to do what your husband says is not wrong. A woman who disobeys her husband, oblivious to righteousness, will fall into the deepest hell. The only chaste woman is the one who does not deviate from her husband's word, her husband's wish, or her true duty."

"That might be so," said Chastity, "But how do you expect me to accept that?"

"My dear young wife, a woman's purity and her virtue rest with her husband. A woman who does not oppose her husband's wishes is a chaste woman. Her husband is paradise, her husband is a heavenly being, and her husband is God. Now my friend wants you and his desire has to be satisfied. You must treat him exactly the way you treat me, but if you should hurt his heart in any way at all, I will kill you and take my own life, I swear this. I'll send him to you and you must be very humble and submissive. Do whatever he wants."

And then he went to Manokaran, "My beloved friend, my beloved companion, I have summoned that girl to the house so you can carry out the affair you've been thinking about. Go to the girl and enjoy yourself, amuse yourself with her until daybreak." Ananda gestured to Manokaran to go inside while he himself remained at the doorstep. "Go in and gratify your desires."

Lying on the fragrant and freshly made quilt mattress Manokaran said, "My dear, come to me."

Chastity's whole body was perspiring, shaking, and trembling in fear. She thought to herself, "If I go against my husband's wishes I don't know what he'll do to me. My chastity is certain to be lost either way." Sighing and holding out her hands in prayer, "O my mother, O God of chastity and virtue, only You can protect me," she prayed.

"Come my dear," he said again, but as Manokaran drew her close to him and looked up at her, his glance strayed to the roof where he saw Ananda's name on the quiver hanging from a rafter. "A ha! This is my friend's house indeed, and she is my friend's wife. What a horrible sinner I am! He made his wife offer herself to me. What must he think? How patient he must be, how wise he must be, how full of peace he must be! My own brothers would never do such a thing for me. O God! *Aiyo!* O my God! I am such a terrible sinner, how can I ever look him in the face again, how can I ever speak to him again? I am the worst of all sinners! *Aiyo!* How can I ever show my face to my virtuous, dutiful mother again, how can I ever look at her again? I'll be haunted by this humiliation and disgrace till the end of the world. O my God, please be patient with my faults and grant me the grace of Your forgiveness. I can no longer live in this world."

As he said this he seized an arrow, grasped it tightly in his hands, and prepared to stab himself in the chest. *"Aiyo!"* Chastity cried out, "Don't! What will I tell my husband? How would I explain this to him?" and she grabbed his hands.

"My lady, I am a terrible sinner, let go of my hands. It is not right for such a virtuous woman to touch me. Mother!" He stabbed himself in the chest with the arrow crying, "O my mother, O my brother!" and he fell dead on their bed.

Chastity began to scream, "What will I tell my husband? O God, when day breaks my husband will return. What will I tell him?" she cried beating her head in grief. "When he returns he'll say, 'Instead of taking care of my brother as I told you to, you have stabbed him and killed him.' He will be so angry there'll be no end to his rebukes, and I'll deserve his anger. Certainly, it would be better for me to die." She pulled the arrow from Manokaran's chest. "O my God, light of my virtue, my husband, my deity, light of my eyes, your feet alone are my refuge. I am blameless, please forgive me. O my dearest one, my lord." She stabbed herself in the chest and the life left her body.

When dawn broke Ananda thought, "It's dawn and I haven't seen Manokaran and Chastity." He went home, knocked on the door, and called out, but there was no sound in return. "O ho! They probably made love and played and laughed all night, and now they must be sleeping blissfully. Let them have a good sleep; they'll awaken later. It wouldn't be right for me to interrupt their rest. Oh well, let them doze on, I'll wait till they wake up." Then he went back to the old woman's house, had her make some food, and waited until about ten o'clock in the morning. "It's already ten o'clock and still they are not to be seen," he thought as he went to his own house and knocked on the door. There wasn't a sound within. Wondering what could have happened he broke the door open, saw his wife dead near the door and his friend on the bed.

"Sinful woman, you killed my brother, you have stabbed him and killed yourself too," he shouted kicking his wife's body out of the way with his feet. He lifted up the corpse of his friend Manokaran, embraced him, and wept with grief, "O my eye, my gem, this evil woman killed you!" He placed his cheek on Manokaran's, "How can I go on living? I am coming with you."

As Ananda took the arrow from his wife's chest and was about to stab himself, he heard the sweet and loving voice of God, "My son, virtuous child, stop! My son, the dead will rise up and return to life. Don't be sad, and don't have any doubts about your wife. Her chastity and her sense of duty are most exalted, she is a truly chaste, virtuous woman. Your beloved friend longed for her because he didn't know she was your wife. You are a truly loving child because you thought of your friend's longing as your own, you wanted his desire satisfied. No one else in the world has ever done such a noble thing, no one has ever offered his own wife to relieve the sadness of a friend. You sent her to him because he yearned for her. While she was contemplating her virtue and her duty, your friend beckoned to Chastity and said, 'Come lady,' calling her to him. But when he looked up at her face, he saw the quiver hanging from a rafter of the roof. 'A ha! That is my brother's quiver, his name is on it, that is his! This woman must be his wife! Who else in the world would have been good enough to have thought of doing this? Is there anyone else who would have given his wife to someone else? How can I ever look at the faces of these sweet flowers of righteousness again? How will I ever be able to look at this chaste woman's face, this woman I ought to have treated as my mother?'

As he was thinking this, preparing to stab himself with an arrow, Chastity said, '*Aiyo,* what will I do? What will I tell my lord?' She grabbed his hands but Manokaran said, 'Mother, please do not defile yourself by touching me,' and he stabbed himself. Your wife didn't know what to tell you, and she was so afraid you would be very angry, she decided it would be better to kill herself. She seized the arrow, stabbed herself and died.

All three of you acted from a perfect sense of duty. If you can really understand this, you'll see that no one did anything wrong. May you all live a long time in true friendship, may Chastity's virtue remain untouched. You three will be chaste friends shining with honor in this world." And then God blessed them saying, "Let the world see it is possible for such people to exist. May they emulate your noble actions."

Now the hunter said to Vandi Puluhan and Kandi Puluhan, "The people of the world who heard of them followed their example. This is the end of the story the Sheikh told me to tell you."

"Whew! You crazy man, are there any women like that left in the ABCD world?"

"Yes," said the hunter, "There are."

"Where? Show us!"

"You must come to eat with us and invite your wives too. Please let my wife Virtue serve food to the four of you, and while you are eating, I'll show you that secret."

"All right, we'll do that," they said, "But if you don't show us, we'll swallow you up."

The hunter brought them the water pitcher, set out four leaves as plates for them, and called to his wife, "You must serve some rice on these leaves and stand here ready to wait on them." When Virtue finished putting out the food the hunter glanced at Vandi Puluhan and Kandi Puluhan, "Please ask your wives to come too," he invited. They called inside themselves to their wife Maya, but she didn't appear. They called her two or three times, but she still didn't come. "Maya, what was all that you promised before, why won't you come now?"

"*Aiyo* Vandi Puluhan! *Aiyo* Kandi Puluhan! Virtue's chaste and pure state are powerful weapons which won't let me come near her. They scorch me, they burn me on all four sides like flames from *akini asthiram*, the flame-throwing weapon of the realm of fire itself. I'm even suffering here inside your bodies. If I can't tolerate this much, the brilliance of her purity would burn me to ashes if I were to come out."

"You told us you were so accomplished," they said, "You told us you could take millions and millions of forms, you told us you could make this world quake and tremble. Maya, you told us all kinds of stories, and now you refuse to come out because you are afraid of one girl!"

"Gentlemen," she replied, "I can make the world quake, I can take many forms, I can conquer everyone, but I cannot defeat chaste, virtuous women, dutiful, virtuous men and women who have integrity, and *gnānis*. As soon as I see such people I have to disappear. If I oppose them I would be consumed by fire. You'll have to believe this because I can't even endure this pain here inside your bodies. Only that blind God knows how much I'm suffering."

"Maya," they asked, "Are there many women like her in the world?"

"My lords, women like her are very rare, so instead of wasting time on people like her, let's gather the multitudes who are eager to join us, to be our followers. Let's leave without wasting any more time here."

After that Vandi Puluhan and Kandi Puluhan ate in silence, not saying a word except to boast once again about their valiant, glorious deeds as they prepared to leave. Finally they said, "Well then hunter, all right, we'll leave now and come again some other time."

"Why are you in such a hurry?" asked the hunter, "Have you gone crazy, do you have some obsession? You asked if there were virtuous women with integrity. I hope you've found the answer, imbeciles! Do you know now that there *are* chaste and faithful wives in the world? Idiots! Do you also know that there are many excellent, even perfect men and women in the world? You total fools, the woman you call Maya bragged she would make the world dance and quake, she said she would bounce the world upside down, she said she would dance in different costumes and turn the world around. For all her exaggerated talk, that female who said she would dance has admitted she couldn't even come into the presence of an insignificant woman. *Aday,* you dogs who don't know the difference between good and evil, realize that!

Now listen you immodest, ignorant beasts of loathsome conduct, you dogs with four feet and a tail in the middle, you five-mouthed beasts without wisdom, you arrogant demons living on trees in the jungle, the darkness of ignorance spreads across your foolish hearts and enshrouds them with the blackest night. You're hypnotized and fascinated by the circus tricks of Maya, you dull-witted, amoral animals." And he rebuked them over and over again, finally saying, "*Aday,* you are fools who are ignorant of your own fate. There are many perfect men and women, and there are those with divine wisdom who are going to destroy you. Always remember that. Now I'm going to sing you a song, and then you can leave after you've heard it."

THE HUNTER'S SONG

O my heart, search for the truth.
If the angel of death comes to seize you tomorrow,
Your fate will be certain ruin.

Painful suffering comes in the grave.
If you don't use it wisely,
Time passing brings countless woes.

Treacherous ruin
Befalls those who have lost their patience.
Fathomless hell awaits all those who do wrong.

O my heart, search for the truth.
If the angel of death comes to seize you tomorrow,
Your fate will be certain ruin.

If you stop worshiping God, sorrow will be yours.
Pain is the consequence of desire for women.

Though they weep and weep tears,
Rivers of tears after death,
God's trials will come in abundance.

O my heart, search for the truth.
If the angel of death comes to seize you tomorrow,
Your fate will be certain ruin.

If you give up your intentions, your austerities,
You will understand tomorrow
When you go to God, how
Difficult your lot will be.
This body which spoke with such pride
Will be scorched in the fire.
All that you saved
Will be quickly spent.

O my heart, search for the truth.
If the angel of death comes to seize you tomorrow,
Your fate will be certain ruin.

Those who do not understand their duty here
Will learn it in the grave.
When they go to face God's judgment,
They will be swallowed by hell.
Those shameless creatures,
Caught by lust for lewd women,
And trapped by greed for gold
Will become firewood for hell.

O my heart, search for the truth.
If the angel of death comes to seize you tomorrow,
Your fate will be certain ruin.

A ruinous, deserted hell awaits
Treachery with money.
Those who hurt their mothers and fathers
Will crawl into hell.
Those who comply with

*The desires of their mind
Will be scorched in a living hell.
Great suffering will reward
Those who hurt others with their tongue.*

*O my heart, search for the truth.
If the angel of death comes to seize you tomorrow,
Your fate will be certain ruin.*

*There will be trouble for those
Who take the possessions of the poor.
Vengeance and treachery
Will corrode wisdom.
If your words are not pure,
Heaven will leave you far behind.
If you put your trust in the world,
Sorrow will hound you.*

*O my heart, search for the truth.
If the angel of death comes to seize you tomorrow,
Your fate will be certain ruin.*

*The evil people who destroy families
With their sinful treachery
Will have worms and smoke
Stuffed in their mouths tomorrow,
And will burn in all seven hells.
If you act deceitfully,
You will lose your honor.*

*O my heart, search for the truth.
If the angel of death comes to seize you tomorrow,
Your fate will be certain ruin.*

*As you advance in meditation
The world will despise you,
Your family and friends will desert you,
Titles and wealth will depart.
But your good and evil actions will be known in the grave.*

*O my heart, search for the truth.
If the angel of death comes to seize you tomorrow,*

Your fate will be certain ruin.

All your possessions will leave you,
And worries will assail you till the very end,
Important people will ignore and forget you,
You will open the door and enter the grave.

O my heart, search for the truth.
If the angel of death comes to seize you tomorrow,
Your fate will be certain ruin.

Your house and property will remain
Here on earth, your attachments
Will make you suffer.
The angel of death will drag you to the grave,
And when the breath has left,
Crows and vultures will pick the body to shreds.

O my heart, search for the truth.
If the angel of death comes to seize you tomorrow,
Your fate will be certain ruin.

The usurer's wealth can't travel
With his corpse, and beautiful women
Forget soon. When his body leaves
Dressed in a shroud, only the whores
Who preyed on him have any passing regret.

O my heart, search for the truth.
If the angel of death comes to seize you tomorrow,
Your fate will be certain ruin.

Gluttony makes you drowsy,
And laziness brings you sorrow.
When the breath leaves, you are
Placed in a burning fire,
And all your intense but worldly
Prayers are in vain.

O my heart, search for the truth.
If the angel of death comes to seize you tomorrow,
Your fate will be certain ruin.

If you believe in God your sorrows
Will be scorched, but if you seek wealth alone,
Blame and disgrace will follow,
Death will triumph over your body
In that burning fire, and immense
Sorrow will hound you forever.

O my heart, search for the truth.
If the angel of death comes to seize you tomorrow,
Your fate will be certain ruin.

"*Aday!*" Vandi Puluhan said, "Stop your singing you idiot!"

"This song is full of bliss only for people like you," said Kandi Puluhan.

"Yes, yes," said the hunter, "You are *quite* right. A brainless idiot says others are fools. Together we've learned about idiocy which can be inherited. You imbecile, remember there is a conqueror for every conqueror in the world, you numbskulls who don't know the difference between good and evil! This is the story my Sheikh told me to tell you. This is the true meaning of what my Sheikh said, and you are, indeed, abysmal sinners not to understand the meaning of this teaching. I've also learned the value of that teaching just from looking at you. All right then, come back some other time." And that was the end of what he had to say.

"Well then, little brother," Vandi Puluhan and Kandi Puluhan said to each other, "Now we know there are such people, even in the ABCD world under our very own rule. Somehow we must destroy them," and off they went.

As they walked along Kandi Puluhan glanced at Vandi Puluhan, "Brother, the hunter talked about a conqueror for every conqueror. Let's go and find that conqueror."

"Yes, let's go do that."

As they continued their journey, walking along, they came upon a shepherd grazing his goats. He was bent over leaning on his staff, peering intently at an anthill. They greeted him, "Hey shepherd, you're watching that anthill with great concentration. What's in there?"

"Why do you want to know what I see?" asked the shepherd.

"So that we can know the secret of what you're looking at," mocked Vandi Puluhan. "What's inside? What are you staring at?"

"I am looking at a very rare, wonderful scene of ecstasy," said the shepherd.

Vandi Puluhan laughed and asked, "What on earth can you see in an anthill?"

"Just listen, Sir, and I'll tell you."

Not very far away, on this side of the anthill, there is an ocean, and on the shore of the ocean is a mountain, and at the foot of the mountain is the Sheikh of divine luminous wisdom. He lives in a very beautiful forest glade. Many celestial beings wait upon him there. Jinns, fairies, true *gnānis*, honest men, virtuous women, foreigners, poor folk, and others who have come in search of the Sheikh also serve him there. The delicacy and beauty of that forest are so exquisite they are impossible to describe. At the forest's edge are three overflowing rivers, a river of milk, a river of honey, and a river of sweet nectar. Those who serve the Sheikh bathe in the river of milk, eat the different kinds of wild fruit on the trees, and drink freely from the rivers of honey and sweet nectar. They play on swings set with diamonds, cinnamon-stones, and various precious gems. Their seven-storied houses, each with seven terraces, have unimaginable loveliness. On those terraces men and women speak affectionately to each other, living in carefree gaiety, singing and dancing.

Now these people live this way, but at the same time there is a certain boy who swore to his father some time ago that he would kill God. "I swear, Father," he said, "Father, I swear I will kill that God, or else I'll swallow Him. If I can't do that I'll never come here again and you can disown me. Once I have swallowed Him up I will look at your face again." After a difficult journey he arrived at the forest glade and sought out the Sheikh. "*Aday* beggar," he said, "I'm going to swallow you."

"That's amazing," said the Sheikh, "How can you swallow *me* when the One who created the world exists?"

"You crazy man," said the boy, "The whole world is mine, and moreover, there certainly isn't anyone here who can conquer me. I have the power to create or destroy this world, and I'm going to swallow you."

"You cannot swallow me," replied the Sheikh, "There is a God."

"Yes," said the boy, "That's who I'm looking for. If you point Him out to me you'll escape. If not, I'll swallow you instead. So if you want me to let you off you'd better show Him to me."

"Can you really swallow Him? Well then, I'll show Him to you, but first, what is your name, what is your father's name, what is your mother's name, and where do you come from?"

"My father's name is Kandi Puluhan and my mother's name is Maya. Mine is The Boy Who Swallows The Flesh Of The Fruit But Leaves The Skin Intact. My uncle's name is Vandi Puluhan. The Puluhans rule this ABCD world, and I swore to them I would either swallow God, or kill Him, or conquer Him. I swore that and went to so much trouble getting here, but you're the only one I've seen. It occurred to me if I swallowed you it would then be very easy to swallow your God who would come to protect you. But hey beggar, show Him to me now! I want to swallow Him."

"Is that so?" asked the Sheikh, "Do you really think you can swallow Him?"

The Boy Who Swallows The Flesh Of The Fruit But Leaves The Skin Intact said, "Yes, I'll swallow Him fast."

"In that case," said the Sheikh, "I'll show you where God lives," and he pointed out an ant crawling in front of him, "Look at this tiny, crawling ant. God is in that ant too, and if you can swallow it, that will amount to the same thing as swallowing God."

"Your son jumped up, and he jumped down," said the shepherd to Vandi Puluhan and Kandi Puluhan, "He laughed, he leaped up and down, he pulled up a huge tree by the roots and crushed it to dust. He looked at the ant, leaped very skillfully to catch and swallow it, but that tiny creature tossed him with its nose and caught him with its legs, and threw him here and there, scattering him in little pieces all over the countryside. No one can describe his pain and difficulty, and this is the wonder I'm watching."

"This shepherd spoke our names in that story," said Kandi Puluhan and Vandi Puluhan, "And therefore that boy must have been our son. We did name him The Boy Who Eats The Flesh Of The Fruit But Leaves The Skin Intact; so it must definitely have been our son, and we somehow have to kill that Sheikh to save him." They took this decision and called the shepherd, "Come, show us that place."

"Gentlemen," pleaded the shepherd, "I make my living by caring for goats and taking them out to feed. I earn my food as a shepherd, grazing the animals and taking them back to their owners. If I didn't return on time the owners would beat me to death. That's why I can't come with you, but I will give you directions to guide you there."

"Very well then," they replied, "Show us the right path."

"If you go south from here you'll see an ocean," said the shepherd. "Through the center of that ocean winds a small, narrow footpath, and if you follow this path with caution, it will take you to the foot of a mountain. To the west of the mountain another path will appear, and that will take you where you want to go. But if you do take this road to the Sheikh, remember you will meet some very tricky people on it, and if you speak to them at all you may never get there. On the path between these clever people and the Sheikh there is also a river. When you cross that river you'll find seven lakes as big as seven oceans. When you cross the seven lakes there is a mountain, and in those three places there'll be three very clever men. Now be careful if you do speak to them—as a matter of fact, if you say anything at all to them, I don't know what will happen. Be very wary."

The two of them listened to the shepherd's words and took that path until they came to the ocean. They saw the very narrow footpath which wound through its center and followed it. As they were walking they saw the mountain the shepherd had mentioned. "There is the path west of the mountain he told us about," they said to each other. And then the river the shepherd had described appeared. They went up to its banks and stopped to look. At that very moment they saw a man pull up a huge banyan tree from the river shore and brush his teeth with it. Vandi Puluhan and Kandi Puluhan were both shocked. Shaking with fear they looked at each other, "What is he, a demon or a devil?" There they stood, worried, with quivering hearts.

Finally, they gathered a little courage, "Hm, brother Vandi Puluhan, we could get closer to him and have a better look," said Kandi Puluhan.

So they went closer and asked, "Cousin, who are you? You seem to be very strong and clever, even mighty. Is anyone anywhere as strong as you?"

The man looked at them and said, "You seem so surprised, but there are people much cleverer than I am. Every strong man in this world has someone stronger than he is. And there is a Conqueror of all the conquerors in the world."

Kandi Puluhan addressed him, "*Appa,* will you take us across this river?"

"Wait a minute," said the man, "Let me wash my face first." He dammed up the water in the river with one hand and washed his face with the other. After washing his face he drank all the water in the river and belched. "Follow me. There's no water here now. We can walk."

"What on earth!" they exclaimed. "There's not a drop left—he drank it all. Let's see some more of this world."

The three of them climbed down into the riverbed and began walking. As they walked they saw someone inhale and pull a mountain more than forty leagues away towards himself. Then they saw him crush that mountain with two fingers and brush his teeth with the powder. And all three said, "You've turned such a huge mountain into powder, and now you're brushing your teeth with it!"

"You can scarcely imagine my powers," said the second man. "I can take all the waters of the ocean into my mouth, gargle with it, and spit it out. This mountain I just brushed my teeth with was more than forty leagues away. I pulled it towards me with my breath, powdered it between two fingers, and brushed my teeth."

"He is cleverer and stronger than we are," the three of them said. "He even looks like a small mountain."

Kandi Puluhan asked, "Is there anyone else as talented as you?"

"There is a Conqueror of all the conquerors in this world," replied the second man.

"Brother, please show Him to us," said Vandi Puluhan.

"All right, just a moment, let me wash my face first," the second man said, and with one breath he drew in an ocean of water and gargled. Now there was no water left to wash his face, and he leaped over to the next ocean, scooped up all the water with his hands, washed his face and came back to the other three men who trembled and shivered with great fear.

"Show us the One you spoke of," they said.

"Very well, come on, let's go," he answered. The four of them set out on their travels, and soon came upon someone eating all the animals in a jungle, and drinking all the water with everything in it from seven lakes, each as big as an ocean. After he finished eating and drinking, he stuffed millet and straw in his behind as a plug, and then he went to sit on top of a huge mountain. He seemed like a huge mountain sitting on top of another mountain. "Brothers," announced the second man, "The path we're on goes around this mountain. If we have to walk around that way it will take a long time, but if I pick up the mountain and move it aside we can journey much faster," and he began to lift the mountain.

Feeling the mountain below him move, the third man remarked, "This mountain is moving. It feels like a worm boring a hole in the earth underneath." So saying, he pulled out the plug of millet and straw from his rear-end, and immediately, out cascaded the water of seven oceans destroying many villages and sweeping the four of them five or six miles away.

Vandi Puluhan, Kandi Puluhan, and the other two men picked themselves up thinking, "What's this? Not only did seven oceans rise up in a tidal wave and carry us here, but many villages and lives were destroyed as well!" As they stood there unable to get over their surprise, a man came by. The four of them addressed him, "Sir, where have you come from, where is your home?" but because he was deaf he continued to walk away without answering.

"Don't you know who we are?" asked Vandi Puluhan and Kandi Puluhan rudely. "We can make this ABCD world quake and dance for you. We are the rulers of the world, yet you keep going without answering when we call you!" they yelled at him being as unpleasant as they could.

Now the man who had used up all the water in the river and the second man who had inhaled and pulled a mountain towards himself, crushed it to powder, and brushed his teeth with it, were looking on and spoke to each other. "Vandi Puluhan and Kandi Puluhan seem to be very bad-natured and stupid. They have caught hold of a poor deaf man whom they are beating just to display their strength. Those two are total fools, and we shouldn't stay with them." And so they went back the way they had come.

Later, after Vandi Puluhan and Kandi Puluhan finished beating up the poor man, they saw their two companions had left, and grabbed the poor man again, boasting and bragging, putting up their fists saying, "Hey, come and fight with us!"

"Gentlemen," said the deaf man, "I am a poor man. When you call me to fight with you, I don't know what to do because I don't have anyone to help me—O God, You alone are my help—but you two strong people should pick on people your own size, shouldn't you? Look, there is a very strong man in that jungle, and if you overcome him, you can claim to have conquered the whole world." He said that and went away.

"Let's take a look at him," Vandi Puluhan and Kandi Puluhan said to each other as they set out. While they walked along there were no villages to be seen at all. "The man said he would be here, but we don't see anyone." Then a house appeared. "O ho! There's a house now. Let's go and inquire there." As they went towards it they saw a man with a young deer seated on the path between themselves and the house. "Who are you?" they asked.

"Gentlemen," he replied, "I am just one of those created by the King who feeds all eighty-four million kinds of creations, from the tiniest of flies and ants to all the other living beings in the world. I've waited here for you many days according to His instructions.

"What's that you crazy man, just who are you waiting for?"

"According to the instructions of God, the ruler of this world, I have been looking for two people," said the man with the deer.

"And who are they?" asked Vandi Puluhan.

"Their names are Vandi Puluhan and Kandi Puluhan," he answered. "They call themselves the rulers of the ABCD world, and claim to be the mightiest of all. Engulfed in the darkness of ignorance they say there is no one greater than they are, there is no eternal, omnipresent God, Creator of the world, and that they are God. They praise themselves copiously, but in fact, they are ruining the world and its people with the fear they inspire in them. These two depraved creatures of evil are signs of destruction and decay, and the King is waiting to disgrace and destroy them. The two of you must be those wretched, degenerate forms. Yes, I'm certain you are Vandi Puluhan and Kandi Puluhan. God who is eternal and absolute is waiting to destroy you and the ten demons who have caught you. Aren't you the two who answer to those names?"

"Who's ruling the world aside from us?" yelled Vandi Puluhan and Kandi Puluhan. "Just show Him to us and we will burn Him to ash immediately," and gave the man with the baby deer a kick.

Accepting the kick he said, "All right, come and I'll show Him to you," and led them to a hut.

"*Aday* man, where is He? Show Him to us now."

The man with the deer said again, "See, I'll show you." He raised both his hands and looked up at the heavens. "O my God, eternal and absolute One, form of bliss, O God, will You not burn these signs of worldly destruction to ashes? O my God, only Your grace is truth." Then the man with the young deer showed them a small earthen chamber the size of a chicken coop on the floor of the hut. "Hey Vandi Puluhan! Kandi Puluhan! Look, this is where He is."

"O ho!" they shouted, "This place in which your King lives appears to be a chicken coop. You called him the King of the world, but what is He, a chicken, a stork, a bird? Your King's palace seems to be an underground room. Look at the opening, not even a man's head can get in! Now we see how big the palace of your King of justice is. You said He rules this world, but how could anything be ruled by Him? The stupid people of the world believe in such a tiny One, calling Him different names, calling Him Father and Lord. *Aday* man, is this the size of your King? Is this your King's palace?'' and they mocked and ridiculed the man with the deer.

"You two evil creatures seem to have taken the degenerate birth of asses,'' he answered. "Within all lives, within flies and ants and insects, within all created lives and beings in the world, there is a palace for God, our King.

Listen, I'll tell you more. He dwells in shrubs, vines, grasses, ripe and unripe fruit, but you two wild monkeys who know only monkey tricks, you say you are going to kill God. This is indeed the place where He lives, but it has only a very small doorway. Stand near it, bend your heads down, look, and you *will* see Him. You will see your cleverness and His.''

"Ha ha!'' laughed Vandi Puluhan and Kandi Puluhan, "Your King is in a chicken coop!'' They mocked him, leaping up and down, singing and dancing. "Hey look, we're going to shove you and your King right down beneath the seven worlds!'' The two of them leaped a great leap into the skies and landed back on the earth. When Vandi Puluhan jumped up, he pulled a mountain from the earth and returned with it on his shoulders. Kandi Puluhan came back carrying a great banyan tree. "Look, we are going to crush that King to dust!'' Roaring, they jumped back in front of the tiny chamber, and looked at the man with the deer again. "Hey man, is the King who dwells in the chicken coop in there or not? Tell us quickly.''

"He is indeed there,'' said the man, "Bend down, look carefully inside that earthen room, and you'll see Him.''

Kandi Puluhan and Vandi Puluhan said to each other, "That man could be lying. How could a King live in this little room?'' and they put down the tree and the mountain they had been carrying.

Vandi Puluhan glanced at Kandi Puluhan and said, "*Aday* brother, once we make sure He's in there or not,'' and they both looked around, "We could smash the chicken coop with this tree and the mountain, but He might slip away. So you pick up your tree, stand outside and watch the doorway of the hut carefully. If He comes out, hit Him with the tree. I'll bend down and look. Just in case He has heard of us and tries to trick us and run away in fear, smash Him. Be very careful.'' Vandi Puluhan crouched down with great caution and put his face near the opening. While Kandi Puluhan stood outside the hut with the tree, inside the chicken coop the formless King formed within love seized Vandi Puluhan's nose and cut it off. As soon as that happened Vandi Puluhan covered his face with both hands and hurried out, running past Kandi Puluhan without saying anything.

"What's this?" wondered Kandi Puluhan, "My brother Vandi Puluhan was given a present and he's trying to hide it, leaving without telling me." He went to the small earthen chamber and bent down. From within, the formless King took hold of Kandi Puluhan's nose and cut it off as well. With his nose cut off he too covered his face with both hands and felt very embarrassed. Although they didn't dare look at each other they were both thinking, *"Aiyo!* What will we do, how can we be kings of the world from now on, how can we even show our faces in this world? *Aiyo!* We wanted to make this world dance and quake with fear. We were the cleverest in the world until now, but not any longer."

As they walked along, each with his own thoughts, Sandakumaran, the Prince of Peace appeared on the path in front of them.

"Who are you?" asked Sandakumaran, "Why are you standing there covering your noses?"

Vandi Puluhan thought, "He resembles that Sandakumaran we encountered before," and then he spoke aloud to him. "Worthy, honorable Sandakumaran, Prince of Peace, we met you earlier in the ABCD world and tried to destroy you so many times. We changed men into cattle and cattle into men in that world, we changed sinful actions into justice, and justice into a sinful act. We turned all the laws upside down.

Using the ABCD language we took good behavior, good conduct, good language, good religion, good men, good actions, good qualities, patience, virtue, tranquillity, steadfastness, peacefulness, duty, all four religions, men and women of integrity, wise men, sages, heavenly beings, God, all beautiful actions, all loving words, and we degraded all that was good and elevated all that was bad. We did all this in the ABCD name so we could rule the world. We destroyed righteousness and made unrighteousness rule, and that's why our noses were cut off. Sandakumaran, Prince of Peace, we would like to tell you a story. Will you listen?"

The Song of One Who Weeps Forever In the Name of Sheikh Sultan Muhaiyaddeen of Baghdad

Have you abandoned me at this moment,
Permitting my body's destruction?
Have you made all my struggles and suffering useless,
So that I sigh with frustration
Like a man longing for fruit beyond his reach?
Yā Muhaiyaddeen, may Allah be pleased with you.

I do not know the destiny written for me.
Have my words not reached your holy ears?
O grace, you have come as the gracious one,
Have mercy on me.
Come, take me to the palace of the King,
Yā Muhaiyaddeen, may Allah be pleased with you.

Come to this world and make me your own,
So that I see your state in this cage
Before death comes.
I am just a wicked man singing songs,
Come, take away my suffering, console me,
O great Muhaiyaddeen, may Allah be pleased with you.

There is no one else to help me,
Why do you not have pity
On me? I arrived at this sad state
Because of my parents' faults.
Come to me before I am put into an earthy grave,
Yā Muhaiyaddeen, may Allah be pleased with you.

If you do not have pity on me even after saying all this
Whom can I tell of my kinship with you,
O great King Muhammad, *Rasūl,* Messenger
From whom the fragrance of *kastūri* emanates,

Please remove the suffering of a sinner,
Great Muhaiyaddeen, may Allah be pleased with you.

At your feet I weep and beg
That all the faults of this tormented sinner be forgiven.
To whom can I confess my sins?
Please come immediately, take away my sorrows,
Yā Muhaiyaddeen, may Allah be pleased with you.

At this moment take pity on me.
I have unwittingly had what is in the crown of your head.
Forgive my faults before my body is destroyed,
Keep me at your feet,
Muhaiyaddeen, may Allah be pleased with you.

Endless treachery and falsehood have lived
In my heart as intoxicants. I am such a sinner,
But I know you are the only refuge for this poor wretch.
Please remove the treachery from my heart,
Muhaiyaddeen, may Allah be pleased with you.

If you who know everything
Should abandon me at this moment,
Where can I turn?
There is no one to help me.
Please come, dwell in my heart,
Save me from the torment of my sorrows,
So I will yearn for your divine feet,
Yā Muhaiyaddeen, may Allah be pleased with you.

If you leave my heart, I will become so evil,
I will become a sinner wasting my time,
I will melt and burn like wax in a fire.
Appear before me this very moment,
Our Muhaiyaddeen, may Allah be pleased with you.

I was cheated when I worshiped the earth,
I was possessed by a demon when I worshiped women.
As my mother and father would, take pity on me, your slave.
Is there anyone else who can help me?
Muhaiyaddeen, may Allah be pleased with you.

Please forgive all the faults I have committed,
Draw me to your feet, protect me.
I swear in the name of God who permeates heaven and earth
I have told the truth as I see it.
Please hear me,
Yā Muhaiyaddeen, may Allah be pleased with you.

Radiance of the pure one
Who shone like light from a cradle of beautiful gems
In the throne of God, even in the time of darkness before creation began,
Is there any other truth to praise or sing about?
Protect me, have compassion, jeweled light of my eyes,
Yā Muhaiyaddeen, may Allah be pleased with you.

Even though I keep your holy name within,
And I try to establish that inner light of perfect purity,
Why do I still waver and make mistakes?
I am a sinner whose bodily cage may be destroyed before I ever see
    the King.
I have no one to help me except you,
Yā Muhaiyaddeen, may Allah be pleased with you.

I am telling the absolute truth,
And the time is right.
Appear before me,
Appear in my heart, at this moment take pity on me,
Make me victorious
In the field of devotion, in the countryside
Where the golden rain of grace falls,
Yā Meera Muhaiyaddeen, may Allah be pleased with you.

Meera Muhaiyaddeen, may Allah be pleased with you,
You imprisoned that jinn in a small phial
And rescued a golden princess.
Will I ever find myself
And dedicate my life to God
Before death comes to seize me?
Meera Muhaiyaddeen, may Allah be pleased with you.

9

The City of Sokku

Vandi Puluhan and Kandi Puluhan tell Sandakumaran the amazing story of the city of Sokku.

The city of Sokku was ruled by King Mahendiran who had a daughter called Vastira Alangaram. When she was three years old her mother died, and after that, their servant Sandirapadi brought her up as if she had been her own child. When she was older, the king arranged a huge assembly to show off his daughter's dancing and artistic ability, and sent invitations to the kings of many lands. As a compliment to his daughter's dancing, the king decreed that anyone who could accompany her with great inspiration on the drums would win a minister's title in his kingdom, but he also announced if the contestant's skill did not match the excellence of the dancing, his head would be cut off.

In a suburb of Sokku there was a boy named Kunamayjayan who came from a very poor family. Even though his parents were extremely poor they had taught him many disciplines and music of a very high order. Everyone praised him highly. When Kunamayjayan heard of the king's proclamation and its conditions, he decided to take part in the assembly and win that title. He went to his parents and asked for their permission, but they opposed his wish when they heard the stipulations.

"*Appa,* Son," they said, "According to his rules that fierce king will kill you if you lose."

Although they pleaded and pleaded with him, he was not dissuaded. He knelt in front of them begging, "Mother, Father, God will not forsake me. Your loving permission is sufficient protection for me, please let me go."

Finally, his kind-hearted parents relented, "Son, God who is eternal and absolute will protect you. Do not forget your parents or God during the musical competition. Remember there are five things you must never be involved with, intoxicants, falsehood, theft, lust, or murder. God will protect you, and if you learn to love the lives of others as much as you love your own, you will always be victorious. May you return safely, child!" They gave him their blessing, Kunamayjayan prayed to God, and left for the assembly.

The kings of many countries had gathered and were being entertained lavishly in the palace and courtyards. When Kunamayjayan arrived at the palace gates the guards stopped him. "Please Sir, don't stop me. My name is Kunamayjayan. I've come here to display my talent and take part in the king's musical competition. Please take me to him."

But the guards took one look at him and shouted, "Hey, you're crazy, there's no place for you here!"

Then Kunamayjayan sang this song.

KUNAMAYJAYAN'S SONG

Crazy am I, with the craziness which
Comes from the destiny God has given me,
The craziness for that all-pervasive One
Who dances through the universe.
The world does not understand goodness.
In all four directions
Anyone good is considered crazy.
To all those who yearn
For the divine feet of the Lord
His grace is their craziness,
If His heart so wills
In His melting clemency.

The sound of his song reached the ears of the king.

THE KING: Who is that singing there? Guards, bring him here.

[*The guards enter with Kunamayjayan.*]

THE KING: [*Considers Kunamayjayan*] Now then boy, why have you come here?

KUNAMAYJAYAN: O king, I have come to show my skill in the art of singing and drama, to win the contest and earn that job you promised in the proclamation.

THE KING: [*With surprise*] Do you know the punishment if you don't win? Your head will be chopped off!

KUNAMAYJAYAN: My lord, I knew that very well when I came here.

[The king orders arrangements to be made.
The contest begins. Vastira Alangaram sings.]

VASTIRA ALANGARAM'S SONG

So sublime, ah
This world is so sublime.

*May our king live a long time
And rule with splendor,
May his reign prosper,
May our subjects live a long time,
May they prosper,
May this city of Sokku
Live forever and ever.
May your compassionate justice
Reign forever,
Everywhere,
May your wonderful world
Live on,
May the mountain rivers
Flow forever full,
May the goddess of the arts
Live forever more.*

THE MAHARAJAH OF MANTIRAPUR: I am filled with admiration for the incomparable excellence King Mahendiran's worthy daughter has acquired in the art of singing and dancing. In praise of her rare, wonderful performance which has filled my heart with ecstasy, I offer this string of pearls as my gift. The beauty of her song and dance has immersed us all in a deep ocean of bliss.

After these words of congratulation from a visiting king the assembly dispersed, and Kunamayjayan, who had also shown his excellence, earned the king's praise and the prize he had promised, a minister's role in the government.

Now at this time there was also a poor boy named Visittira Layka going to school in Sokku. The day after the assembly that boy was returning home from school as usual when Vastira Alangaram spoke to him, "Well beggar boy, what's your name?" she asked.

"My name is Visittira Layka," he replied.

"Are your parents living? What is your racial origin?" she asked next.

"Yes, my lady, my parents are living, and I am a member of the male race."

"*Aday*, what is your lineage?"

"Mendicant," he replied and then immediately began to sing.

VISITTIRA LAYKA'S SONG

There are many religions in the world,

But I don't know what race is, my lady.
Joyfully one day
I asked my mother and father
What race means,
So that my heart would know.
Happily my mother and father answered,
"Male and female are the only races
Which exist in this world.
In the world we are all one race.
Understand this."
I don't know my race, you peacock.

VASTIRA ALANGARAM'S SONG

Idiot, you don't know anything about race or religion,
Your words make me laugh.
You're an idiot who doesn't understand race or religion.
You talk like a eunuch
Who doesn't know anything about the place of birth.
What you say is crazy,
Even a madman doesn't talk like that,
And the way you act is certainly crazy.
You say we are all one race.
Shoo, dog! Go away, fool!

"My lady," said Visittira Layka, "I am not a fool, I am not crazy, I am not a eunuch. Why are you so angry with me?"

"Ah, what a pity! You are a foolish idiot who doesn't understand race or religion," she answered.

"My lady doesn't seem to have realized that virtue, patience, wisdom, good qualities, and compassion towards all lives are indispensable for a woman. You're the one babbling as if you were crazy. My lady appears to have nourished only her anger all this time instead of her wisdom."

"*Aday* beggar, do you dare preach to the king's daughter in the city of Sokku? Just remember if my father knew of it you would lose your head."

Just then a wayfarer came down the road and heard their argument. "My goodness, this is a strange world indeed. How can the rain fall when such women exist in this world?" and he breathed a deep sigh at the thought.

Now the poor boy Visittira Layka, studied the princess and said, "There are three things I must ask you. First my lady, since you have gone to school and studied hard, tell me what learning is. The second is a riddle: you're riding a horse, a horse which can go ten miles a minute, and you hold the reins without seeing the horse. What is it? And third my lady is this, the fortress in which you live is gigantic. It has twelve openings and four doors facing the four directions. You have placed guards on all sides, but what is the treasure this fortress holds? Now my lady, if you can answer these questions then I certainly am a fool."

Vastira Alangaram looked at the poor youth and shouted with uncontrollable anger, "You dog, you beggar! You wait, I'll teach you a good lesson." Promising this, she stormed home in a rage and sat in a corner with a set expression on her face, not taking care of her usual duties.

THE KING: [*Observing his daughter's distress*] My child, why is your face so sad?

VASTIRA ALANGARAM: [*Remains silent*]

THE KING: [*Embracing her*] Alangaram, my dear child, if you tell me what the trouble is, I will see that it is attended to immediately.

VASTIRA ALANGARAM: [*Sobbing and speaking with great sorrow*] Father, today as I was coming home I met some new kind of fool I've never seen before. Not only did he argue with me, but he asked me three questions and humiliated me.

THE KING: [*Speaking with unrestrained anger*] I will give that beggar the punishment he deserves. Do not grieve my dear child. Send for the Prime Minister!

[*The Prime Minister enters.*]

A fool has distressed my honorable daughter Vastira Alangaram by asking her three questions, and he's embarrassed her as well. I want him arrested and brought here immediately.

THE MINISTER: So be it, my lord.

The minister sent out soldiers in all directions, but they were beset with great difficulties as they went through the forest in search of the boy. The wandering, searching soldiers were tormented by exhaustion and sat down to rest under a tree. Then one of the soldiers sang a song from the despondency which filled his heart.

SOLDIER'S SONG

Is my sin merely being here on earth

Or is this the destiny God has decreed for me?
Is it my plight
To roam the world?
Thirst constricts my throat, I feel faint,
My body is parched and it trembles.
I fear I cannot last,
Save me O Lord, O glorious One,
Please save me, I am so afraid.

While the soldier sang this song a hunter was running quickly in that direction chasing a deer. When he came to the tree he was startled by the sight of the king's guards and stopped running. "Who are you, Sir?" asked the soldier.

"I just hunt for my living in this wide forest, and I would be very grateful if you could tell me who you are," said the hunter. "Why have you come here?"

"We'll tell you all that later," said the soldier. "Right now, we are parched with thirst. Please give us some water." The hunter immediately invited the soldiers to his hut, and gave them food and water with great courtesy. While the soldiers were eating the food and drinking the water the hunter had given them so lovingly, they heard a sweet song coming from somewhere.

"*Appa,* are there other cottages around here?" asked a soldier.

"No," replied the hunter.

"Then where is that song coming from?" asked the soldier.

"It is surprising," said the hunter, "Let's go and find out," and he accompanied the guards.

Soon they came upon Visittira Layka, sitting with a holy man under a tree singing his remembrance of God with an overflowing heart.

VISITTIRA LAYKA'S SONG

Is it fair
That You who are not separate
Are separate from me?
O God, light of awareness,
Majestic, unconquerable ray of light,
Rising within me, not filling me,
You who cannot be too full,
Be always at my side
Protecting this lowly one.

O inner meaning of religion,
O true meaning of the scriptures,
O ultimate sound, pure treasure,
O Father, protect me with Your grace.

While he was singing, the soldiers saw Visittira Layka. "Look, there's the crazy boy, the one we've been looking all over for," and they seized him by the arms.

"O please Sir, why are there so many of you holding me down?" he cried. "What have I done wrong? Please let go of me," he begged.

"Soldiers," said the holy man, "Why have you surrounded this little boy, why are you detaining him, what has he done to any of you? The poor boy, please let him go."

"Holy one," they replied, "He may be small, but in fact, he's much too big. He humiliated Vastira Alangaram, our king's daughter, and caused her so much pain. Now he is pretending to be a renunciate spending his time on the path to God. He is a hypocrite, a scoundrel, and a traitor."

"Don't say such things about one of God's poor devotees, one who seeks Him in the belief that love, grace, and truth are the only treasures that endure. You have already concluded he is bad, a scoundrel, an enemy, without a proper investigation. The evil of what you're doing will engulf you, in fact it already has," said the holy man.

Fear crept into the hearts of the soldiers, "Holy one, we must take him with us because it is our king's command. Please don't stop us."

"Holy one," wailed Visittira Layka with a trembling heart, "What cruelty, what injustice is this? What have I done wrong? Is there no justice for a poor, helpless man?" and he fell crying at the feet of the holy man.

"My sweet child," said the holy man blessing the poor youth, "Don't be afraid, everything is part of God's graceful plan. I'm here, don't be afraid of anything. Listen carefully to these five things, impress what I say firmly in your heart because it's the only thing there is to guide you properly.

The first thing you must know is that all the actors on this worldly stage who live with pride and vanity will go to a bottomless hell. They are possessed by a horrible demon whose name is desire. Now, when that demon tries to attach itself to you, drive him away with all your strength. Second, there are prostitute demons who resemble Satan, always lying in wait for men, trying to lure them into a deep pit of hell. They pursue you throwing maya's net of enchantment around you. Don't become entangled in that net—kick the mayic demons away. And then there are three other very horrifying evils, the monkey-devils known as lies, theft, and murder. Their most important function is to devastate good people. Those three monkey-devils approach you very insidiously, they try to deceive you and torment you, but don't fall into their clutches. Be very careful not to let them in. My child, there is a mantra which will destroy these five demons. Listen, I'll teach it to you," and the holy man began to sing.

THE HOLY MAN'S SONG

Faith is the only mantra.
For the Lord who dances
The dance of the universe,
The mantra of wisdom's eye
Is the luminous light
In the ray of bliss.

If you merge with Him
At every moment
Like fire swallowed by water,
At any moment of danger He will protect you.
Faith is the only mantra,
It is indeed the mantra
Nothing can conquer.
Firm, perfect faith is the only mantra.

"Even your song and its purity can't make up for our thirst and the king's command. We must take Visittira Layka with us. That was the king's order, wise sage, and we don't dare disobey." As they said this they took Visittira Layka by the arm and began to pull him away. He fell at the feet of the holy man and paid obeisance to him.

"Sweet child," said the holy man blessing him, "Go now and come back when you can. God will never forsake you," and he sent him off with the soldiers who took the boy to the palace.

That day happened to be Vastira Alangaram's birthday, and there was a celebration with very extravagant, beautiful festivities. The guards took the youth before the king.

THE KING: [*With great anger to the soldiers*] Who is he? Why did you bring him here?

THE SOLDIERS: My lord, he is the boy we went in search of. He's the one who caused such distress to our princess, but when we found him he was with a holy man pretending to be a devotee of God. . . . .

THE KING: [*Interrupting before they can close their mouths*] *Aday* you dog, you beggar, you have fallen into my hands today, and you'll never escape me now! Tomorrow we'll have an inquiry. Lock him up in the dungeon. When this day is done, tomorrow your turn will come.

[*A court of inquiry is convened first thing next morning.
The king's four ministers enter:
Mandayveengee or Swollenhead, the first minister
Mahasooran or Big Demon, the second minister
Kudialitan or Homewrecker, the third minister
Kunamayjayan or Triumphant Virtue, the fourth minister.
Kunamayjayan's analytic ability and the quality of his justice
and wisdom seem superior.*

The king enters.]

THE KING: [*With uncontrollable anger seeing Visittira Layka*] *Aday* you dog, you beggar, you demon! You and your three questions upset my daughter. We shall, therefore, have you whipped as the first part of your punishment.

KUNAMAYJAYAN: O my king, please be patient for a moment. It's neither just nor fair to become angry so quickly with your subjects. What is just is to inquire into a case, analyze all the circumstances and details, find out who is at fault, and then pronounce sentence. Then when the guilty parties are identified, their punishment should be carried out in the appropriate place. If we depart from this procedure and administer the punishment right here in the king's court, that would bring disgrace to your reign.

THE KING: Very well, but I've been waiting many days to pronounce the most terrible punishment on him. The four of you should address yourselves to this case, and then devise an appropriate sentence for him.

VISITTIRA LAYKA: My king and my lords of the city of Sokku, what you said is very true, but there is a subtle point to understand. Now you called me a dog, but a dog has four legs and people have two legs. You also called me a demon, but the feet of demons don't even touch the ground, so wise men say. And let me tell you, dogs and demons are eternal enemies. Even if you kick and beat a dog he won't give up, he won't run away until the life leaves his body. There is a prayer to destroy a demon, a prayer which is a resplendent, omnipresent light, an eternal, wide open space. None of you in this assembly seem to know this, and your cruel government doesn't appear to be aware that this prayer is always waiting, open-mouthed, to devour evil demons. Not only that, this government believes in culture and thinks that amusements and entertainments are very important. If your people really believe amusements give splendor to their lives, how long do you think it will be until the king and his subjects are destroyed? Remember that day is not far off. There's no point sniffing a bouquet of flowers which has no fragrance, or hankering after food which has no taste. This is a saying my teacher taught me when I was young, and now, after observing you today, I know its meaning.

[*When they hear this, the ministers and others become extremely angry at the youth, and prepare to behead him.*]

KUNAMAYJAYAN: [*Stopping them*] My lord, this boy's words are very profound, and we must analyze them minutely to understand it all. Once we have done that, then we can think about the right punishment for him. The ocean of patience has no waves. We must really understand that if we act without forethought we will bring suffering upon ourselves which will be a living death. As I said earlier, it could bring disgrace to our country. It is not just for the government to favor one side: a king's rule must be completely impartial or else that government will acquire a reputation for tyranny, sin, and wrongdoing. Therefore, I sincerely beg that the inquiry be stopped for today and continue tomorrow.

THE KING: Very well. Put the boy in the dungeon and we will take this up tomorrow for further inquiry.

When the assembly dispersed Swollenhead, the Prime Minister, went home. As soon as he got there his wife Poyandal asked, "Why are you so late today?"

"Today," he answered, "We began an inquiry in which a youth named Visittira Layka was charged with upsetting the princess. That's why I am late."

"Did that wretch have to insult the princess of all people? That's as ignorant as an escaped convict trying to hide in the magistrate's house. Now don't let him go, he must be punished severely," she said.

"A ha! You do know your husband, don't you? This minister can turn falsehood into truth and truth into falsehood. That youth will not escape, apple of my eye, you don't have to worry."

Then their daughter Kamamohasuntari who was listening to them said, "The boy's name seems to indicate he might be a good person."

Instantly Swollenhead became angry with his daughter, "Shoo dog! What do you know, anyway? Can we simply judge people on the strength of their names?"

Cynically his daughter answered, "Father, if the city of Sokku had four other people as good as you are, it would flourish and prosper! Even I know there is no room here for good, truthful people. In my opinion, a good person seems like a dog to all of you."

"Keep quiet child," said Swollenhead, "You don't understand this world. We have to go along with whatever it wants."

"All right, Father," said Kamamohasuntari, "Beat him like a dog. You will suffer the consequences later." Eventually, they all settled down to sleep, and the next day Swollenhead went back to the palace for the trial. The assembly gathered again to hear the case against the boy.

[*The princess enters and the inquiry begins.*]

THE KING: [*Addresses Visittira Layka*] What is your name?

VISITTIRA LAYKA: My name is Visittira Layka. It always has been.

THE KING: What is your native country?

VISITTIRA LAYKA: My native land is the whole, wide splendid world.

THE KING: Are your parents alive?

VISITTIRA LAYKA: Yes, my parents are living.

THE KING: Is it true you upset my daughter?

VISITTIRA LAYKA: Upset someone? Who? I've never distressed anyone in the past, nor will I ever in the future.

THE KING: *Aday* youth! Keep to the point and don't volunteer anything else.

VISITTIRA LAYKA: Yes, my lord, I'll do just that.

THE KING: Come now, Visittira Layka, are you guilty or not guilty?

VISITTIRA LAYKA: My lord, I am not guilty.

THE PRIME MINISTER: O king, he looks like just a little boy, but he seems full of arrogance. We must devise a severe punishment.

THE SECOND MINISTER: O king, he might be small, but I've never heard anyone speak so rudely before. Because he's a slanderous traitor to our government, he should be locked in the dungeon.

THE THIRD MINISTER: O king, I have never seen anyone like him in all the time I have served you. Not only has he been rude to the princess, he has also insulted you and your government. Therefore we should execute him.

KUNAMAYJAYAN, THE FOURTH MINISTER: O king, please excuse me for speaking. What they said may be true, but all of them seem angry at the boy's words. They didn't ask about the circumstances of the incident, whether it really happened, why he asked the three questions, what he did to embarrass the princess, or what actually did happen. It would not be right, not worthy of the king's justice if we came to a conclusion without knowing the truth. Therefore, it is our duty to analyze this incident, bit by bit, and then when we understand it we can pass judgment. That will be just, fair, and lawful. Since we should question both the plaintiff and the defendant minutely, it would be reasonable to ask a few questions of our princess. Only then will a just verdict be possible. It is my firm opinion that would be the most exalted and just thing to do.

THE KING: That seems acceptable to a certain extent. Let us question the princess. Alangaram, among many other things the youth said he was not guilty. What do you say?

THE THIRD MINISTER: [*Interrupts*] My lord, there is another subtle point. If he did not commit any wrong, why did he have to go to the forest and put on an ascetic's disguise?

THE KING: Yes, yes, that is a very pertinent question. He is truly guilty. There'll be no saving him now. His punishment will be death by hanging. [*Looks at the youth*] *Aday* beggar, you villain, your punishment is death by hanging. You will be executed six days from today.

Send for the executioners!

[*The executioners enter paying obeisance to the king.*]

He must be hanged six days from now. Until then, lock him up in the dungeon without food.

THE EXECUTIONERS: So be it, my lord.

KUNAMAYJAYAN: [*Humbly entreats the king, showing him a small book*] My lord, you must grace me with your pardon. I would like to read you a small story, a true story I learned from this book.

THE KING: What is it? Tell us the story, let's hear it.

Advice to Intellect

You talk like an enemy,
Are you a human being?
You don't understand the eight, the two,
Or yourself, you cowardly fool!

Search for the kingdom of heaven,
Go there. Millions have come
From this earth to that bliss.
Search for that luminous ray of light,
Find it and become a true, perfect man.
I sing this.

You talk like an enemy,
Are you a human being?
You don't understand the eight, the two,
Or yourself, you cowardly fool!

Go, without argument,
Says God from the *'arsh,*
His throne in the crown of the head,
Go, why keep bragging about yourself?
Go, don't rant like a madman.

You talk like an enemy,
Are you a human being?
You don't understand the eight, the two,
Or yourself, you cowardly fool!

You will be disgraced, I warn you.
Come, God lives in your *'arsh.*
I sing this. Now search for it,
Find that rare, precious thing,
And you will find bliss and grace,
You foolish creature.

You talk like an enemy,
Are you a human being?

You don't understand the eight, the two,
Or yourself, you cowardly fool!

Countless millions like you
Talk on, not even searching for it.
You fool, you don't know your own mother,
Can the five letters become one?

You talk like an enemy,
Are you a human being?
You don't understand the eight, the two,
Or yourself, you cowardly fool!

Fools without knowledge of subtle form
Roam aimlessly. There are millions in the world
Who fail to understand this does no good.
A lowly being on this earth, I sing this.

You talk like an enemy,
Are you a human being?
You don't understand the eight, the two,
Or yourself, you cowardly fool!

10

Kunamayjayan

In the Puluhan's story of the city of Sokku, Kunamayjayan, the good minister, tells the King of Sokku a story which may come true.

KUNAMAYJAYAN: My loving prayers and respectful greetings to my good king and his court.

[*He begins reading the story.*]

There was a city known as Kothipore or angry town, where there was a very honored sage with four disciples who had been given the titles The Fault-Finder, The Singer of Songs, The Entertainer, and The Divider of Spoils. All the people in that city were famous for their pride in themselves, and whenever they encountered true followers of God it was their nature to ridicule them, insult them, and chase them away. Ananda Atchaypan, an untouchable who was one of God's devotees, came to Kothipore from the city of Devapore, or God's town. Since he really wanted to stay there a while and had no place to live, he asked a poor man named Tondan if he could stay with him.

Tondan studied Ananda and decided that he looked like a follower of God. "You honor me, holy one," he said, "This is where I live. It's only a hut, but if you find it acceptable, I would be pleased," and he stood there in humble reverence.

"Sir," said Ananda Atchaypan, "There is something I must tell you. I am a *pulaiyan,* an untouchable."

"Master," replied Tondan, "I am a poor man without awareness of caste or racial or religious differences. Any caste, race, or religion, they're all the same to me."

Ananda thought to himself, "He really is a man of duty whose name is witness to his good qualities," and he willingly accepted a corner of the hut as his dwelling place.

"Master," said Tondan, "Your stay here is the greatest wealth my heart could know. My body, my possessions, and my soul belong to you." He folded his hands together in a prayerful salutation and paid obeisance to him.

During his stay there Ananda Atchaypan treated some of the sick people in the area very successfully and he soon became well-known because of this. The people in nearby villages came to love him and have great faith in him. There were many other wonders connected with him as well.

As his reputation to cure terrible diseases with his powers and his herbs grew, the local sage and his faction watched the people of their own town, of neighboring towns, and even of other countries come to Kothipore to pay obeisance to this lowly Sheikh. When they considered his healing ability and the way his following was increasing, they wanted to be rid of him and began to plot and scheme to drive him away. Others equally wicked joined them and created all sorts of trouble and difficulty for the Sheikh, hoping to force him out. Although they placed many obstacles and dangers in his path they didn't have the power to cause the slightest harm to the Sheikh or his followers. They themselves were tolerant and forbearing of any trouble or hardship, keeping strictly to themselves. But soon the Sheikh realized the kind of people the sage and his group were, and in accordance with the old adage 'Don't look for trouble,' he decided to leave the city. He had earned the kind words, the respect, and the devotion of all the people, and left with a heart full of love.

In the course of time the evil intentions which aimed at the downfall of a great being took their toll. There is an old saying, 'Don't even unwittingly think of hurting others. If you do, justice will exact retribution from you.' And since there is an undying truth in this saying, God who is within engulfed those schemers and wiped them out. In the end the sage and his entire family were destroyed, and that whole faction was disgraced, impoverished and humbled.

[*Kunamayjayan finishes reading.*]

KUNAMAYJAYAN: [*Handing the book to the king*] This book will prove to you, my lord, that we must not persecute wandering mendicants. Although it's not easy to establish, this poor boy may really be a devotee of God. His words did have great depth and meaning, and it's possible that many difficulties might beset us, that we could be humiliated, even destroyed because of what we do to him. Therefore, we must analyze all this carefully. If we have love and compassion for all living beings, righteousness will flourish, the government will prosper and earn the respect and praise of our people.

THE KING: [*Reflecting and understanding the truth of what he had heard*] What Kunamayjayan said is true. There is real meaning in his words.

I hereby commute the death sentence pronounced earlier on Visittira Layka to perpetual imprisonment in the dungeon.

This inquiry is concluded.

The next day the investigation was reported in the daily newspaper. Two passers-by went to a newsstand, bought a paper, and read the news. Their names were Vayloo and Soopoo, and both were staggeringly drunk.

"I say cousin, here's an old saying, 'Don't let go,'" said Vayloo.

"What's the meaning of that?" asked Soopoo.

"*Aday,* you're a real fool," said Vayloo, "All this time you've been drinking and getting drunk, and yet you still don't know the meaning of 'Don't let go.'"

"*Aday,* you're crazy," said Soopoo. "All right, tell me what it all means, tell me as much as you can."

"'Don't let go' means hang on to this bottle."

"*Adada,*" sang Soopoo, "That's part of a song from ancient times sung by a wise old woman called Awwayar, and a poet named Poyyamoli. And that isn't the true meaning of this saying either."

"Well all that's in the past, but in today's terms that stuff is like a mountain already climbed. What *I* said is the real meaning for today. Now, after you've been drinking, haven't you ever looked around at the world, Soopoo?"

"Yes, I have. Down rolls up and up rolls down. I don't move but the whole world seems to whirl. I walk straight but the ground sways and rolls, and much, much more."

As they walked along a song came to them, and they sang in a lofty, commanding style.

VAYLOO AND SOOPOO'S SONG

Adada, *ah the ecstasy of drunkenness gets you high!*
Edada, *when will we conquer this heart?*
Padada, *sing, you'll slip and fall right into the earth itself.*
Vidada, *give up and swear allegiance to our religion of drunkenness.*

Our eyes are dancing and rolling,
Meanings are tottering,
The glory of intoxication without end
Cannot be told in words.
What, oh what can be done
To overcome our inhibitions,
And murder the awareness of goodness
Which is torturing us?

If you drink our sweet-tasting wine
Your perceptions will change.

*All lifeless things will
Rise up and take form,
Your eyes will be destroyed,
Your sight will be ruined,
You will vomit black vomit,
And swear to give up drinking.*

But adada, *ah the ecstasy of drunkenness gets you high!*
Edada, *when will we conquer this heart?*
Padada, *sing, you'll slip and fall right into the earth itself.*
Vidada, *give up and swear allegiance to our religion of drunkenness.*

They sang as they walked along, and then later sat down to read the newspaper again. In the papers they read all about the case of the king's daughter, her humiliation, Visittira Layka's conviction, and the sentence of perpetual imprisonment. They wondered who Visittira Layka was, and thought very carefully about the fact he was a wandering mendicant. Both of them thought and thought, and Vayloo realized that Visittira Layka was the son of Ramu, a pilgrim in this world. He mentioned this to Soopoo who couldn't remember him, and Vayloo had to remind him of the day they had gone to Ramu's house to buy a goat. They decided to visit him again.

But meanwhile, Visittira Layka was singing in his dungeon.

VISITTIRA LAYKA'S SONG OF SUPPLICATION TO THE KING, THE GREAT KING

*What can I do now?
What should I do?
Is this my fate? I can't say.*

*Divine form,
Divine precious Sheikh, my God,
Please protect me with Your grace.*

*What can I do now?
What should I do?
Is this my fate? I can't say.*

*Is it right to close Your eyes to my fate?
Please save me.
There is nothing I can do.*

Do not brush me aside or forsake me,
Indeed You must embrace me and protect me,
Grant me refuge from starvation, disease, and death.

What can I do now?
What should I do?
Is this my fate? I can't say.

Was it something I did wrong in this lifetime,
Or has this misfortune befallen me
Because of what I did before?
You are the Polestar,
The real meaning which guides the whole world.
Protect this disciple with Your grace,
Even as a voice from heaven.

What can I do now?
What should I do?
Is this my fate? I can't say.

When he finished singing this song he heard a voice, "Don't be afraid my child, don't be disturbed! This dungeon is not your destiny, and besides, in this exalted state, what can it do to you? Home or a dungeon makes no difference to you. Don't forget that God protects His devotees in this world with unceasing vigilance. It would be a grave mistake to think that His eyes might be closed or that He has no compassion. No matter what happens, don't be afraid." A sweet voice whispered this in the boy's ear.

Visittira Layka jumped up in shocked surprise, "Yes, yes, it does sound like the voice of my Sheikh. Yes, it is he!" And his mind was composed and comforted. The guards had been serving Visittira Layka stale, leftover food after the other prisoners had eaten, and that day when they brought him his bits of food, because of his sincere devotion he received that food and ate it willingly with the faith that it was the food of grace from his Sheikh.

Just then Vastira Alangaram was riding past on her way to the flower garden, and she glanced into the dungeon. She laughed when she saw Visittira Layka eating the rotten food, "Oh, you look like Visittira Layka."

"Yes, my lady," he replied, "I am Visittira Layka."

"A ha!" she laughed scornfully, "How is the dungeon, or is it more fun to give advice to the king's family, ask them questions, and make fun of them?" Visittira Layka remained silent. "What? You seem to have learned perfect silence! Only the other day you asked me so many questions, yet today I don't hear any reply at all to *my* question."

As an answer, Visittira Layka sang this song.

VISITTIRA LAYKA'S SONG

Honored dancing lady,
The words you use
Blend nicely with
The songs and dances of the world.

Woman,
Don't you realize even now
That everything is destroyed
By our thoughts?

Honored dancing lady,
The words you use
Blend nicely with
The shrill words of the world.

Can the world foretell
What will happen tomorrow?
When you know,
You, with your own mouth
Will lament.

Honored dancing lady,
The words you use
Blend nicely with
The shrill words of the world.

A blissful kingdom will be destroyed
Because of you, and then
You will understand your own pride.
Your joyful dancing and all your indifference
Fly away at the mere
Glance of a poor boy.

Honored dancing lady,
The words you use
Blend nicely with
The shrill words of the world.

*Good advice to the royal family
Can only come from wandering mendicants.
You will see,
Alangaram, O woman,
This kingdom will not be saved
By your actions.
Only the grace of the omnipresent Lord
Will save it now.*

Meanwhile, Soopoo and Vayloo arrived at Ramu's house. Soopoo said to Ramu, "My brother Vayloo and I have had so much trouble."

"*Adada!* Why should that be? You came here once before, didn't you?" asked Ramu.

"Yes, we did," said Vayloo, "But you know, in old age we easily become tired and forgetful."

"That's quite true," said Ramu, "Come in please and be seated." He called his wife, "Ay, Tangam, Tangam, dearest wife, come here, some old friends have come."

"Coming!" answered Tangam, "But I don't remember either one!"

"What Tangam?" reminded Ramu, "This is Soopoo, and that is Vayloo."

"O ho! I guess I do remember," she said.

"Tangam, please bring them some of the good tea," said Ramu.

"Yes, I'll do that right away."

"All right," said Ramu looking over at his friends, "Now, about the purpose of your visit?"

"The business we have come about is very, very serious," said Soopoo.

"What is very serious?" asked Ramu.

"It is very serious," said Soopoo, "But never mind, where is your son?"

"He went to Ayoti Forest to hear the divine teachings of a holy man."

"A ha!" said Soopoo, "When did he go?"

"It's been about a month and a half since he left."

"Isn't his name Visittira Layka?"

"Yes, why the doubt?"

"There is no doubt," replied Soopoo, "There's news. Today I read in the papers that your son was imprisoned in the dungeon."

"*Aiyo!* My son? In the dungeon? Why in the dungeon? Why did he have to go?" Ramu cried and wailed as he suffered torment in his heart, not knowing what to do. "Oh no!" he cried hugging his friends, falling to the ground and rolling around in unbearable agony.

His wife Tangam heard the sound of his wailing and came running. "O God, what's wrong? Why are you crying?"

"Mother," said Soopoo, "We told him the newspapers say your son has been imprisoned in the dungeon, and he's crying now because of the pain in his heart."

Ramu said, "I will go first to Ayoti Forest, then see my boy, find out everything I can, and return here."

"My brother, if that's what you are going to do, we'll join you," said Soopoo.

The three of them set off on their journey to the Forest.

[*Vastira Alangaram enters, returning from the flower garden, tense and distressed.*]

THE KING: Baby, what's wrong? Why are you so upset?

VASTIRA ALANGARAM: Father, I visited the flower garden today, and on the way I went past the dungeon. That beggar made fun of me again, even more so this time.

THE KING: What's that? The sinner! Does a mere beggar who sings for his supper have that much arrogance? He dares to do this even while in prison? Just see what I will do with him!

[*The king shouts and walks away in great anger.*]

Commander-in-chief, that beggar in the dungeon has mocked our own Vastira Alangaram once again. He must not escape! There can be no reprieve for him this time. Keep him in a dark cell for three days and put him to death the next day. This is my decision.

SWOLLENHEAD, BIG DEMON, HOMEWRECKER: [*Together*] My lord, we agree with your pronouncement!

KUNAMAYJAYAN: [*Dissenting*] O King, I beg your indulgence. It is neither proper nor fair nor just to permit yourself to be deceived by the words and acts of a vengeful, cunning woman. And it is not right to change the judgment, to increase the punishment against a defenseless man without another inquiry.

Many great kings and emperors have perished because of a woman's tricks. King Rama, for instance, lost his country and his crown, and had to live in the jungle, suffering intensely because of Kuni, the hunchbacked woman. And mighty King Ravana, prodded by his sister, committed unjust acts and knew great suffering too. Finally, he was killed by Rama's arrows and his kingdom was devoured by fire.

As king, it is your duty to inquire, to think deeply, to assess and judge impartially in all circumstances. You should also see that no judgment based on hastiness, cruelty, or anger, no judgment causing hardship to the people can be righteous. The great sages tell us that a true king behaves like a mother and father, like God to all lives. You should realize that a king, his subjects, and his country must cooperate like the muscles of the body, that a kingdom flourishes when the king and his subjects are united like the fingernail and the finger. A kingdom which is ruled with a club is a cruel kingdom. It would do you good to reflect on this and think about what it means.

THE KING: [*With an angry stare*] Ha, minister! You are ruining this government's affairs. The other day when the boy was being sentenced you thought that judgment was wrong, and you refused to agree with the other ministers. Since there really is a vast difference between my opinions and yours you are no use to us as a minister, and it would be better if you resigned your post.

KUNAMAYJAYAN: No matter what you say, you are a cruel, demonic, unrighteous king! There is indeed a difference between fire and water, and that is the difference between an unjust king like you and myself.

[*Kunamayjayan takes off his ministerial robes and flings them down in front of the king.*]

Foolish man to obey the dictates of a woman, would a tiger eat grass even if it were starving? Certainly not. Many of the crowned kings who ruled this world have been disgraced and killed. Don't think you can rule this country forever. You only have a few days left and then your kingdom will fly away from you in a truly amazing way.

THE KING: [*Shouting*] Guards! Here is a minister who is cleverer than his king! Give him five minutes to leave the country. He is banished!

[*Immediately the guards seize Kunamayjayan and start to drag him away.*]

KUNAMAYJAYAN: [*With anger*] O King, you can banish me to the forest now, but I'll see you and your equally evil ministers driven there before you kill that poor boy. My lord, before I leave I am going to sing you a few verses from a song. Listen to it carefully and understand what it means.

KUNAMAYJAYAN'S SONG

What use is it
To pursue the monkey of the mind
As it runs fleetingly through
The limitless forest and sands of the mind?
To receive the grace, the light, the victory of compassion
Which exists as One, as many, as life to life,

Search for that state of devotion and surrender,
Search for Him.

People of the world, come merge with Him.

Those who are in the fellowship of purity
Are in the fellowship which
Bestows indescribable blessings.
Even if worldly success seems to fall into your hands,
Leave the court where only outer meanings are conveyed.
Do not be part of a fellowship
Which lets lies creep in.
Come see the fellowship of God.

People of the world, come merge with Him.

If you are friendly to crows,
All you will see is blackness
Until your life comes to an end.
Only in the cascading flood of divine luminous bliss
Will the purity of open space be reached.

Before the body is swallowed by the grave,
People of the world, come merge with Him.

THE KING: All right, all right. Now disappear!

Swollenhead's daughter Kamamohasuntari saw Kunamayjayan leaving the palace and spoke to her father as soon as he came home. "Father, I hear that Kunamayjayan left the palace and went away. Why is that?"

"He was the minister who refused to conform to the king's court," said Swollenhead. "What else could the king do but dismiss him?"

"Is he guilty then?" asked his daughter.

"Why are you asking this?"

"Father!" exclaimed Kamamohasuntari, "Can a government which mistreats innocent people be just?"

"You mind your own business," said Swollenhead. "It's not right to question each and every thing that happens. If you don't stop talking about it you'll have to be banished from this kingdom too."

"Very well, Father," she replied. "When a father tells his own child to leave the house, it's unconditional farewell."

"Girl!" he exploded, "You are impudent to your mother and father! Go then! Why should we keep a daughter who won't listen to us?"

Kamamohasuntari left the house and began a journey of many hardships. Finally she came to the forest and met a band of gypsies who took her in and cared for her.

[*The king enters with his first minister.*]

THE KING: Minister! I understand you had to banish your own daughter because she was evil enough to side with that beggar.

SWOLLENHEAD: Yes my lord, my feeling is that any daughter who refuses to listen to her father, and any minister who thinks he is greater than the king should not be allowed to stay in this city.

THE KING: You are the most appropriate minister for this kingdom!

Meanwhile, Soopoo, Vayloo, and Ramu, after many hardships, came to the holy man in the forest and paid obeisance to him. "Children, sit down and rest," he invited them. "There, quench your thirst at the spring."

"Holy one, we have come to ease our suffering minds," they said.

"I know all about why you have come," he answered, "I will tell you everything you need to know, but please refresh yourselves first."

Now, while this was going on the band of gypsies protecting Kamamohasuntari were celebrating a religious festival in honor of Lord Krishna. The women sang and danced around and around in circles.

THE SONG OF THE GYPSIES

This is the end of the year, friends,
And this is the land of the gypsies.
The angel of death might come any time, gypsies of the forest,
Clap your hands, devotees of Lord Krishna,
Declare your devotion.
This is our beloved gypsy land,
This is the land of Lord Krishna
Who ate the curd out of pots
Hung from the rafters.

This is the land of Lord Krishna.
The gypsy festival and the fragrance
Of our simmering milk and rice fill the forest
Like the tree which grants all wishes.
Red snakes and birds come and dance,
This is the gypsy festival,

Cook fragrant milk and rice,
Let us dance and play and rejoice.

Now let us catch cobras,
Remove their poisonous fangs and train them,
Let's show our snakes to city people
And take their money.
We'll show them the snakes
And sell them stones, making them believe
They'll cure snake bite.

We'll sell them medicines too,
And swear to their effectiveness
On the heads of our tame snakes.
Let us all celebrate with joy,
And always come back to the forest
Before the sun sets each day.

The band of gypsies sang and celebrated and observed their festival ecstatically. When Kunamayjayan came walking along the path which went past their village he saw them singing and dancing, and stopped to watch. One gypsy woman noticed him, pointed him out to another, then the whole band turned as one to kill him. He hid in a thicket but one gypsy saw him and raised his sword. Instantly, Kunamayjayan picked him up with the sword still raised in his hand and threw him down. Then he jumped on him, sat on his chest, punched him, and took the sword. When the others saw that, they surrounded him on all four sides and attacked with swords and lances. Kunamayjayan fought them all fearlessly, but without hurting anyone seriously. The chief, a huge man named Donjon, saw that and jumped on Kunamayjayan, attacking like a lion. Kunamayjayan parried with his short sword; the chief's sword broke and fell to the ground, then they fought hand to hand for many hours. Finally, Kunamayjayan dealt a great blow, Donjon unsheathed a knife which had been concealed in his clothes and tried to stab Kunamayjayan. Quick as a tiger Kunamayjayan jumped him, grabbed his knife, struck and killed him.

Then Caracone, who was second-in-command, said to him, "Now you must marry Kamamohasuntari, the most beautiful woman in our band, and remain with us as our leader."

And so they were married, and Kunamayjayan spoke to his bride for the first time. "My beloved, precious wife, blessed being who has come to share the joys and sorrows of my life, now that I can really see your qualities and appreciate your beauty, you seem so different from the other gypsies. Who are you?"

Then Kamamohasuntari told her story, "I am the daughter of Swollenhead, the Prime Minister of Sokku. I wanted to live a righteous life, but my father was persistently unjust, there was a great separation between us, and I was forced to leave. I came walking along this forest path when the gypsies found me and took me in."

"Oh, that's so good," he said, "Your destiny and mine are the same. Do you know who I am?"

"No, I don't."

"I was the king's fourth minister, Kunamayjayan. I was chased out of the country too."

"The two of us do have the same fate!"

"My dear, let me tell you something," said Kunamayjayan, "In this curiously wrought world there is a money demon known as a *pay* who presides over caste and religious differences. Anyone who has a money *pay* belongs to the highest caste, anyone who doesn't have one belongs to a lowly caste, occupies an inferior place in his religion, and finds himself generally oppressed. That demon has turned this strange world into the city of Sokku. Because of that *pay*, duty, charity, generosity, mercy, compassion, surrender to God, and all the other characteristics of virtue are disappearing. There is no justice, there are no good intentions, and lies, murder, theft, treachery, and vengeance, those five hideous evils, are exalted by the money *pay*. Let's make a plan to destroy that terrible demon. Let's dress in thieves' clothing, take money from the rich people who are bad, give it to those who are good but poor, and try to make everyone equal that way. We may need many different disguises to do this, but don't be afraid. We must dedicate our lives to the poor. That's my idea, what do you think?"

"Exactly the same idea occurred in my heart," said Kamamohasuntari, "Let's follow your plan."

Then they happily sang these songs.

KAMAMOHASUNTARI'S SONG

Inseparable lord of my life,
You are my heart's delight.

With mind and heart
So pure and beautiful,
You speak such sweet words
Even stones will melt.

Inseparable lord of my life,
You are my heart's delight.

Like the rarest flower
And its exquisite fragrance,
Like an intricate song
And its precious meaning,

Inseparable lord of my life,
You are my heart's delight.

Filled with pure happiness,
Let us live our love
In this enchanting forest.
Bless us, O God.

Inseparable lord of my life,
You are my heart's delight.

Have mercy, O God.
May I live with my treasure
Here in this forest
Filled with every pleasure.

Inseparable lord of my life,
You are my heart's delight.

Grant Your grace and Your strength
To carry out all our plans.
You are my Father, you are my Mother,
Bless me, O God.

Inseparable lord of my life,
You are my heart's delight.

KUNAMAYJAYAN'S SONG

Nothing in the world can be quite
Like God's creation of you and me,
One soul in two separate bodies.

The blissful way we live,
With clear understanding,
With love and joy,
Is like sweet honey.

*Nothing in the world can be quite
Like God's creation of you and me,
One soul in two separate bodies.*

*There are warriors
Who praise your strength,
There are brave men
Who praise your courage.*

*Nothing in the world can be quite
Like God's creation of you and me,
One soul in two separate bodies.*

*You are gentle as a deer,
Your face is like the moon.
You are the four virtues,
Modesty, reserve, restraint,
And sincerity are yours.*

*Nothing in the world can be quite
Like God's creation of you and me,
One soul in two separate bodies.*

KAMAMOHASUNTARI'S SONG

*You were born a truly exalted being
With the ability to rule,
The sign of true manliness.
You are a warrior, born to lead.
Noble husband, so abundantly wise,
Excellent and understanding,
Protect your fragile wife.*

KUNAMAYJAYAN

*My wife, jeweled light of my eyes,
You are naturally beautiful and good,
You are my most precious treasure.
Your delicate eyes
Are life to me.
Come let us walk to our forest home.*

KAMAMOHASUNTARI

Like the soul to my body,
You are life to my life.
Everything, my body, my soul,
All are yours,
My loving husband.

When their songs were over they went to the mountain cave of the gypsy band.

At that very moment, the Sheikh was taking care of Soopoo, Vayloo, and Ramu. When they had rested he said, "Ramu, while your son Visittira Layka was studying divine wisdom with me, soldiers under orders from the king of Sokku came to take him away."

"*Aiyo,*" cried Ramu in a loud voice, "He is my one and only son, what will we do? I can no longer live in this world. Oh my son, Visittira Layka!" He fell unconscious at the feet of the Sheikh.

"Soopoo, bring a little water from that pool." Soopoo brought water to the Sheikh who woke Ramu by splashing his face with it, telling him not to be afraid. He reassured him, led him into the forest, and just then Kunamayjayan came into view chasing a deer. "My child," he called to him, "Come here! Do you remember what you said earlier?"

"What did I say?" asked Kunamayjayan, "I don't understand what you mean."

"Indeed, don't you have any recollection of the vow you took in front of everyone at the palace?"

"Wise Sheikh, now I remember."

"Well then, I'll give you a few weapons to help you keep your promise. Come with me," and they went to his ashram where Kunamayjayan fell at his feet and paid obeisance to him. "My child, please get up. Now here, take these invincible weapons. Take this sword, and as long as you have it no one can defeat you. Here is a flute which has the power to create the music of vinas, drums, cymbals, and songs and dances to go with the music exactly as you imagine it. Take this ring which will materialize anything you can think of. If you wear it in battle all the soldiers and weapons you might want will appear the moment you think of them. Nothing can stop them from appearing. May you destroy all the evil people you meet, liberate the poor, and return victorious. God bless you. Now take this sword, this flute, and the ring, and guard them carefully."

Then Kunamayjayan asked the Sheikh's permission to depart. "Master," said Kunamayjayan, "I will leave now and return when my work is done." They went back to the gypsies and Kunamayjayan called them all together. "Go into this peculiar world, plunder all those who are evil, ruin them, and come home."

The gypsy band journeyed into the world, traveling in all four directions, badgering and robbing the evil people they encountered. The guards of Sokku reported their action to the king, and he ordered them to capture the rebels. He also sent out spies everywhere, but none of the rebels could be caught because they trounced the spies soundly and ran away each time. Then Kunamayjayan sent Soopoo and Vayloo into the strange and curious world to find out what was happening and report back.

Now Vayloo had a wife named Sokki who had taken the sorcerer Somasuntarum as her lover. Knowing that Vayloo, Soopoo, and Ramu had joined the forest gypsies, and concerned that they might have difficulty carrying on their affair, Somasuntarum proposed a scheme to Sokki. "You must dance violently as though you were possessed by a demon, and when the news reaches Vayloo he will call on me for help as an exorcist. Then leave the rest to me." The sorcerer left and as soon as Vayloo returned home, his wife started her devil's dance. Immediately Vayloo took Soopoo and went hurrying to Somasuntarum, told him what happened, and asked him to come home with them.

"Your wife!" exclaimed the sorcerer, "How awful!"

"Yes, it's my wife," said Vayloo, "Please come quickly!"

In the meantime the three days' respite given to Visittira Layka came to an end, and the king called his ministers, his guards, and the executioners to the place of execution. *"Aday* wretched beggar, how do you feel now?" asked the king. "In five minutes you will be decapitated. Look, the executioners stand ready to cut off your head!"

"My lord," said Visittira Layka, "Please give me those five minutes, and then they can chop away. But I have something to tell you first."

"What's that!" protested the king, "Very well, you have five minutes—talk fast!"

"I will sing you a song."

VISITTIRA LAYKA'S SONG

God, O ruler of beginningless beginning
Whose heart knows no fear,
Father, treasure of reality
Who rules this slave with compassion,
Before this eight-span body perishes,
Come to me and burn away
My evil attachments, O Father!

*Please come fearlessly, destroy
Those traitors who have
The five evils firmly entrenched
In their hearts.
O God,
Even though I've kept that formless form
Who has no mantras in my heart,
Is this my fate,
To have the eight-span body sliced in two?*

*Almighty One,
O my Sheikh, my God,
Have pity, please come.
Is this helpless child
To be destroyed?
When the evil act is done, O Father,
Be the refuge for my body.*

As he completed this prayer he placed his head on the block, and the king gave the command. At the moment the executioners had their swords raised to cut off Visittira Layka's head, he heard the sound of a voice from heaven within his ears, "My child, your body will be turned to stone as soon as the sword touches it. Later, all these evil people will be cursed and turned to stone, and you will resume your natural form." This sound reached Visittira Layka's ears only, then the executioners swung their swords, and Visittira Layka's body became stone. The king and the executioners were furiously angry and tried to knock the statue over, but it couldn't be moved.

"Ministers," said the king, "He is probably a magician who will change back to his original form when we leave. Place two guards here to catch him when he does."

"Yes, my lord," they answered, "He does indeed seem like a terrible magician. We will keep two guards here."

Song of Ecstasy

Do not forget God my mind,
And you will know liberation, I promise you.

God is the life of this body.
If you look within carefully
You will see Him.
I tell you the truth with certitude.
Find Him before this evil body is destroyed.

Do not forget God my mind,
And you will know liberation, I promise you.

If the fortress of the body
Where those five live is destroyed,
It will be revolting to look at.
If you find your real home before this house is torn apart,
That is eternal bliss.

Do not forget God my mind,
And you will know liberation, I promise you.

Close the nine gateways,
The hidden dwelling of the Sheikh is within.
Search for it with wisdom,
Sing the glory of God with love.
If you find His palace, you will have a house of bliss.

Do not forget God my mind,
And you will know liberation, I promise you.

Sing the songs of divine wisdom with fervor.
There is an imperishable King, search for Him,
Search for His sound with your heart.
Gaze up intently,
You will find the house of liberation.

Do not forget God my mind,
And you will know liberation, I promise you.

Give up attachment to house and family,
When death calls, this cage will not last a moment longer.
The cremation ground will be our domain.
Those who roam without reflecting on this
Will someday come to grief.

Do not forget God my mind,
And you will know liberation, I promise you.

All those who come to the marketplace,
See, when the sun sets they return home.
Does this place belong to us?
Believe this if you have any sense,
People of the world.

Do not forget God my mind,
And you will know liberation, I promise you.

This house is alive as long as it breathes,
But it's of no use when the breath leaves.
Look at this house with two legs—
In the crown of your head
Is the house of liberation.

Do not forget God my mind,
And you will know liberation, I promise you.

If you trust the world, destruction will follow.
When the breath stops, this cage will be worthless.
Search before this corpse is buried,
If you know your heart,
You will find the house of bliss.

Do not forget God my mind,
And you will know liberation, I promise you.

11

Kamamohasuntari

In the continuation of the Puluhan's story to Sandakumaran, the unjust king of Sokku prepares for his daughter's wedding, but he is unprepared for what happens.

By this time Vayloo, Soopoo, and the sorcerer arrived at Vayloo's house. When the demon inside his wife Sokki saw them, it danced and jumped around violently. "Ho!" said the sorcerer, "This demon is a vicious one. You'll have to give it goat meat, chicken meat, coconuts, fruit, and incense as an offering. Bring all that to me and I'll drive it out."

Addressing the demon he said, "*Ayyy* demon, stop! Don't come back till I call you." The convulsions induced by the fake demon stopped at the command of the sorcerer, and Vayloo and Soopoo went to the store to buy the things he asked for.

While this was going on King Mahendiran was back at the palace calling his three remaining ministers together to talk about a husband for his daughter. "I have arranged a marriage. What do you think about Visittira Kedu, the son of the Maharajah of Mantirapur marrying my daughter Vastira Alangaram?"

"Yes, that's a good idea," said Swollenhead, "It's a very appropriate marriage. I would be very happy if they were married."

"Visittira Kedu is a man of very good qualities," said Big Demon, "He is the right person for our kingdom and for Vastira Alangaram. I would also be very happy if this marriage were concluded."

Homewrecker said, "O Maharajah, you are getting on in years, if this marriage were performed during your lifetime everyone would be happy. It would be very good for all of us."

"This makes me really happy," said the king, "Call the palace astrologer." To the astrologer he said, "Look at these two horoscopes carefully and analyze their compatibility. Tell us what you see."

"This one looks like your daughter's," he said.

"Yes, go on," said the king.

"Well, first of all their names are compatible, and everything else seems rather harmonious too. It is a suitable match, but there is a little saturnic influence in their planets. You must perform a really good *pūjā*, make many offerings, bathe the image of the goddess Kalika, and then the blemish will disappear."

"Very good, what day can the marriage take place?" asked the king.

"Make the offering to the goddess next Saturday, then the Saturday after that will be a very auspicious day for the wedding."

"Ministers, the astrologer says there are many compatibilities between the two horoscopes. We must be ready by the day he has recommended for the marriage. We not only have to make the arrangements for the *pūjā,* but we also have to invite the kings, the ministers, the nobility, and all our relatives from other countries. Send out the wedding invitations and a scroll to the King of Mantirapur asking him to make preparations there. See what has to be done and take care of it."

While the king was talking to his ministers, the princess Vastira Alangaram was in the flower garden picking blossoms and singing gaily.

VASTIRA ALANGARAM'S SONG

This ornamental pleasure grove is
Filled with beauty, fragrance,
And the scent of joyful flowers.

This orchard in the city of Sokku
Is so lofty, so like our minds,
So filled with truth.

This ornamental pleasure grove is
Filled with beauty, fragrance,
And the scent of joyful flowers.

For heavenly beings and celestial beings,
This is an exquisitely adorned
Pleasure grove beyond compare.

This ornamental pleasure grove is
Filled with beauty, fragrance,
And the scent of joyful flowers.

This is a pleasure grove
Formed in the world of pleasure.
No one else has such graceful
Dancing peacocks and singing cuckoos.
O pretty pleasure grove, ah, ah, ah.

This ornamental pleasure grove is
Filled with beauty, fragrance,

And the scent of joyful flowers.

*Eyes that see it are dazzled
By the ecstasy of so many flowers.
Ah, ah, ah, beautiful pleasure grove.*

*This ornamental pleasure grove is
Filled with beauty, fragrance,
And the scent of joyful flowers.*

*My ladies gathered here,
Come running,
We'll dance and sing without restraint.*

*This ornamental pleasure grove is
Filled with beauty, fragrance,
And the scent of joyful flowers.*

*Now let us dance, come my partners,
Nothing can compare with our dance
In this abundant pleasure grove,
This grove so full of gaiety.*

*This ornamental pleasure grove is
Filled with beauty, fragrance,
And the scent of joyful flowers.*

Sil, sil, sil *the little streams leap
In this ornamental pleasure grove,
Ah, ah, ah.*

*This ornamental pleasure grove is
Filled with beauty, fragrance,
And the scent of joyful flowers.*

Now the king and his commander-in-chief, disguised as commoners, went walking around the countryside to spy out the secrets of the land. They noticed Soopoo and Vayloo bringing the ingredients for the sorcerer's magic to Vayloo's house. Then the sorcerer assembled the offering and called up the demon. The king and his commander stopped to listen and watch as the sorcerer sat Vayloo's wife in front of him, beating a drum and singing to call his swami.

THE SORCERER'S SONG

Father, Karupanna Swami,
Come, come, come.
        Dunn dunn dunn *is the sound of the drum.*

O mighty spirit,
Come, come, come.
        Dunn dunn dunn

Father, Sangili Mada, unconquerable mighty one,
Come, come, come.
        Dunn dunn dunn

You have a white horse with a stringy tail
That beats like a whip,
A horse perfect for you.
        Dunn dunn dunn

Tie up your loincloth tight,
Wrap your turban with a flourish.

Father, mighty one, come now.
        Dunn dunn

Mighty one, you make all the demons
Dance to your tune,
        Dunn dunn

You make all the demons coursing through us
Run away, O mighty one.
        Dunn dunn

    The sorcerer, now in a trance, told the demon to dance. Addressing Sokki he said, "Eh demon, where did you come from? Tell me quickly."
        dunn dunn
    Speaking through Vayloo's wife the demon said, "I will tell you, I will tell. West of the palace there is a temple."
    The sorcerer said, "Don't lie, tell the truth."
        dunn dunn
    "I am the family goddess of the king," said the demon.

"Why are you bothering this woman? Are you a goddess or a demon?" asked the sorcerer.

dunn dunn

"*Aday,* I'm not a demon, I am the goddess Pada Patirakali. Listen, let me tell you this woman's husband is a traitor to the king."

"Hmm," said the sorcerer, "What treachery did he commit?"

dunn dunn dunn dunn

"*Aiyo!*" cried Vayloo, "What have I done wrong?"

"*Aday,* I will pluck out your liver," said the demon, "You haven't done anything wrong, you say? You're a traitor to the king. Three of you went to the holy man for his blessing, for help in killing the king. *Aday,* you cannot kill the king who is my child. *Aday!*"

"Oh no, Mother, were they really going to do something like that?" exclaimed the sorcerer, "Anyhow, please Mother, show mercy and leave this woman!"

"You want me to leave, do you? Only after you've told the king, and these three men are sent to jail will I leave. If you force me to go I'll take her liver with me." After listening to this, the king and the commander-in-chief rushed into the house, seized Vayloo and Soopoo, and dragged them off to prison. When the king asked where Ramu was they said they didn't know.

"Well how was my acting?" asked Sokki. "I certainly chased those fellows away. Did you see that?"

"That's right," said the sorcerer. "Now we can enjoy ourselves, we don't have to worry about anything."

SONG

Sokki

Let's live with love,
My chosen love.
I put on an act,
I put on a demon-dance.
For my chosen love,
I put on an act.

The Sorcerer

You little peacock,
I put on an act, too.
Now we will never be parted,
Now we will live together in love.

By this time Ramu, Kunamayjayan, and Kamamohasuntari were worried because Vayloo and Soopoo hadn't returned yet.

"My dear husband," said Kamamohasuntari, "They went to the city and haven't come back yet. Now since we don't know whether anything has happened to them or not, it really is our duty to go look for them."

"Yes," replied Kunamayjayan, "That's true, we must go."

"Wait," said Ramu, "I have an idea. We shouldn't go as we are. If we do and the king sees us, he'll put us all in jail. Let this lady dress as a fortuneteller, and we'll disguise ourselves as snake charmers, then we can enter the city safely and learn all the secrets." They put on their disguises in the forest, then set out to look for Vayloo and Soopoo in the city.

That night the king had a dream. He saw one demon coming to strangle him and another one threatening to behead him, then a certain holy man turned him to stone. Startled, he awakened and summoned his ministers and the nobility. "Ministers and nobles, last night I had a dream I am very worried about."

"What kind of dream?" asked the ministers. "Would Your Royal Highness be pleased to tell us about it?"

"It is hard to describe. My heart is trembling even now while I'm talking to you. I saw one demon coming as if it were going to strangle me, and another one coming to behead me. Then a holy man appeared and turned me to stone with a curse. Figure out what this means and explain it to me."

"My lord, there is only one meaning," a minister answered, "Our goddess Kali appeared as a demon in your dream and showed what happened to the beggar; the death sentence you pronounced was well deserved."

"That sounds right, but my mind is not quite at peace. Just to be sure, call a fortuneteller," ordered the king.

Two soldiers were sent out to look for a fortuneteller and met Kamamohasuntari walking down the road in gypsy clothing. "Fortunes told, fortunes told!" she called out.

"Hey fortuneteller, stop!" said the soldiers. "Come here. Can you tell us what took place at the palace and explain it too?"

THE FORTUNETELLER'S SONG

All the secrets of the world,
        Lay lay langadee lay lo
All the secrets of your thoughts,
        Lay lay langadee lay lo
I can tell by reading minds.
        Lay lay langadee lay lo

All the women in the world,
      Lay lay langadee lay lo
I can bring by casting spells.
      Lay lay langadee lay lo

"All right," the soldiers said, "Come to the palace," and they led her to the king.
"Woman, are you good at reading fortunes?" asked the king.
"Oh yes, Your Majesty," said Kamamohasuntari, "I do that very well."
"Then tell me what I am thinking of," said the king.

THE FORTUNETELLER'S CHANT

I will tell the secret of the king
      Lay lay langadee lay lo
Who is renowned in the world.
      Lay lay langadee lay lo
You had a dream, yes a dream,
      Lay lay langadee lay lo
You saw a black demon approaching,
      Lay lay langadee lay lo
With a sword in its hand,
      Lay lay langadee lay lo
You saw it about to cut your throat,
      Lay lay langadee lay lo
You saw yourself turned to stone.
      Lay lay langadee lay lo
I will tell you about those horrors.
      Lay lay langadee lay lo
What you saw was not good,
      Lay lay langadee lay lo
One more thing I will tell you,
      Lay lay langadee lay lo
In this good city itself,
      Lay lay langadee lay lo
You tried to kill someone that way.
      Lay lay langadee lay lo
You tried to murder an innocent young beggar,
      Lay lay langadee lay lo

But he was turned to stone,
                Lay lay langadee lay lo
You were cursed at that moment,
                Lay lay langadee lay lo
And your body will turn to stone.
                Lay lay langadee lay lo

The king interrupted, "Who will turn to stone?"
Kamamohasuntari continued, singing now.

Here in this city you expect
                Lay lay langadee lay lo
To have your daughter married,
                Lay lay langadee lay lo
To another king.
                Lay lay langadee lay lo
Trouble will come at the wedding,
                Lay lay langadee lay lo
There will be fighting at the wedding.
                Lay lay langadee lay lo
While they are fighting at the temple,
                Lay lay langadee lay lo
Everyone's clothes will fly away.
                Lay lay langadee lay lo
Your guards will do their duty,
                Lay lay langadee lay lo
A terrible war will begin.
                Lay lay langadee lay lo

"Well," said the king, "Are you certain that's the way it will all happen?"
"Yes," she said, "It will happen exactly that way."
"What if it does not?" asked the king.
"Then kill me if you want, but whatever comes from my mouth is the truth. Now I am going to travel from village to village telling fortunes, and then I'll be at the inn near the temple of Kali, your family goddess. What I say always comes true."
"No!" exclaimed a minister, "She is just saying anything she can think of to escape. It makes sense to put her in jail, and then if what she predicted does not come true we can easily put her to death."

"Yes, that's right, said the king, and had her put in jail. When Kunamayjayan and Ramu discovered what happened they approached the palace as flute playing, gypsy snake charmers, and came up to the guards.

"We would like to show the king our artful snake charming. Please get his permission to admit us."

"Stay here," one of the guards said, "We will let the king know you are here and bring his reply." He went inside to the king, "My lord, there are two snake charmers outside who want permission to display their powers."

"Snake charmers?"

"Father," said Vastira Alangaram, "I would love to see the snake charmers!"

"Very well then," said her father, "Call them." The guard brought them in and they bowed to the king.

"What kind of snakes do you have?" asked the king.

"We have a huge cobra, and if we make it dance the whole world will be frightened."

"Well then have it dance, let's see."

One of them played the flute and the other one sang as the snake began to sway to the music.

THE SNAKE CHARMER'S SONG

Dance snake, dance nicely snake,
Dance in this strange world, snake,
Dance snake, and do your act well.
Dance on this civilized world, snake,
Drive fear into their hearts, snake.
Dance Siva's ornament.
Dance snake,
Hold up the earth and sky, snake.
Descendent of Adi Shaydan,
Dance snake,
Dance snake, dance snake.
Spread your hood of bliss
And dance cobra,
You will amaze this land.
Dance snake, dance,
Make this land prosper.
Dance snake,
Dance in bliss,
Dance snake, dance.

> *May this palace last forever,*
> *Dance, dance, snake.*

When the snake charming was over the king praised their skill, and ordered his ministers to give them an appropriate reward. They accepted it, bowed to the assembly, and left. Now Kamamohasuntari who was down in the dungeon still dressed as a fortuneteller took out the ring the Sheikh had given them, and thought of her husband. Immediately, he appeared in front of her, and she told him everything that had happened in the palace, and how she had been locked up. Kunamayjayan was very angry, took the ring from her, and left for the Kali temple promising to make all her predictions to the king come true.

The king, his ministers, Vastira Alangaram, and their attendants proceeded to the temple where all the arrangements for the *pūjā* had been made. At the same time, masses and masses of the rich and poor people of the city had come together awaiting the arrival of the king. When the king and his retinue reached the temple the offering began. Vastira Alangaram thought about the goddess and sang this song.

VASTIRA ALANGARAM'S SONG

> *You are the goddess of our family,*
> *O mother.*
> *You shine with justice,*
> *O goddess of our family,*
> *O mother,*
> *O goddess who fills my heart*
> *Forever within the letter* om,
> *O my lady, my mother.*
>
> *I am a woman,*
> *Poor and ignorant,*
> *Protect me.*
>
> *Almighty one of many forms,*
> *Gazing with a thousand eyes,*
> *Protect me.*
> *O mother, you are strength,*
> *I am your slave.*
> *Protect me.*

While Vastira Alangaram was singing Kunamayjayan walked quickly in the direction of the temple meditating on the ring, and asked that all his wife's predictions come true. At once the clothes of the king, the royal families, and the nobility flew off to the poor people, and the poor people's clothing sped to the king and his retinue. When that happened the people began to fight among themselves. There was chaos, everyone calling everyone else a thief, tugging at each other's clothes until the king had to call out the guard to subdue the riot. When the disturbance was quelled, the king, the king's daughter, the ministers, and the rich merchants all rushed back to the palace.

"Ministers," said the king, "That beggar was the cause of what happened at the temple."

"Yes he was," replied one of them, "And he wasn't the only one either. That gypsy fortuneteller should not be let out of jail, my lord."

"Yes," said the king, "Disasters have indeed befallen our country. At any rate, let's leave that for now while we make the preparations for Vastira Alangaram's wedding."

O Ultimate Unique One

Whoever worships with the faith
That You alone will protect him with Your grace
Cannot suffer any more in the detestable sea of illusion,
O refuge of my soul,
O ultimate unique One.

Now that You have seen my ignorance, will You not come
As the Sheikh of grace to remove my sufferings?
In Your state of perfect purity, You
Have placed the universes in Your grace,
O ultimate unique One.

Whoever has left a life of illusion in the world
To search for life in You, swims in the ocean of Your grace.
I am in the seven worlds of hell—to erase my ignorance,
Please look at me with Your sixth face of divine wisdom,
O ultimate unique One.

Am I in the right state to see Your compassion
Which hides in my heart governing me?
Why am I tortured like the fish in a pond
Where they have directed poisonous flood waters,
O ultimate unique One?

For the devotees who love You in their souls
Like the honeybee which ecstatically turns and turns
In the lotus of the pond, You give refuge.
I'm like a grass seller in a flower shop,
Let me not wrong You, O God, O ultimate unique One.

Tears fall down my chest like a mountain stream
Rushing down a steep slope.
Have You not seen my flood of love, O God, O state of peace?
O God of bliss, the four religions sing their hymns to You,
O ultimate unique One.

Have You not seen my tired heart and face
Looking for the company of Your true devotees?
You alone know the songs I sing everywhere
In praise of the grace I have been seeking,
My God, O ultimate unique One.

Lasting companion of my soul,
In my innermost heart You have always whispered,
"Believe; fear not!" You have taken away my anguish.
Who am I to offer thanks in the proper way?
My God, O ultimate unique One.

If I praise You often with my intellect,
I become a fool who does not ask for liberation.
What shall I do to find the truth?
Please turn Your face towards me, show me how to serve
Your devotees, O ultimate unique One.

I have not seen You, I have not heard You.
My heart does not know the state in which You will be revealed.
Is this the time for liberation?
I am ignorant of true service.
I cannot speak of Your beginning, You alone know the past,
Please speak, O ultimate unique One.

12

Sandakumaran Marries Mutavalli

Sandakumaran, the Prince of Peace, reconciles the ABCD world to live in peace and justice.

The following week Vastira Alangaram's wedding ceremony began with great pomp and ceremony. The wedding necklace was put on the bride, the couple sat on a decorated dais, and a celebrated dancer kept the crowd enthralled. Kunamayjayan and Ramu, standing at the palace gates, concentrated on the ring and wished Soopoo, Vayloo, and Kamamohasuntari were there. They appeared at once and it occurred to them that the five of them needed horses. Everything they needed was instantly given to them. Kamamohasuntari put on male clothing, the others adopted their own disguises, and then Kunamayjayan gave these instructions, "You four stay at this gate and watch for anyone who comes out. I'll storm the palace on my flying horse and do battle with those inside. If the fight becomes too much for me, I'll give the battle cry *Donjon!* in a loud voice, and you come to my assistance. Any time you find yourself in danger, summon me in the same way, and I'll be there at once to help you."

As soon as he said that he flew off into the palace unnoticed by any of the guards. Then, invisible, he hovered in the air and willed the king's crown to fly off. "Ah ha ha!" he chortled, "My lord, how is your kingdom now? Your crown has just flown away. Your kingdom will take flight in the same way." Next the king's robes all soared aloft, and Kunamayjayan laughed again, "How is your mighty strength now? How is your unjust government now?"

The king, the ministers, and the crowd all blinked their eyes in disbelief, looking around. "What strange omen is this?" everyone asked. "It happened at the temple, and it's happening again in the palace. This is really terrible."

"This is really good," said Kunamayjayan. Then the clothes of everyone in the palace sailed around, and they all ended up wearing poor people's clothing.

"What else can this be but the work of that youth, the beggar? He must be a great magician to have called up the demons themselves!" said the king.

Kunamayjayan laughed, "King Mahendiran, I'm no demon. You forfeited wisdom, you forsook righteousness and persisted in evil. What do you think of your strength now?" Visible again, he sailed down into the king's followers who were by now thoroughly agitated.

"Guards!" yelled the king, "Pounce on that vicious tiger! Catch him!"

"You false, cowardly king," called Kunamayjayan, "I have come to fight you, you lovely eunuch! Come, get ready to face me in single combat." When they heard that the king's warriors all rushed to fight Kunamayjayan. He leaped high and he leaped low; he stood alone and fought ferociously. Both sides fought intensely, then Kunamayjayan shouted the signal *Donjon!* and the other four charged in. Now there was a tremendous battle. Disguised in male clothing, Kamamohasuntari engaged in a desperate sword fight with her father Swollenhead, until, at last, he was defeated and the fighting died down. Then Kunamayjayan and his four companions left, but as the king's soldiers chased them, they disappeared. The soldiers came back and Mahendiran renewed their courage to turn about and get ready to fight again.

Visittira Kedu, the king's new son-in-law, and his wife Vastira Alangaram went home to Mantirapur, gathered their battalions, and returned to the city of Sokku where the king welcomed them. Now all their forces were gathered around the palace in readiness.

Back in Ayoti Forest Kunamayjayan took out his ring and considered the swordsmen, the cavalry, the artillery, and supplies he needed. All his forces appeared immediately. With Kunamayjayan as commander-in-chief, Kamamohasuntari as leader of the cavalry, Soopoo as principal swordsman, Vayloo the artillery chief, and Ramu as the courier, they marched from the forest to the battlefield. With the power of the ring they erected tents to rest their soldiers on the way, and Kunamayjayan sent Ramu on ahead with a message written on a scroll. King Mahendiran of Sokku read this message:

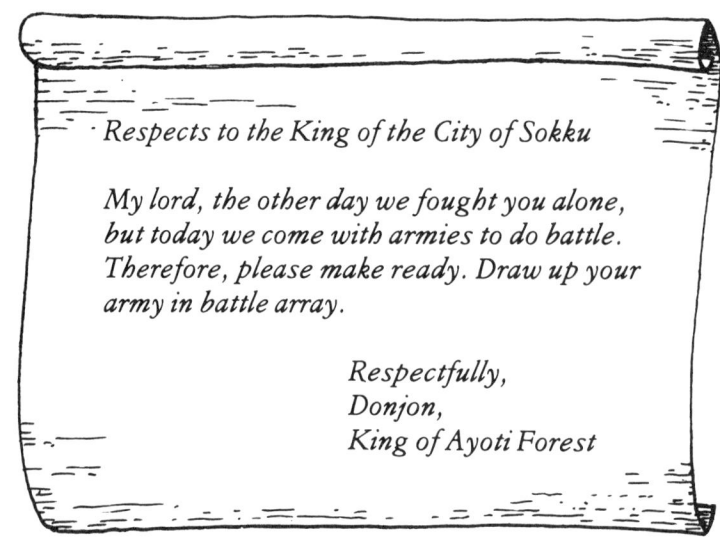

Respects to the King of the City of Sokku

My lord, the other day we fought you alone, but today we come with armies to do battle. Therefore, please make ready. Draw up your army in battle array.

Respectfully,
Donjon,
King of Ayoti Forest

The king sent this answer back with the messenger:

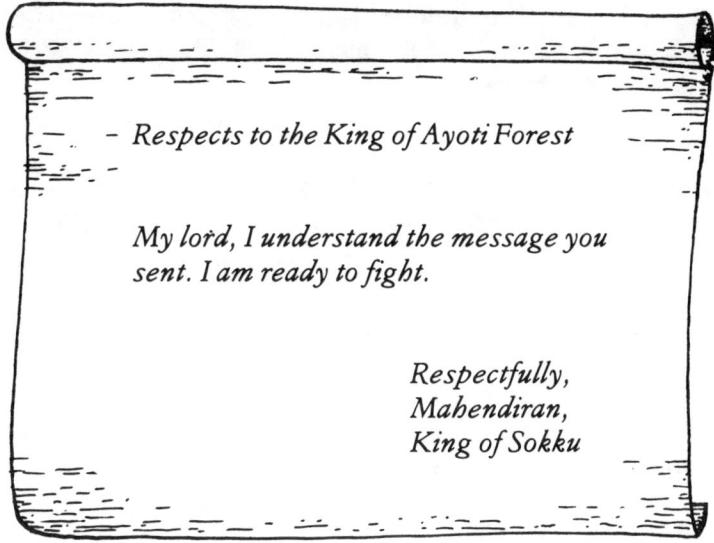

- Respects to the King of Ayoti Forest

My lord, I understand the message you sent. I am ready to fight.

Respectfully,
Mahendiran,
King of Sokku

That night Swollenhead's wife Poyandal had a dream. A figure exploding from her stomach went into the forest and brought someone back who turned Swollenhead into a statue. She howled in fear. "What is it?" asked her husband, and she described her dream. The next day Mahendiran placed his son-in-law's troops on guard at the palace, drew up his own forces outside, and pitched tents near the palace for himself and his forces.

When Kunamayjayan's army arrived the two armies clashed and a violent battle began. The cavalry and foot soldiers of the king of Sokku were crushed and Mahendiran, Swollenhead, and many of the other military leaders were taken prisoner by Kunamayjayan. The remainder of Mahendiran's forces retreated and ran far away, chased by Kunamayjayan's cavalry. The tent which had been Mahendiran's headquarters went up in flames. Then whole families of ghouls appeared and did what they liked with the corpses. They loaded the dead on their shoulders and danced and played exclaiming, "Aah, ooh, what sinners!"

Some of the defeated soldiers made their way back to Visittira Kedu, told him what happened, and the next day his soldiers ran swiftly to the battlefield. Again the two forces began to fight fiercely. Kamamohasuntari, still wearing male clothing, engaged Vastira Alangaram in a sword fight, and Kunamayjayan shot Visittira Kedu who fell at his wife's feet. She wailed with grief at the death of her husband, while her own soldiers were being conquered. Kamamohasuntari left the battlefield with scorn for Vastira Alangaram's lack of judgment, and dragged her off to the dungeon. As the battle ended Kunamayjayan, surrounded by his conquering forces, entered the city victorious to the accompaniment of triumphal drums. The prisoners were brought along after them.

"Long live justice!" shouted the soldiers, "Death to injustice." They raised the victory flag in front of the palace while the people of the city who had assembled there cheered.

Then Kunamayjayan entered the palace. Seated on a throne, he called the guard, "We are victorious in what we set out to do. Our reign must be just forever, our country must flourish, and we must never do anything to hurt our people. Now all the evil here must be eradicated. Arrest Swollenhead's wife Poyandal, Vayloo's wife Sokki, and the sorcerer. Bring them to me."

As the guards were searching for them, the sorcerer and Vayloo's wife discussed the government. "I hear the government has changed now," said Sokki.

"Yes it has, but that doesn't matter. What's that to us?" he asked.

"But what if my husband escapes and comes here?"

"Will you be sad if I tell you this? He must be dead by now," said the sorcerer. They were still talking when the guards came to arrest them. Then these two, Swollenhead's wife, and King Mahendiran were all summoned to be tried.

Back at the execution ground, Visittira Layka who had been turned to stone was awakened by the holy man for a moment, "My child you must remain a statue a little while longer. In a few moments a man of virtue whose name is Kunamayjayan will touch you. As soon as he does, you will return to your original form." The Sheikh disappeared and Visittira Layka became stone again.

Kunamayjayan, his wife, and all their troops, arrived at the execution ground with their prisoners. Kunamayjayan thought of the holy man, touched the statue, and Visittira Layka became himself again. He greeted everyone respectfully, and then Kunamayjayan spoke to him, "Child, I have known many hardships for your sake, and now you must accept this kingdom and rule it. But first, if there is anything on your mind, you may ask these sinful people standing before you now."

Visittira Layka turned to Vastira Alangaram and the king, "You loud-mouthed woman, do you remember how you mocked me and called me a sinner in your garden? Who is the sinner now? And you proud king, you called me a criminal. Now tell me, who is the criminal, who is the sinner?"

"You paragon of virtue," Vayloo said to his wife Sokki, "You had your own husband sent to jail with your tricks and your cunning. Why are you blinking at me as if you were wondering who I am? I'm your husband," he said flinging off his snake charmer's disguise, revealing his true identity.

"Great big Swollenhead of King Mahendiran," said Kamamohasuntari, "Minister who converted truth into falsehood and falsehood into truth, you drove justice away and fostered injustice. You banished your own daughter from this country for counseling justice. You thought I died, but here I am, alive."

And Ramu added, "Now you minister of piercing intellect, foul-mouthed destroyer of the people, you mule who advised the king to put my son in jail, did truth or falsehood win in the end? Stop shaking and look at me. I am the poor boy's father."

"Obscene, false woman," Soopoo said addressing Swollenhead's wife Poyandal, "You are the embodiment of lies. When your child spoke of duty you didn't stop to think she was your own child, you and your husband just chased her out of the country. And now tell us freely what you got out of that!"

"King Mahendiran," said Kunamayjayan, "The other day you banished me from this country because I defended righteousness. The two-faced wretches you used as ministers made your reign poisonous to the frightened villagers. Their loathsome treachery burned the hearts of your people. You treated the dangerous statements of your daughter as pure gold and condemned this beggar to death. You tortured the hearts of the poor and tormented them by doing away with the just laws given to us by the grace of God and His compassion, laws for the protection of millions of souls. You forgot the pure qualities a king should have. Haven't you heard the saying, 'Righteousness will save your life, unrighteousness will take you to your death'? Look at me, and look at this poor boy you pronounced the death sentence on."

When he said that Visittira Layka was suddenly transformed into a prince. "From now on he will be king of this strange and curious world. Mahendiran, just as you abandoned justice and promoted injustice, so the limbs of your body will be turned backwards, reversed from their natural position. You will face the rear, the back of your body will become the front. You will be completely changed so the people in this peculiar world can learn a lesson from this. May they follow laws of pure justice from now on. All of you, turn to stone!"

The four of them instantly became stone statues, and then the rest of the people led Visittira Layka to the palace where he was crowned in the midst of happy celebrations and festivity. The poor were fed to their hearts' content, and while they were eating Visittira Layka discussed their problems and difficulties with them. He noticed a poor woman there dressed in tatters whose name was Darmavadi or justice.

"Who are your mother and father?" asked the new king.

"My lord, I am a poor woman without mother, father, brothers, or sisters," answered Darmavadi.

"You are the one who must be my wife, my queen in this palace," he said.

"King Visittira Layka, that is a peculiarly inappropriate thing to say. How could a foolish, ragged beggar woman roaming in search of her next meal be suitable for a king?" she asked.

"You dear virtuous woman, I am not a prince. Like you, I'm just a poor wandering mendicant in this land." Visittira Layka took Darmavadi into the palace and they were married. Then Kamamohasuntari sang this song.

KAMAMOHASUNTARI'S SONG

Happy days have come now
That all the evil karma is destroyed.
This is the right time to establish
The justice destined for this land.
The time has come,
The evil people are destroyed,
The time has come for us
To join together and live as one.
We will join together
And live in happiness.
May we uproot and drive away
Our karma,
May we suffer and strive for the sake
Of this land,
May we live merged with God
Who rules the beginning, the end,
Everything.

The next day Visittira Layka chose the ministers he needed, with Kunamayjayan as his first minister, Soopoo his second minister, and Vayloo as third minister. The town crier and his drum summoned all the people to an enormous meeting in front of the palace, and waves and waves of people came from all over the countryside. The new king and queen appeared on the dais and the people cheered, "Long live the king! May our king live forever!"

Then Visittira Layka addressed the throng, "Beloved people, my greetings to you. Because our people have been held prisoner by the money demon until now, this city has been known as Sokku, the city of lures and traps. Now I wish to erase that name and call it Sattiapur, the city of absolute truth. In managing the affairs of Sattiapur, we must be absolutely truthful, and act with love, mercy, compassion, generosity, non-violence, and every good quality. We must be virtuous, leave the five deadly sins behind us, and live without racial, social, or religious differences.

Listen all people in all lands, we must live as brothers! God looks upon the wandering ascetic who truly believes in God as His own child. He bestows His grace upon sages, upon those who pray faithfully to God, and upon dutiful, virtuous women. Let us live virtuously, let us praise God and worship Him, let us fly the triumphant flag of absolute truth and make Sattiapur shine with purity. We must realize that a life of truth is a life of eternal freedom. May God bless you and grant you all His treasures. My greetings to all of you."

The people acclaimed the king's speech joyfully and shouted in jubilation, "Truth will be victorious!" Then they returned to their homes.

Just then two passers-by came along. "My friend," asked the first one, "What will our life be like now?"

The other one answered, "Our life? It will be very peaceful. There will be no poverty at all. May our new king live a long time." And indeed the king and all his subjects continued to live there happily and at peace, the king shining as a friend to his people.

This was the end of the story Vandi Puluhan and Kandi Puluhan told Sandakumaran. "Therefore, Sandakumaran," they continued, "We pray that you never act as we have, that you continue to live a good life, that you cherish all four religions, that you live correctly with peace, and patience. We have one other thing to tell you—Mutavalli has been praying many years for you on a mountaintop. You should marry that chaste, virtuous woman. God will grant you measureless grace if you do.

We will not live in the world any longer. If God the eternal and absolute One grants us His grace to be born again as human beings, we will try to live as human beings, to grow up as human beings, to do our duty as human beings, and praise only Him. May He grant us His grace. All praise belongs to Him.

Appa Sandakumaran, for anyone born as a man, deception, vengeance, and witchcraft are the worst sins. Anyone who commits these sins will suffer the worst fate, and this is absolutely true. Because we wouldn't give up our evil ways God cut off our noses to disgrace us. All the people of the world must know this and really understand how we lived. Anyone who summons demons, who practices witchcraft, treachery, vengeance, envy, deception towards the human family, anyone who has anger, who lies or acts with egoism, possessiveness, or arrogance, anyone who murders or commits any other evil will be totally destroyed. These are God's words and this is absolutely true.

Sandakumaran, anyone born as a man must not harm any other life. May you teach true wisdom, wise precepts, and good conduct to everyone. May you show them how to live a good life, and just as we now know that

God exists, may you make the people of this age realize that truth too. Pray to God for us and for the world, pray that He will forgive our faults."

They fell at Sandakumaran's feet, paid obeisance to him, leaped into a well and drowned. The Prince of Peace gave the two evil creatures a decent burial, and then traveled through many, many countries teaching God's truth. Finally, he came to the mountain where Mutavalli lived.

As he climbed the mountain, night was falling and Mutavalli, who had just finished her prayers, was playing in the flower garden when he came upon her. "Who are you?" he asked, but she was too shy to look at the face of a man, and thought immediately of her Sheikh. He appeared before them. Both Mutavalli and Sandakumaran fell at his feet and paid obeisance to him.

The Sheikh said, "This is Sandakumaran, the Prince of Peace I spoke of." Then he summoned angels and heavenly beings as witnesses and married them. "May you live a long time. May you live forever," he said blessing them.

Mutavalli and Sandakumaran prayed to God, were joyously engaged in service to the world, and lived happily together. May the people of the world follow in their footsteps.

THE SHEIKH'S SONG

Everything is God's grace.
Listen people of all lands,
We are all one family,
There is only one faith.
May the peace of God be with you.
May the peace of God be with you.
May the peace of God be with you.

The central branch of the Bawa Muhaiyaddeen Fellowship is located in Philadelphia and serves as Bawa's residence while he is in the United States. The Fellowship also serves as a meeting house and as a reservoir of people and materials for all who are interested in the teachings of M. R. Bawa Muhaiyaddeen. For information, write or call:

The Bawa Muhaiyaddeen Fellowship
5820 Overbrook Avenue
Philadelphia, Pennsylvania 19131

Telephone: (215) 879-8631